W9-BZP-361

EYEWITNESS TRAVEL GUIDES

# EUROPEAN
## PHRASE BOOK

DK Publishing

LONDON, NEW YORK, MUNICH, MELBOURNE, AND DELHI

Produced for Dorling Kindersley by
g-and-w PUBLISHING 47A High St, Chinnor, OX9 4DJ, UK

First American Edition, 2001
Reprinted with corrections 2003
4 6 8 10 9 7 5

Published in the United States by DK Publishing, Inc.
375 Hudson Street, New York, New York 10014

Dorling Kindersley books can be purchased in bulk quantities at discounted
prices for use in promotions or as premiums. We are also able to offer special
editions and personalized jackets, corporate imprints, and excerpts from all of
our books, tailored specifically to meet your own needs. To find out more, please
contact: Special Markets Department, Dorling Kindersley Publishing, Inc.,
375 Hudson Street, New York, NY 10014; Fax: 212-689-5254.

Library of Congress Cataloging-in-Publication Data

European phrase book.-- 1st American ed.
     p. cm. -- (DK travel guides)
Includes index.
     ISBN-13:  978-0-7894-9486-3 (alk. paper)
     ISBN-10:  0-7894-9486-8 (alk. paper)


     1. Polyglot glossaries, phrase books, etc. I. Dorling Kindersley Publishing,
Inc. II.
Dorling Kindersley travel guides.

PB73 .E894 2001
413'.21--dc21

Printed and bound in China by Leo Paper Products Limited

see our complete catalog at
**www.dk.com**

**Picture Credits**
Jacket photography © Corbis/Georgina Bowater (c)
All other images © Dorling Kindersley.
For further information see:  www.dkimages.com

# CONTENTS

| | |
|---|---|
| About this book | 4 |
| Czech | 5 |
| Danish | 33 |
| Dutch | 61 |
| Finnish | 89 |
| French | 117 |
| German | 145 |
| Greek | 173 |
| Hungarian | 201 |
| Italian | 229 |
| Norwegian | 257 |
| Polish | 285 |
| Portuguese | 313 |
| Spanish | 341 |
| Swedish | 369 |

## ABOUT THIS BOOK

The *Eyewitness Travel Guide European Phrase Book* has been compiled by a team of language experts to provide all the key vocabulary you need to survive in the 14 main European countries. Each language section begins with a guide to pronunciation and special grammatical points, followed by general words and phrases (greetings, numbers, days of the week etc.), and features on communications, hotels, shopping, and eating out. Finally, a menu guide supplies core vocabulary for everyday foods and beverages, as well as regional specialities.

Typical replies to questions you may ask during your journey, and the signs or instructions you may see or hear, are shown in tinted boxes. In the main text, the pronunciation of words and phrases is imitated in English sound syllables – the unique, easy-to-use, "say it as you see it" system.

Other language and travel guide titles from Dorling Kindersley are shown at the back of this book.

# CZECH

## CONTENTS

| | |
|---|---|
| INTRODUCTION | 6 |
| USEFUL PHRASES | 8 |
| DAYS, MONTHS, SEASONS | 13 |
| NUMBERS | 14 |
| TIME | 15 |
| COMMUNICATIONS | 17 |
| HOTELS | 20 |
| SHOPPING | 24 |
| EATING OUT | 25 |
| MENU GUIDE | 29 |

# INTRODUCTION

**PRONUNCIATION**

When reading the imitated pronunciation, stress the first syllable of each word. Pronounce each syllable as if it formed a part of an English word and you will be understood sufficiently well. Remember the points below, and your pronunciation will be even closer to the correct Czech.

| | |
|---|---|
| *a* | as in the "u" in "up" except when it is followed by an *h* and is pronounced like the long "a" in "lather" |
| *ay* | as in "pay" |
| *e* | as in "bed" except when it is followed by *h* and the sound is longer |
| *g* | as in "get" |
| *h* | as in the English "h" in "hand" |
| H | is similar to the "ch" in the Scottish word "loch" |
| *i* | as in "bit" |
| I | as the "i" sound in wine |
| *o* | as in "hot" except when it is followed by an *h* and is pronounced *oh* |
| *u* | as in "put" |
| *y* | always as in "yes" apart from *ay* above |
| *zh* | like the "s" in "leisure" |

It is important to remember that when **e** comes at the end of a word, it must be pronounced as a separate syllable. For example, the word **moře** should be pronounced *morzheh*. The pronunciation guide in the phrase sections adds an *h* to a final *e* in cases where confusion could arise.

## Summary of Special Characteristics in Czech

| | |
|---|---|
| a | similar to the "a" in "ant" or the "u" in "up" |
| á | is a long "a" as in "lather" |
| c | as the "ts" as in "cats" |
| č | as the "ch" in "church" |
| d' | as the "d" in "duty" |
| é | is similar to the "e" in "bed" but longer |
| ě | as the "ye" in "yet" |
| h, ch | as the "ch" in the Scottish word "loch" |
| í | as the "ee" in "weed" |
| j | as the "y" in "yes" |
| ň | as the first "n" in "companion" |
| ó | as the word "awe" |
| ř | is similar to the Scots rolled "r" run together with the "s" sound as in "leisure" |
| š | as the "sh" in "ship" |
| t' | as the "t" in "tune" |
| ú, ů | as the "oo" in "moon" |
| w | as the "v" in "van" |
| ý | as the "ee" in "weed" |
| ž | as the "s" in "leisure" |

The alternatives indicated by (*man*) and (*woman*) in the phrases show the forms to be used by a male or female speaker.
Similarly, (*to a man*) and (*to a woman*) indicate the forms to be used when addressing a man or a woman.

# USEFUL PHRASES

**Yes/no**
Ano/ne
*ano/neh*

**Thank you**
Děkuji
*d-yeku-yi*

**No, thank you**
Ne, děkuji
*neh d-yeku-yi*

**Please**
Prosím
*prosseem*

**I don't understand**
Nerozumím
*nerozoomeem*

**Do you speak English/French/German?**
Mluvíte anglicky/francouzsky/německy?
*mlooveeteh anglitski/frantsohski/n-yemetski*

**I can't speak Czech**
Nemluvím česky
*nemluveem cheski*

**I don't know**
Nevím
*neveem*

**Please speak more slowly**
Mluvte pomalu, prosím
*mloovteh pomaloo prosseem*

**Please write it down for me**
Napište mi to, prosím
*napishteh mi to prosseem*

**My name is …**
Jmenuji se …
*y-menoo-yi seh*

**How do you do, pleased to meet you**
Těší mě
*t-yeshee m-yeh*

**Good morning**
Dobré ráno
*dobreh rahno*

**Good day** (*common general greeting*)
Dobrý den
*dobree den*

**Good evening**
Dobrý večer
*dobree vecher*

**Good night**
Dobrou noc
*dobroh nots*

**Goodbye**
Nashledanou
*nas-ʜledanoh*

**How are you?**
Jak se máte?
*yak seh mahte*

**Excuse me, please**
S dovolením
*zdovoleneem*

**Excuse me?** *(pardon?)*
Prosím?
*prosseem*

**Sorry!** *(apology)*
Promiňte!
*promin-yteh*

**I'm really sorry**
Je mi to moc líto
*yeh mi to mots leeto*

**Can you help me?**
Můžete mi pomoci?
*moozheteh mi pomotsi*

**Can you tell me …?**
Můžete mi říci …?
*moozheteh mi rzheetsi*

**May I have …?**
Mohu dostat …?
*mo-hoo dostat*

**I would like …**
Rád *(man)*/ráda *(woman)* bych …
*raht/rahda* biн

**Is there … here?**
Je tam … tady?
*yeh tam … tadi*

**Where can I get …?**
Kde mohu dostat …?
*gdeh mo-hoo dostat*

**How much is it?**
Kolik to stojí?
*kolik to sto-yee*

**What time is it?**
Kolik je hodin?
*kolik yeh hodin*

**I must go now**
Už musím jít
*oozh moosseem yeet*

**I've lost my way**
Zabloudil (*man*)/zabloudila (*woman*) jsem
*zablohdil/zablohdila ysem*

**Cheers!** (*toast*)
Na zdraví!
*na zdravee*

**Do you take credit cards?**
Berete karty?
*bereteh karti*

**Where is the restroom?**
Kde je záchod?
*gdeh yeh zaнot*

**Go away!**
Jděte pryč!
*yd-yeteh prich*

**Excellent!**
Výborně!
*veeborn-yeh*

**I've lost my money/traveler's checks/credit cards**
Ztratil jsem peníze/cestovní šeky/kreditní karty
*stradil ysem peneezeh/tsestovnee sheki/kreditnee karti*

**I've lost my passport**
Ztratil jesm pas
*stratil ysem pas*

**Where is the US embassy?**
Kde je americká ambasáda?
*gdeh yeh ameritskah ambasahda*

**Is there wheelchair access?**
Je tam bezbariérový přístup?
*yeh tam besbari-yehrovee przheestup*

**Are guide dogs allowed?**
Má sem přístup slepecký pes?
*mah sem przheestup slepetskee pes*

**I'm deaf**
Jsem hluchý *(man)*/hluchá *(woman)*
*ysem hlutlee/hluttah*

**I'm blind**
Jsem slepý *(man)*/slepá *(woman)*
*ysem slepee/slepah*

---

### Things You'll Hear

| | |
|---|---|
| **Ahoj** | Hello, Hi |
| **Díky** | Thanks |
| **Dobrý den** | Good day |
| **Dobré ráno** | Good morning |
| **Jak máte?** | How are you? |
| **Nashledanou** | Goodbye |
| **Na zdraví!** | Cheers! |
| **Není zač** | You're welcome; Not at all |
| **Nerozumím** | I don't understand |
| **Nevím** | I don't know |
| **Omluvte mě** | Excuse me |
| **Pozor!** | Look out! |
| **Prosím vás** | Excuse me |
| **Správně** | That's right |
| **Vítáme vás** | Welcome |

## DAYS, MONTHS, SEASONS

| | | |
|---|---|---|
| Sunday | neděle | *ned-yeleh* |
| Monday | pondělí | *pond-yelee* |
| Tuesday | úterý | *ooteree* |
| Wednesday | středa | *strzheda* |
| Thursday | čtvrtek | *chuhtvuhrtek* |
| Friday | pátek | *pahtek* |
| Saturday | sobota | *sobota* |
| | | |
| January | leden | *leden* |
| February | únor | *oonor* |
| March | březen | *brzhezen* |
| April | duben | *dooben* |
| May | květen | *kv-yeten* |
| June | červen | *cherven* |
| July | červenec | *chervenets* |
| August | srpen | *suhrpen* |
| September | září | *zahrzhee* |
| October | říjen | *rzhee-yen* |
| November | listopad | *listopat* |
| December | prosinec | *prosinets* |
| | | |
| Spring | jaro | *yaro* |
| Summer | léto | *lehto* |
| Fall | podzim | *podzim* |
| Winter | zima | *zima* |
| | | |
| Christmas | vánoce | *vahnotseh* |
| Christmas Eve | Štědrý večer | *sht-yedree vecher* |
| New Year | Nový rok | *novee rok* |
| New Year's Eve | Silvestr | *silvestuhr* |

# NUMBERS

| | | | |
|---|---|---|---|
| 0 | nula *noola* | 5 | pět *p-yet* |
| 1 | jedna *yedna* | 6 | šest *shest* |
| 2 | dvě *dv-yeh* | 7 | sedm *sehduhm* |
| 3 | tři *trzhi* | 8 | osm *ossuhm* |
| 4 | čtyři *chuhtirzhi* | 9 | devět *dev-yet* |

| | | | |
|---|---|---|---|
| 10 | deset *desset* | 11 | jedenáct *yedenahtst* |
| 12 | dvanáct *dvanahtst* | 13 | třináct *trzhinahtst* |
| 14 | čtrnáct *chuhtuhrnahtst* | 15 | patnáct *patnahtst* |
| 16 | šestnáct *shestnahtst* | 17 | sedmnáct *sehduhmnahtst* |
| 18 | osmnáct *ossuhmnahtst* | 19 | devatenáct *devatenahtst* |

| | |
|---|---|
| 20 | dvacet *dvatset* |
| 21 | dvacet jedna *dvatset yedna* |
| 22 | dvacet dva *dvatset dva* |
| 30 | třicet *trzhitset* |
| 40 | čtyřicet *chtirzhitset* |
| 50 | padesát *padessaht* |
| 60 | šedesát *shedessaht* |
| 70 | sedmdesát *sehduhmdessaht* |
| 80 | osmdesát *ossuhmdessaht* |
| 90 | devadesát *devadessaht* |
| 100 | sto *sto* |
| 110 | sto deset *sto desset* |
| 200 | dvě stě *dv-yeh st-yeh* |
| 300 | tři sta *trzhi sta* |
| 400 | čtyři sta *chtirzhi sta* |
| 500 | pět set *p-yet set* |
| 600 | šest set *shest set* |
| 700 | sedm set *seduhm set* |
| 800 | osm set *ossuhm set* |
| 900 | devět set *dev-yet set* |
| **1,000** | tisíc *tiseets* |
| **100,000** | sto tisíc *sto tiseets* |
| **1,000,000** | milion *mili-on* |

# TIME

| | | |
|---|---|---|
| today | dnes | *dness* |
| yesterday | včera | *fchera* |
| tomorrow | zítra | *zeetra* |
| this week | tento týden | *tento teeden* |
| last week | minulý týden | *minulee teeden* |
| next week | příští týden | *przheeshtee teeden* |
| this morning | | |
|   (*early*) | dnes ráno | *dness rahno* |
|   (*late*) | dnes dopoledne | *dness dopoledneh* |
| this afternoon | dnes odpoledne | *dness otpoledneh* |
| this evening | dnes večer | *dness vecher* |
| tonight (*early*) | dnes večer | *dness vecher* |
|   (*late*) | dnes v noci | *dness vnotsi* |
| last night (*early*) | včera večer | *fchera vecher* |
|   (*late*) | včera v noci | *fchera vnotsi* |
| in three days | za tři dny | *za trzhi dni* |
| three days ago | před třemi dny | *przhed trzhemi dni* |
| late | pozdě | *pozd-yeh* |
| early | časně | *chassn-yeh* |
| soon | brzy | *buhrzi* |
| later on | později | *pozd-yay-i* |
| at the moment | právě | *prahv-yeh* |
| second | sekunda | *sekunda* |
| minute | minuta | *minuta* |
| one minute | jedna minuta | *yedna minuta* |
| two minutes | dvě minuty | *dv-yeh minuti* |
| quarter of an hour | čtvrt hodiny | *chuhtvuhrt hodini* |
| half an hour | půl hodiny | *pool hodini* |
| three quarters of an hour | tři čtvrtě hodiny | *trzhi chuhtvuhrt-yeh hodini* |
| hour | hodina | *hodina* |
| that day | ten den | *ten den* |
| every day | každý den | *kazhdee den* |
| the next day | příští den | *przheeshtee den* |

## TELLING TIME

"It's one o'clock" is **je jedna hodina** (*yeh yedna hodina*); for "it's two/three/four o'clock" use **jsou** (*yuhsoh*) followed by the number and **hodiny**; the remaining hours to twelve o'clock are simply **je** plus the appropriate number and **hodin**.

For time past the hour always refer to the next hour. For "half past" use **půl** (*pool*) and specify the next hour. For example, "half past one" is **půl druhé** (*pool drooheh*) literally "half of the second." Similarly for "quarter past" use **čtvrt na** (*chuhtvuhrt na*) and specify the next hour. For example, "quarter past one" is **čtvrt na dvě** (*chuhtvuhrt na dv-yeh*). For "quarter to" use **tři čtvrtě na** (*trzhi chuhtvuhrt-yeh na*) and specify the next hour. For example, "quarter to eight" is **tři čtvrtě na osm** (*trzhi chuhtvuhrt-yeh na ossuhm*).

Any of the expressions given above can be used with **v** meaning "at," for example, "at half past one" is **v půl druhé**.

| | | |
|---|---|---|
| **am** (*midnight to 5 am*) | v noci | *vnotsi* |
| **am** (*5 to 9 am*) | ráno | *rahno* |
| **am** (*9 to 12 am*) | dopoledne | *dopoledneh* |
| **pm** (*12 to 5 pm*) | odpoledne | *otpoledneh* |
| **pm** (*5 to 10 pm*) | večer | *vecher* |
| **pm** (*10 to 12 pm*) | v noci | *vnotsi* |
| **one o'clock** | jedna hodina | *yedna hodina* |
| **ten past one** | jedna hodina deset minut | *yedna hodina a desset minut* |
| **quarter past one** | čtvrt na dvě | *chuhtvuhrt na dv-yeh* |
| **half past one** | půl druhé | *pool drooheh* |
| **twenty to two** | za dvacet minut dvě | *za dvatset minoot dv-yeh* |
| **quarter to two** | tři čtvrtě na dvě | *trzhi chuhtvuhrt-yeh na dv-yeh* |
| **two o'clock** | dvě hodiny | *dv-yeh hodini* |
| **midday** | poledne | *poledneh* |
| **midnight** | půlnoc | *poolnots* |

# COMMUNICATIONS

### Useful Words and Phrases

| | | |
|---|---|---|
| **code** | předčíslí | *przhetcheesslee* |
| **collect call** | hovor na účet volaného | *hovor na oochet volaneh-ho* |
| **dial tone** | volací tón | *volatsee tawn* |
| **directory assistance** | informace | *informatseh* |
| **emergency** | případ nouze | *przheepat nohzeh* |
| **extension** | linka | *linka* |
| **fax machine** | fax | *fax* |
| **internet** | internet | *internet* |
| **mobile phone** | mobilní telefon | *mobilnee telefon* |
| **number** | číslo | *cheesslo* |
| **operator** (*exchange*) | ústředna | *oostrzhedna* |
| **phone card** | telefonní karta | *telefonee karta* |
| **receiver** | sluchátko | *slooHahtko* |
| **telephone** | telefon | *telefon* |
| **telephone booth** | telefonní budka | *telefonee bootka* |
| **website** | web site | *web site* |
| **wrong number** | špatné číslo | *shpatneh cheesslo* |

**Where is the nearest phone booth?**
Kde je nejbližší telefonní budka?
*gdeh yeh nayblizhshee telefonee butka*

**I would like a number in …**
Chtěl (*man*)/chtěla (*woman*) bych číslo v…
*Ht-yel/Ht-yela biH cheesslo v*

**I would like to speak to …**
Rád (*man*)/ráda (*woman*) bych mluvil/mluvila s …
*raht/rahda biH mluvil/mluvila s*

**My number is …**
Mé číslo je …
*meh cheeslo yeh*

**Could you leave him a message?**
Můžete mu nechat vzkaz?
*moozheteh mu neнat fskas*

**Sorry, wrong number**
Promiňte, mám špatné číslo
*promin-yeteh mahm shpatneh cheesslo*

**What's your fax number/email address?**
Jaké je tvé faxové číslo/e-mailová adresa?
*yakeh yeh tveh faxoveh cheeslo/e-mailovah adresa*

**May I send a fax/email from here?**
Mohu odtud poslat fax/e-mail?
*mo-hu odtud poslat fax/e-mail*

---

### THINGS YOU'LL HEAR

**Koho voláte?**
Whom would you like to speak to?

**Máte špatné číslo**
You've got the wrong number

**Kdo je u telefonu?**
Who is speaking?

**Mluví. Počkáte si?**
The line is busy. Will you wait?

**Není tady**
He's not in

**Nezavěšujte!**
Don't hang up!

**Řeknu mu, že jste telefonoval**
I'll tell him you called

**Vrátí se v … hodin**
He'll be back at …

---

## THINGS YOU'LL SEE

| | |
|---|---|
| fax | fax (machine) |
| informace | directory assistance |
| kopírka | photocopier |
| meziměstský hovor | long-distance call |
| mezinárodní hovor | international call |
| místní hovor | local call |
| ohlašovna poruch | repair service |
| poplatky | charges |
| porucha | out of order |
| předvolba | code |
| přímá volba | direct dialing |
| případ nouze | emergency |
| telefon | telephone |
| telefonní budka | telephone booth |
| telefonní kabina | telephone booth (at post office) |
| telefonní seznam | phone book |
| ústředna | exchange (operator) |
| webová stránka | website |
| záloha | deposit |

# HOTELS

## Useful Words and Phrases

| | | |
|---|---|---|
| balcony | balkón | *balkawn* |
| bathroom | koupelna | *kohpelna* |
| bed | postel | *postel* |
| bedroom | ložnice | *lozhnitseh* |
| breakfast | snídaně | *sneedan-yeh* |
| check | účet | *oochet* |
| dining room | jídelna | *yeedelna* |
| dinner | večeře | *vechehr-zheh* |
| double room | pokoj s dvojlůžkem | *pokoy z dvoyloozhkem* |
| elevator | výtah | *veetaн* |
| lobby | předsálí | *przhetsahlee* |
| full board | plná penze | *puhlnah penzeh* |
| half board | polopenze | *polopenzeh* |
| hall of residence | studentská kolej | *stoodentskah kolay* |
| hotel | hotel | *hotel* |
| key | klíč | *kleech* |
| lounge | hala | *hala* |
| lunch | oběd | *ob-yet* |
| manager | ředitel | *rzheditel* |
| reception | recepce | *retseptseh* |
| receptionist | recepční | *retsepchnee* |
| restaurant | restaurace | *restowratseh* |
| room | pokoj | *pokoy* |
| room service | donáška do pokoje | *donahshka do poko-yeh* |
| shower | sprcha | *spr-на* |
| single room | jednolůžkový pokoj | *yedno-loozhkovee pokoy* |
| toilet | záchod | *zaнot* |
| twin room | dvoulůžkový pokoj | *dvohloozhkovee pokoy* |

**Do you have any vacancies?**
Máte volné pokoje?
*mahteh volneh poko-yeh*

**I have a reservation**
Mám rezervovaný pokoj
*mahm rezervovanee pokoy*

**I'd like a single/double room**
Chtěl (*man*)/chtěla (*woman*) bych jednolůžkový pokoj/pokoj s
   dvoulůžkem
*Ht-yel/Ht-yela biH yedno-loozhkovee pokoy/pokoy s dvoyloozhkem*

**I'd like a twin room**
Chtěl (*man*)/chtěla (*woman*) bych s dvěma lůžky pokoj
*Ht-yel/Ht-yela biH s dvyema loozhki pokoy*

**I'd like a room with a bathroom/with a balcony**
Chtěl (*man*)/chtěla (*woman*) bych pokoj s koupelnou/s balkónem
*Ht-yel/Ht-yela biH pokoy skohpelnoh/sbalkawnem*

**Is there satellite/cable TV in the rooms?**
Je v pokojích satelit/kabelová televize?
*yeh f-pokoyeeH satelit/kabelovah televize*

**I'd like a room for one night/for three nights**
Chtěl (*man*)/chtěla (*woman*) bych pokoj na jednu noc/na tri noci
*Ht-yel/Ht-yela biH pokoy na yednu nots/na trzhi notsi*

**I'm looking for private accommodations**
Hledám ubytování v soukromí
*hledahm ubitovahnee f-sohkromee*

**What is the charge per night?**
Kolik stojí jedna noc?
*kolik sto-yee yedna nots*

**I don't know yet how long I'll stay**
Ještě nevím, jak dlouho tady zůstanu
*yesht-yeh neveem yak dloh-ho tadi zoostanu*

**When is breakfast/dinner?**
Kdy je snídaně/večeře?
*gdi yeh sneedan-yeh/vecherzh-eh*

**Please call me at … o'clock**
Prosím, zavolejte mi v … hodin
*prosseem zavolayteh mi v … hodin*

**May I have breakfast in my room?**
Mohu snídat ve svém pokoji?
*mo-hu sneedat veh svehm poko-yi*

**I'll be back at … o'clock**
Vratím se v … hodin
*vrateem seh v … hodin*

**My room number is …**
Číslo mého pokoje je …
*cheesslo meh-ho poko-yeh yeh*

**I'm leaving tomorrow**
Odjíždim zítra
*od-yeezhdeem zeetra*

**May I have the check, please?**
Mohu dostat účet, prosím?
*mo-hu dostat oochet prosseem*

**I'll pay by credit card**
Budu platit úvěrovou kartou
*budu platit oov-yerovoh kartoh*

**I'll pay cash**
Budu platit v hotovosti
*boodoo platit vhotovosti*

**Can you get me a taxi?**
Můžete mi zavolat taxi?
*moozheteh mi zavolat taksi*

## THINGS YOU'LL SEE

| | |
|---|---|
| **nouzový východ** | emergency exit |
| **obsazeno** | no vacancies |
| **poschodí** | floor |
| **pouze pro personál** | staff only |
| **recepce** | reception |
| **restaurace** | restaurant |
| **sem** | pull |
| **snídaně** | breakfast |
| **sprcha** | shower |
| **tam** | push |
| **tlačit** | push |
| **účet** | check |
| **výtah** | elevator |
| **zadáno** | reservation |

## THINGS YOU'LL HEAR

**Pokoje s dvoujlůžkem už nemáme**
There are no double rooms left

**Jednolůžkové pokoje už nemáme**
There are no single rooms left

**Jak budete platit?**
How will you be paying?

**Lituji, máme obsazeno**
I'm sorry, we're full

**Na kolik nocí?**
For how many nights?

**Platí se předem, prosím**
Please pay in advance

# SHOPPING

**Where is the … department?**
Kde je oddělení …?
*gdeh yeh od-yelenee*

**Do you have …?**
Máte …?
*mahteh*

**How much is this?**
Kolik to stojí?
*kolik to sto-yee*

**Where do I pay?**
Kde mohu zaplatit?
*gdeh mo-hoo zaplatit*

**Do you have anything less expensive?**
Máte něco levnějšího?
*mahteh n-yetso levn-yaysheeho*

**Could you wrap it for me?**
Můžete mi to zabalit?
*moozheteh mi to zabalit*

**May I have a receipt?**
Mohu dostat paragon?
*mo-hu dostat paragon*

**May I have a refund?**
Mohu dostat zpátky peníze?
*mo-hu dostat spahtki peneezeh*

**I'm just looking**
Jenom se dívám
*yenom seh deevahm*

**I'll come back later**
Ještě se vrátím
*yesht-yeh seh vrahteem*

# EATING OUT

Restaurants – **restaurace** (*restowratseh*) – are divided into four price categories. The first category – **cenová skupina** – and some of the second can be fairly expensive. A wide variety of both Czech and international food is available and Chinese and Indian restaurants are popular.

Food in less expensive restaurants varies depending on the season, region, and initiative of the manager or owner. Small pubs in the mountain region of Bohemia often serve interesting local dishes. Roast pork with dumplings and sauerkraut (**vepřová pečeně s knedlíky a se zelím,** *veprzhovah pechen-yeh sknedleeki a se zeleem*) is a popular dish. In big hotels and more upscale restaurants, game is available in season, and haunch of venison in cream sauce (**srnčí kýta na smetane,** *sruhnchee keeta na smetan-yeh*) is recommended. Those who like freshwater fish should try trout in herb butter (**pstruh na másle,** *puhstrooн na mahsleh*). While meat still plays an important role in Czech food culture, some vegetarian dishes are available.

Popular snacks in lower-priced restaurants include tripe soup (**dršťková polévka,** *druhzht-yehkovah polehfka*), goulash soup (**gulášová polévka,** *goolashovah polehfka*), and stewed pork with paprika and rice (**vepřové na paprice rýží,** *veprzhoveh na papritseh s reezhee*). Goulash with dumplings, or just with a roll as a snack, should be of reasonable quality anywhere.

Beer is at its best in Bohemia, but there is some good beer in Brno, and a few locally brewed beers in Northern Moravia and Slovakia are worth trying. A visit to one of the wine cellars in Southern Moravia is recommended. The best wines come from South Moravia. The white wines **Rulandské bílé** (*roolantskeh beeleh*), **Müller Thurgau** and the red **Kláštorné červené** (*klashtorneh cherveneh*) are among the most popular. **Mattoniho kyselka** (*matoniho kiselka*) is the best type of mineral water.

A service charge may be shown on the check, but a tip of about 10% is customary.

## USEFUL WORDS AND PHRASES

| beer | pivo | *pivo* |
|---|---|---|
| check | účet | *oochet* |
| bottle | láhev | *lah-hef* |
| bowl | miska | *miska* |
| cake | zákusek | *zahkoossek* |
| chef | kuchař | *kooнarzh* |
| coffee | káva | *kahva* |
| cup | šálek | *shahlek* |
| fork | vidlička | *vidlichka* |
| glass | sklenice | *sklenitseh* |
| hors d'oeuvre | předkrm | *przhetkuhruhm* |
| knife | nůž | *noozh* |
| menu | jídelní lístek | *yeedelnee leestek* |
| milk | mléko | *mlehko* |
| plate | talíř | *taleerzh* |
| receipt | stvrzenka | *stuhruhrzenka* |
| sandwich | obložený chléb | *oblozhenee нlehp* |
| napkin | ubrousek | *oobrohsek* |
| snack | rychlé | *riнleh* |
| | občerstvení | *opcherstuhvenee* |
| soup | polévka | *polehfka* |
| spoon | lžíce | *lzheetseh* |
| sugar | cukr | *tsookuhr* |
| table | stůl | *stool* |
| tea | čaj | *chɪ* |
| teaspoon | čajová | *chɪ-ovah* |
| | lžička | *luzhzhichka* |
| tip | spropitné | *spropitneh* |
| waiter | číšník | *cheeshneek* |
| waitress | číšnice | *cheeshnitseh* |
| water | voda | *voda* |
| wine | víno | *veeno* |
| wine list | nápojový | *nahpo-yovee* |
| | lístek | *leestek* |

**A table for one, please**
Stůl pro jednoho, prosím
*stool pro yednoho prosseem*

**A table for two, please**
Stůl pro dva, prosím
*stool pro dva prosseem*

**Is there a highchair?**
Mají tam dětskou židličku?
*mayee tam dyetskoh zhidlichku*

**May I see the menu?**
Mohu dostat jídelní lístek?
*mo-hoo dostat yeedelnee leestek*

**Do you have a vegetarian menu?**
Máte vegetariánskou nabídku jídel?
*mah-te vegetari-yahnskoh nabeedku yee-del*

**Call the manager, please!**
Zavolejte vedoucího, prosím!
*zavolayteh vedohtseeho prosseem*

**May I see the wine list?**
Mohu dostat nápojový lístek?
*mo-hoo dostat nahpo-yovee leestek*

**Do you do children's portions?**
Děláte dětské porce?
*d-yelahte d-yetskeh portse*

**Can you warm this bottle/baby food for me?**
Můžete ohřát tuto láhev/kojeneckou výživu?
*moozheteh o-hrzhaht tuto lah-hef/ko-yenetskoh veezhivu*

**What would you recommend?**
Co byste mi doporučil (*to a man*)/doporučila (*to a woman*)?
*tso bisteh mi doporuchil/doporuchila*

**Is this suitable for vegetarians?**
Je to vhodné pro vegetariány?
*yeh to vhodneh pro vegetari-yahni*

**I'm allergic to nuts/shellfish**
Jsem alergický (man)/alergická (woman) na ořechy/korýše
*ysem alergitskee/alergitskah na orzhetti/koreeshe*

**I'd like …**
Rád (man)/ráda (woman) bych …
*raht/rahda biн*

**Just a cup of coffee, please**
Jenom šálek kávy, prosím
*yenom shahlek kahvi prosseem*

**Waiter/waitress!**
Pane/paní vrchní!
*paneh/panee vuhruннee*

**A beer/two beers, please**
Pivo/dvě piva, prosim
*pivo/dv-yeh piva prosseem*

**May we have the check, please?**
Můžeme dostat účet, prosím?
*moozhemeh dostat oochet prosseem*

**I only want a snack**
Chci jenom něco malého k jídlu
*нtsi yenom n-yetso maleh-ho k-yeedloo*

**I didn't order this**
Toto jsem si neobjednal (man)/neobjednala (woman)
*toto yuhsem si ne-ob-yednal/ne-ob-yednala*

**The meal was very good, thank you**
Jídlo bylo velmi dobré, děkuji
*yeedlo bilo velmi dobreh d-yekoo-yi*

# MENU GUIDE

**aperitiv** aperitif
**banán** banana
**bažant** pheasant
**bez ledu** without ice
**biftek s vejcem** steak with an egg
**bílé víno** white wine
**bramborák** potato pancake
**bramborová kaše** mashed potatoes
**bramborová polévka** potato soup
**bramborové hranolky** french fries
**bramborové knedlíky** potato dumplings
**bramborové placky** potato pancake
**bramborový guláš** potato goulash
**brambory** potatoes
**broskev** peach
**brynza** sheep's cheese
**burské oříšky** peanuts
**celer** celery
**celerový salád** celeriac salad
**chlupaté knedlíky se zelím** Bohemian
  potato dumplings with cabbage
  (dumplings made from a mixture of
  raw grated potatoes, flour, and egg)
**chřest** asparagus
**cibule** onions
**cibulová omáčka** onion sauce
**citrón** lemon
**cukr** sugar
**cukroví** cookies
**čaj** tea
**čaj s mlékem** tea with milk
**černá káva** black coffee
**čerstvý** fresh
**červené víno** red wine
**červená řepa** beets
**česnek** garlic
**čočka** lentils
**čočková polévka** lentil soup

**daněk** venison
**datle** dates
**divoký kanec** wild boar
**divoký králík** wild rabbit
**do krvava** rare
**domácí** homemade
**dort** cream cake
**dršťková polévka** tripe soup
**drůbež** poultry
**dušená kapusta** stewed curly kale
**dušené hovězí maso** beef stew
**dušené telecí maso** veal stew
**dušené vepřové maso** pork stew
**dušený** stewed
**džem** jam
**džus** juice
**fazole** beans
**fazole na kyselo** sour beans (beans
  boiled in water, thickened with flour
  and seasoned with vinegar)
**fíky** figs
**guláš** goulash
**guláš z daňčího masa** venison goulash
**guláš z husích žaludků** goulash made
  with goose's stomach
**gulášová polévka** goulash soup (made
  with meat and spices)
**haše** ground beef, hash
**hlávkové zelí** cabbage
**hlávkový salát** lettuce
**hodně vypečený** well done
**holub** pigeon
**horké kakao** hot chocolate
**horký** hot
**hořčice** mustard
**houbová omáčka** mushroom sauce
**houby** mushrooms
**houskové knedlíky** bread dumplings

**hovězí (maso)** beef
**hovězí játra na slanině** calf's liver stewed with onions and bacon
**hovězí maso s houbovou omáčkou** boiled beef in mushroom sauce
**hovězí maso s koprovou omáčkou** boiled beef in dill sauce
**hovězí maso s rajskou omáčkou** boiled beef with tomato sauce
**hovězí pečeně** stewed beef
**hovězí polévka se žemlovým svítkem** meat broth with bread omelette
**hovězí polévka** beef broth
**hovězí polévka s knedlíčky** beef broth with dumplings
**hovězí polévka s masovými knedlíčky** meat broth with meatballs
**hovězí polévka s noky** beef broth with gnocchi (flour and potato dumplings)
**hovězí polévka s rýží** beef broth with rice
**hovězí tokáň** beef stewed in wine
**hrách** peas
**hráškový krém** cream of pea soup
**hroznové víno** grapes
**hruška** pear
**humr** lobster
**husa** goose
**husí játra** goose liver
**chléb** bread
**chuťovky** savories
**játra** liver
**játrová omáčka** liver sauce
**jablko** apple
**jablkový závin** apple strudel
**jahody** strawberries
**jednotlivá jídla** à la carte
**jehněčí maso** lamb
**jelení maso** venison
**kachna** duck
**kachna pečená** roasted duck

**kakao** hot chocolate or cocoa
**kančí (maso)** wild boar
**kapr** carp
**kapr pečený** baked carp
**kapr na rožni** carp on a skewer
**kapr smažený** fried carp
**kapusta** curly kale
**karotka** carrots
**kaše** buckwheat cereal
**káva** coffee
**kaviár** caviar
**kedlubny** kohlrabi
**klobása** smoked sausage
**klopsy na smetaně** stewed meatballs
**knedlíky** dumplings
**koblihy** doughnuts
**koláč** pie
**koláčky** small sweet pies or tartlets
**koprová omáčka** dill sauce
**krém** cream or custard
**krocan** turkey
**krupicová kaše** semolina purée
**krupicové noky** semolina dumplings
**krupicový nákyp** semolina pudding
**křehký koláč s jablky** apple pie
**křenová šlehačka** horse-radish sauce
**kuře** chicken
**kuře na rožni** chicken on a skewer
**květák** cauliflower
**kynuté knedlíky** dumplings made from yeast dough filled with jam
**kyselé zelí** sauerkraut
**lískové ořechy** hazelnuts
**lívance** pancakes with jam
**losos** salmon
**majonéza** mayonnaise
**maliny** raspberries
**máslo** butter
**maso** meat
**masová směs na roštu** mixed grill
**menu** table d'hôte, fixed-price menu

meruňky apricots
minerálka/minerální voda mineral water
mléko milk
mořské ryby salt-water fish
moučník dessert
mouka flour
na jehle on a skewer
na roštu broiled
nanukový dort ice-cream gâteau
ne moc vypečený medium-rare
nealkoholické nápoje soft drinks
nešumivá minerálka still mineral water
noky gnocchi (potato dumplings)
nudle noodles
nudlový nákyp s tvarohem noodle
    pudding baked with cottage cheese
oběd lunch
obložený chlebíček open sandwich
ocet vinegar
okurky cucumber
omáčka sauce
omeleta omelette
opékané brambory fried potatoes
ovoce fruit
párek hot dog
párek s hořčicí sausage with mustard
párek v rohlíku hot dog
paprika pepper (green or red)
pařížský krém whipped cream and
    chocolate cream
paštika pâté
pečená husa roasted goose
pečené hovězí maso roasted beef
pečený roast, baked or broiled
pepř pepper
pivo beer
plněné rajče zapečené stuffed tomato
plněné žampióny stuffed mushrooms
plněný telecí řízek stuffed veal steak
polévka soup
pórek leek

pomeranč orange
pomerančová šťáva orange juice
přesnídávka mid-morning snack
přesnídávková polévka thick soup
přílohy side dishes
pstruh trout
pšeničný chléb white bread
ragú ragoût
rajčatový salát tomato salad
rajská tomatoes
rohlík roll
rybí polévka z kapra carp soup
rybíz currants
ryby fish
rýže rice
rýže dušená stewed rice
řízek fillet
s ledem with ice
s octem in vinegar
salát salad
sekaná pečeně meat loaf
sekané maso ground meat
sekaný chopped
skopová kýta leg of mutton
skopové (maso) mutton
skopové ragú mutton ragoût
sladkovodní ryby freshwater fish
sladký sweet
slanina bacon
sleď herring
slepice chicken
smažené bramborové hranolky
    french fries
smažené bramborové lupínky chips
smažené kuře fried chicken
smažené telecí maso fried veal
smažené vepřové maso fried pork
smažený fried, fried in breadcrumbs
smažený karbanátek fried meatballs
smetana cream, full-cream milk
snídaně breakfast

srnčí (maso) venison
studené předkrmy hors d'oeuvres
studený cold
sůl salt
šumivá minerálka carbonated
  mineral water
sýr cheese
šampaňské champagne
šlehačka whipped cream
špenát spinach
šunka ham
švestkové knedlíky plum dumplings
švestky plums
telecí (maso) veal
telecí řízek přírodní veal steak
teplá šunka boiled ham (served hot)
teplé předkrmy entrées
teplý hot or warm
těstoviny noodles
treska cod
třešně cherries
tvaroh cottage cheese
uzené maso vařené boiled smoked meat
uzené vepřové maso smoked pork
uzeniny smoked meats
uzený úhoř smoked eel
vaječná jídla egg dishes
vařené boiled
večeře supper
vejce egg
veka white French-style bread
vepřové dušené v kedlubnách pork
  stewed with kohlrabi
vepřová kýta na paprice stewed leg of
  pork with paprika
vepřová pečeně roasted pork
vepřová žebírko přírodní stewed
  rib of pork
vepřové na kmíně pork stew with
  caraway seeds
vepřové (maso) pork

vepřové maso uzené smoked pork
vepřové ražniči pork on skewer with
  bacon and onions
vepřový bůček nadívaný stuffed side
  of pork
vepřový guláš pork goulash
vídeňský telecí řízek fried veal fillet in
  breadcrumbs
víno wine
višně morello cherries
voda water
voda s ledem water with ice
zadělávané in white sauce
zadělávané dršťky tripe in white sauce
zajíc hare
zajíc na černo stewed hare in thick,
  dark, sweet and sour sauce
zajíc na smetaně, přírodní hare in
  cream sauce
zapečená šunka s vejci ham and eggs
zapékané brambory se sýrem potatoes
  baked with cheese
zastřené vejce poached egg
zavařenina preserves, jam
zelenina vegetables
zeleninová polévka vegetable soup
zeleninové rizoto rice with vegetables
zeleninový řízek fried vegetable rissole
zelený hrášek green peas
zelná polévka cabbage soup
zelná polévka s klobásou cabbage soup
  with smoked sausage
zmrzlina ice cream
zmrzlinový pohár sundae
znojemská roštěná Znojmo-style sirloin
  (fried, then stewed with onions)
zvěřina game
žampióny mushrooms
žemlovka pudding made from bread,
  apples, cinnamon, eggs, and milk
žitný chléb rye bread

# DANISH

## CONTENTS

INTRODUCTION 34
USEFUL PHRASES 36
DAYS, MONTHS, SEASONS 41
NUMBERS 42
TIME 43
COMMUNICATIONS 45
HOTELS 48
SHOPPING 52
EATING OUT 53
MENU GUIDE 57

# INTRODUCTION

## PRONUNCIATION

When reading the imitated pronunciation, stress the part that is underlined. Pronounce each syllable as if it formed part of an English word, and you will be understood sufficiently well. Remember the points below, and your pronunciation will be even closer to the correct Danish.

| | |
|---|---|
| *ai* | as in "fair" or "stair" |
| *ī* | the "i" sound in "wine" |
| *ew* | like the sound in "dew" (or the French "u") |
| *g* | always hard as in "get" |
| *s* | as in "hiss," never as in "his" |
| *th* | as in "smooth," never as in "smith" |

## DANISH ALPHABETICAL ORDER

In the lists of *Things You'll See* and in the Menu Guide we have followed Danish alphabetical order. The following letters are listed after z: æ, ø, å.

## "YOU"

The informal word **du** *[doo]* has recently become very common, and you may even find yourself addressed with this form by total strangers. All the same, many Danes would still use the more formal **De** *[dee]* to address people they don't know – and this is the form generally given in this book. The verb stays the same whether you use **du** or **De**.

## The Definite/Indefinite Articles

The definite article ("the") in Danish is a suffix: ie **en** or **et** (or **ne** for plural) added to the end of a word. When you see translations given in the form **hus(et)** or **bil(en)**, the form **huset** will mean "the house" and **bilen** "the car." The indefinite article ("a," "an") is again **en** or **et**, but placed as a separate word *before* the noun, as in English: **et hus** ("a house"), **en bil** ("a car"). If the noun is used with an adjective, then the definite article changes to the word **den** or **det** and comes before the noun: eg **den tyske bil** ("the German car"), **det smukke hus** ("the beautiful house").

## USEFUL PHRASES

**Yes/no**
Ja/nej
*ya/nī*

**Thank you/No, thank you**
Tak/nej tak
*tak/nī tak*

**Please** *(offering)*     **Please** *(accepting something)*
Værsgo                      Ja tak
*vairsgoh*                  *ya tak*

**I don't understand (you/it)**
Jeg forstår (Dem/det) ikke
*yī forstor (dem/day) igger*

**Do you speak English/French/German?**
Taler De engelsk/fransk/tysk?
*tahlor dee engelsk/fransk/tewsk*

**I can't speak Danish**
Jeg kan ikke tale dansk
*yī ka igger tahler dansk*

**I don't know**
Det ved jeg ikke
*day vayth yī igger*

**Please speak more slowly**
Vær venlig at tale langsommere
*vair venlee or tahler langsommorer*

**Please write it down for me**
Vær venlig at skrive det ned for mig
*vair venlee or skreever day nayth for mī*

**My name is …**
Mit navn er …
*mit nown air*

**How do you do, pleased to meet you**
Goddag, det glæder mig at træffe Dem
*gohdah, day glaythor mī or treffer dem*

**Good morning/good afternoon/good evening**
Godmorgen/goddag/godaften
*gohmorn/gohdah/goh-aften*

**Good night**
Godnat
*gohnat*

**Goodbye**
Farvel
*farvel*

**How are you?**
Hvordan går det?
*vordan gor day*

**Excuse me, please** *(introducing a question)*
Undskyld
*awnskewl*

**Excuse me** *(trying to move forward)*
Tillader De?
*tillahthor dee*

**Sorry!**
Undskyld
_awnskewl_

**I'm really sorry**
Det må De meget undskylde
_day maw dee mī-et awnskewler_

**Can you help me?**
Kan De hjælpe mig?
_ka dee yelber mī_

**Can you tell me …?**
Kan De sige mig …?
_ka dee see mī_

**May I have …?**
Må jeg bede om …?
_maw yī bay om_

**I would like …**
Jeg vil gerne have …
_yī vil gairner ha_

**Would you like …?**
Ønsker De …?
_urnskor dee_

**Is there … here?**
Er der … her?
_air dair … hair_

**Where can I get …?**
Hvor kan jeg få …?
_vor ka yī faw_

**How much is it?**
Hvad koster det?
*va kostor day*

**What time is it?**
Hvad er klokken?
*va air kloggen*

**Is there wheelchair access?**
Er der adgang for korestole?
*air dair athgang for kurrer-stohler*

**Are there facilites for the disabled?**
Er der handicap faciliteter?
*air dair 'handicap' faseeleetghteh*

**Where is the US embassy?**
Hvor er den amerikanske ambassade?
*vor air den amerikanske ambasather*

**I must go now**
Jeg må afsted nu
*yi maw asteth noo*

**I've lost my way**
Jeg er faret vild
*yi air fahret veel*

**Cheers!**
Skål!
*skawl*

**Do you take credit cards?**
Tager De credit-card?
*tar dee 'credit-card'*

**Where is the restroom?**
Hvor er toilettet?
*vor air toh-ahl<u>e</u>ddet*

**Excellent!**
Fint!
*feent*

---

### THINGS YOU'LL HEAR

| | |
|---|---|
| dav | hello |
| det forstår jeg ikke | I don't understand |
| det går godt | very well, thank you |
| – og De? | – and you? |
| det ved jeg ikke | I don't know |
| farvel | goodbye |
| goddag, det glæder mig | how do you do, |
| at træffe Dem | nice to meet you |
| hvadbehager? | excuse me? |
| hvordan går det? | how are you? |
| højre | right |
| ja (det er rigtigt) | yes, that's right |
| kvinder | women |
| lige et øjeblik | just a moment |
| mænd | men |
| nej | no |
| pas på! | look out! |
| selv tak | you're welcome |
| tak | thanks |
| tillader De? | excuse me? |
| undskyld | excuse me |
| venstre | left |
| vi ses | see you later |
| virkelig? | is that so? |
| værsgo | here you are |

# DAYS, MONTHS, SEASONS

| | | |
|---|---|---|
| Sunday | søndag | _su_rnda |
| Monday | mandag | _ma_nda |
| Tuesday | tirsdag | _tee_rsda |
| Wednesday | onsdag | _aw_nsda |
| Thursday | torsdag | _to_rsda |
| Friday | fredag | _fray_da |
| Saturday | lørdag | _lu_rda |
| | | |
| January | januar | _ya_noo-_ar_ |
| February | februar | _fi_bbroo-_ar_ |
| March | marts | _ma_rts |
| April | april | _apree_l |
| May | maj | mi |
| June | juni | _yoo_nee |
| July | juli | _yoo_lee |
| August | august | _owgaw_st |
| September | september | _septe_mbor |
| October | oktober | _awkto_hber |
| November | november | _nohve_mbor |
| December | december | _disse_mbor |
| | | |
| Spring | forår | _fo_r-or |
| Summer | sommer | _so_mmor |
| Fall | efterår | _e_fter-or |
| Winter | vinter | _vi_ndor |
| | | |
| Christmas | jul | yool |
| Christmas Eve | juleaften | _yoo_ler-_a_ften |
| New Year | nytår | _new_dor |
| New Year's Eve | nytårsaften | _new_dors_a_ften |
| Easter | påske | _paw_sker |
| Pentecost | pinse | _pi_nser |

# NUMBERS

| | | | |
|---|---|---|---|
| 0 | nul *nawl* | 5 | fem *fem* |
| 1 | et *it* | 6 | seks *sex* |
| 2 | to *toh* | 7 | syv *se̲e̲oo* |
| 3 | tre *tray* | 8 | otte *a̲w̲der* |
| 4 | fire *fe̲e̲rer* | 9 | ni *nee* |

10 ti *tee*
11 elleve *e̲lver*
12 tolv *tull*
13 tretten *tre̲dden*
14 fjorten *fyo̲rden*
15 femten *fe̲mden*
16 seksten *si̲sten*
17 sytten *su̲rden*
18 atten *a̲dden*
19 nitten *ne̲dden*
20 tyve *te̲wver*
21 enogtyve *a̲ynor-te̲wver*
22 toogtyve *to̲h-or-te̲wver*
30 tredive *tre̲thver*
31 enogtredive *a̲ynor-tre̲thver*
32 toogtredive *to̲h-or-tre̲thver*
40 fyrre *fu̲r-rer*
50 halvtreds *hahl-tre̲s*
60 tres *tres*
70 halvfjerds *hahl-fya̲irs*
80 firs *feers*
90 halvfems *hahl-fe̲ms*
100 hundrede *ho̲onrerther*
110 hundredeogti *ho̲onrerther-orte̲e*
200 to hundrede *toh ho̲onrerther*
300 tre hundrede *tray ho̲onrerther*
1,000 tusind *to̲osen*
1,000,000 en million *ayn milli̲ohn*

42

# TIME

| | | |
|---|---|---|
| today | idag | *eedah* |
| yesterday | igår | *eegor* |
| tomorrow | imorgen | *eemorn* |
| the day before yesterday | i forgårs | *ee forgors* |
| the day after tomorrow | i overmorgen | *ee aw-wor-morn* |
| this week | i denne uge | *ee denner ooer* |
| last week | sidste uge | *seester ooer* |
| next week | næste uge | *nester ooer* |
| this morning | her til morgen | *hair til morn* |
| (said later in the day) | i morges | *ee mors* |
| this afternoon | i eftermiddag | *ee efdormiddah* |
| this evening | i aften | *ee aften* |
| tonight | i aften | *ee aften* |
| yesterday afternoon | igår eftermiddag | *eegor efdormiddah* |
| last night | i aftes | *ee aftes* |
| tomorrow morning | imorgen tidlig | *eemorn teethlee* |
| in three days | om tre dage | *om tray dah* |
| three days ago | for tre dage siden | *for tray dah seethen* |
| late | sent | *saynt* |
| early | tidligt | *teethleet* |
| soon | snart | *snart* |
| later on | senere | *saynerer* |
| at the moment | i øjeblikket | *ee oyerbligget* |
| second | et sekund | *sikkawnt* |
| minute | et minut | *it minnoot* |
| one minute | et minut | *it minnoot* |
| two minutes | to minutter | *toh minnooddor* |
| quarter of an hour | et kvarter | *it kvartair* |
| half an hour | en halv time | *in hahl teemer* |
| three quarters of an hour | tre kvarter | *tray kvartair* |
| hour | time | *teemer* |

| day | en dag | *dah* |
| two weeks | fjorten dage | *fyorden dah* |
| month | en måned | *mawneth* |
| year | et år | *or* |

## TELLING TIME

In everyday speech, the 12-hour clock is quite common, but the 24-hour clock is preferred for timetables, radio and television programs, and theater performances etc. Using the 12-hour system, the minutes, followed by **i** (to) or **over** (past), come before the hour, eg **fem minutter i/over seks** *(fem minnoodor ee/aw-wor sex)* is "five to/past six" (with the word **minutter** following the minute number). Using the 24-hour clock, the minute numbers (without **minutter**) follow the hour, eg "17.55" is **sytten femoghalvtreds** *(surden femmor-hahltres)*; "18.05" is **atten nul fem** *(adden nawl fem)*. To express the half hour, Danish refers ahead to the next full hour, eg "half past six" is **halv syv** *(hahl seeoo)* – literally "half seven."

| am *(until 10)* | morgen | *morn* |
| *(after 10)* | formiddag | *formiddah* |
| pm *(afternoon)* | eftermiddag | *efdormiddah* |
| *(evening)* | aften | *aften* |
| one o'clock | klokken et | *kloggen it* |
| quarter past one | et kvarter over et | *it kvartair aw-wor it* |
| half past one | halv to | *hahl toh* |
| twenty to two | tyve minutter i to | *tewver minnooddor ee toh* |
| quarter to two | et kvarter i to | *it kvartair ee toh* |
| two o'clock | klokken to | *kloggen toh* |
| 13:00 | klokken tretten | *kloggen tredden* |
| 16:30 | klokken seksten tredive | *kloggen sisten trethver* |
| at half past five | klokken halv seks | *kloggen hahl sex* |
| at seven o'clock | klokken syv | *kloggen seeoo* |
| noon | middag | *midda* |
| midnight | midnat | *meethnat* |

# COMMUNICATIONS

## USEFUL WORDS AND PHRASES

| | | |
|---|---|---|
| **code** | kaldenummer(et) | _kahler-nawmor_ |
| **dial tone** | klartone(n) | _klar-tohner_ |
| **email address** | email adresse(n) | _'email' adrasser_ |
| **emergency** | en nødsituation | _nurth-sittoo-ashohn_ |
| **directory assistance** | oplysningen | _oplewsningen_ |
| **extension** | et lokalnummer | _lohkahl-nawmor_ |
| **mobile phone** | mobiltelefon(en) | _mobeeltillerfohn_ |
| **number** | nummer(et) | _nawmor_ |
| **operator** _(repairs)_ | fejlkontor(et) | _fil-kontor_ |
| _(overseas)_ | udenrigstelefon(en) | _oothenrees-tillerfohn_ |
| **collect call** | en opringning hvor | _oprengning vor_ |
| | modtageren betaler | _mohth-tjoren betahlor_ |
| **telephone** | en telefon | _tillerfohn_ |
| **telephone booth** | en telefonboks | _tillerfohn-boks_ |
| **wrong number** | forkert nummer | _forkairt nawmor_ |

**Where is the nearest phone booth?**
Hvor er den nærmeste telefonboks?
_vor air den nairmerster tillerfohn-boks_

**How much is a call to …?**
Hvad koster en opringning til …?
_va kostor in oprengning til_

**I would like to make a collect call**
En samtale, hvor modtageren betaler, tak
_in samtahler vor mohth-tjoren betahlor tak_

**I'd like to send a fax**
Jeg vil gerne sende en fax
_yī vil gairner senner in fax_

**I would like a number in …**
Må jeg bede om et nummer i …
*maw yī bay om it nawmor ee*

**Hello, this is … speaking**
Hallo, det er …
*hahloh, day air*

**Speaking**
Det er (+ name)
*day air*

**I would like to speak to …**
Jeg vil gerne tale med …
*yī vil gairner tahler meth*

**My number is …**
Mit nummer er …
*mit nawmor air*

**Could you leave him a message?**
Kunne De give ham en besked?
*koo dee gee ham in beskayth*

**I'll call back later**
Jeg ringer igen senere
*yī reng-er iggen saynorer*

**What's your fax number/email address?**
Hvad er dit faxnummer/din email adresse?
*va air dit faxnawmor/deen email adrasser*

**May I send an email/fax from here?**
Kan jeg sende en email/fax herfra?
*ka ya senner in email/fax hairfrah*

## THINGS YOU'LL HEAR

**Hvem ønsker De at tale med?**
Whom would you like to speak to?

**Hvem taler jeg med?**
Who's speaking?

**Hvad er Deres nummer?**
What is your number?

**Han er her desværre ikke**
Sorry, he's not in

**Han kommer igen klokken …**
He'll be back at … o'clock

**Vær så venlig at ringe igen i morgen**
Please call again tomorrow

**Jeg skal sige, De ringede**
I'll tell him you called

## THINGS YOU'LL SEE

| | |
|---|---|
| **drej** | dial |
| **fejlkontoret** | repair service |
| **HJÆLP** | emergency (dial 112) |
| **læg røret** | replace the receiver |
| **mønt(er)** | coin(s) |
| **opkald** | call |
| **optaget** | busy |
| **tag røret** | lift the receiver |
| **ude af drift** | out of order |
| **udenbys-** | long-distance call |
| **udenrigs-** | international call |
| **udenrigstelefonen** | international calls service |

# HOTELS

## USEFUL WORDS AND PHRASES

| | | |
|---|---|---|
| balcony | en balkon | *balkong* |
| bathroom | et badeværelse | *bahther-vairelser* |
| bed | en seng | *seng* |
| bedroom | et værelse | *vairelser* |
| breakfast | morgenmad(en) | *mornmath* |
| check | en regning | *rining* |
| dining room | en restaurant | *restohrang* |
| dinner | en middag | *midda* |
| double room | et dobbeltværelse | *dobbelt-vairelser* |
| elevator | en elevator | *ellervahtor* |
| farmhouse | en bondegård | *bawner-gor* |
| foyer | en foyer | *foh-ah-yay* |
| full board | helpension | *haylpang-shohn* |
| half board | halvpension | *hahlpang-shohn* |
| hotel | et hotel | *hohtel* |
| key | en nøgle | *noyler* |
| lounge | opholdsstue(n) | *opholsstooer* |
| lunch | frokost(en) | *frawkost* |
| manager | direktør(en) | *direktur* |
| reception | reception(en) | *ressepshohn* |
| receptionist (*male*) | portier(en) | *porchay* |
| (*female*) | receptionist(en) | *ressepshohnist* |
| restaurant | en restaurant | *restohrang* |
| restroom | et toilet | *toh-ahlet* |
| room | et værelse | *vairelser* |
| room service | servering på værelset | *sairvairing paw vairelset* |
| shower | et brusebad | *brooser-bath* |
| single room | et enkeltværelse | *enggelt-vairelser* |
| twin room | et to-sengs værelse | *toh-sengs-vairelser* |

**Do you have any vacancies?**
Har De et ledigt værelse?
*har dee it laythit vairelser*

**I have a reservation**
Jeg har bestilt et værelse
*yī har bestilt it vairelser*

**I'd like a single/double room**
Jeg vil gerne have et enkelt/dobbelt værelse
*yī vil gairner ha it enggelt/dobbelt vairelser*

**I'd like a twin room**
Jeg vil gerne have et to-sengs værelse
*yī vil gairner ha it toh-sengs vairelser*

**I'd like a room with a bathroom/balcony**
Jeg vil gerne have et værelse med bad/balkon
*yī vil gairner ha it vairelser meth bath/balkong*

**I'd like a room for one night/three nights**
Jeg vil gerne have et værelse for en nat/tre nætter
*yī vil gairner ha it vairelser for ayn nat/tray neddor*

**What is the charge per night?**
Hvad koster det pr. nat?
*va kostor day pair nat*

**Is there satellite/cable TV in the rooms?**
Er der satellit/kabel TV på værelserne?
*air dair saddeleet/kahbel tay vay paw vairelsorne*

**I don't know yet how long I'll stay**
Jeg ved endnu ikke, hvor længe jeg bliver
*yī vayth ennoo igger vor leng-er yī bleer*

49

**When is breakfast/dinner?**
Hvornår serveres der morgenmad/middag?
*vornor sairvaires dair mornmath/midda*

**Please call me at … o'clock**
Vær venlig at vække mig klokken …
*vair venlee or vegger mī kloggen*

**May I have breakfast in my room?**
Kan jeg få morgenmad på værelset?
*ka yī faw mornmath paw vairelset*

**I'll be back at … o'clock**
Jeg vil være tilbage klokken …
*yī vil vairer tilbah-yer kloggen*

**My room number is …**
Mit værelsesnummer er …
*mit vairelses-nawmor air*

**I'm leaving tomorrow**
Jeg rejser i morgen
*yī rīsor ee morn*

**May I have the check, please?**
Må jeg bede om regningen?
*maw yī bay om rīningen*

**I'll pay cash/by credit card**
Jeg betaler kontant/med credit-card
*yī betahlor kontant/meth 'credit card'*

**Can you get me a taxi?**
Kan De skaffe mig en taxa?
*ka dee skaffer mī in taxa*

## Things You'll See

| | |
|---|---|
| bad | bath(room) |
| betjening | service |
| brandtrappe | fire escape |
| bruser/brusebad | shower |
| dobbeltværelse | double room |
| enkeltværelse | single room |
| fuldt optaget | no vacancies |
| ingen adgang | no admittance |
| kro | country inn |
| nødudgang | emergency exit |
| opholdsstue | lounge |
| oplysning | information |
| tryk/træk | push/pull |
| udgang | exit |

## Things You'll Hear

**Vi beklager, alt er optaget**
I'm sorry, we're full

**Vi har ikke flere enkeltværelser**
There are no single rooms left

**For hvor mange nætter?**
For how many nights?

**Hvad er Deres navn?**
What is your name?

**Hvordan vil De betale?**
How will you be paying?

**Betal venligst forud**
Please pay in advance

# SHOPPING

**Where is the … department?**
Hvor er … afdelingen?
*vor ai … owdayling-en*

**Do you have …?**
Har De …?
*har dee*

**How much is this?**
Hvad koster det?
*va kostor day*

**Do you have any more of these?**
Har De flere af disse her?
*har dee flairer ah disser hair*

**Where do I pay?**
Hvor er kassen?
*vor air kassen*

**Do you have anything less expensive?**
Har De noget, der er billigere?
*har dee nawth dair air beeleeyorrer*

**Could you wrap it for me?**
Vil De godt pakke det ind?
*vil dee got pagger day in*

**May I have a receipt?**
Kan jeg få en kvittering?
*ka yï faw in kvittairing*

**May I have a refund?**
Kan jeg få det refunderet?
*ka yï faw day reffoondairet*

**I'm just looking**
Jeg kigger bare
*yï keeggor bar*

# EATING OUT

Denmark has several kinds of eating establishments. There is the **restaurant** (*restohrang*), which serves a wide variety of dishes including the famous **koldt bord** (*kult bor*), or cold buffet, and **smørrebrød** (*smurrerbrurth*) or garnished open sandwiches. If you feel like **smørrebrød** ask the waiter for the **smørrebrødsseddel** (*smurrerbrurths-sethel*) – the sandwich list.

A **bodega** (*bohdayga*) is less formal and has a less ambitious menu. The **cafeteria** (*kaffertair-ya*) is similar to its American equivalent but with a larger choice of cold food and a very reasonably priced **dagens ret** (*dahns ret*), or dish of the day. Cafeterias are often found in department stores and large supermarkets.

A country restaurant or inn is called a **kro** (*kroh*) and these are much frequented by Sunday visitors wanting afternoon coffee (which can be quite an elaborate affair). Many **kroer** also have a local reputation for their **kroplatte** (*kroh-pladder*), which is an assortment of marinated herring, beautifully garnished cold meats, a small hot dish and cheese.

Danish cafés serve snacks such as quiches, patés, and sandwiches. If you have a sweet tooth, go to a **konditori** (*kondiddoree*) where you can enjoy delicious cakes, sumptuous gateaux, and mouth-watering pastries with your tea, coffee, or hot chocolate (with whipped cream, of course). Service is always included in your check.

The most common drink by far is beer or **øl** (*url*). In Denmark this normally means **pilsner** lager (*peelsnor*). A bottle of Carlsberg (*karlsbair*) and a bottle of Ceres (*saires*) are known as **en hof** (*in hof*) and **en top** (*in top*) respectively. Draft lager is called **fadøl** (*fath-url*).

Beer (or cold soft drinks), never wine, accompanies a **koldt bord**, and it is normal to enjoy one or two ice-cold **snaps** at the beginning with **sild** (*seel*), or marinated herring, and often at the end with the **ost** (*awst*), or cheese. **Snaps**, sometimes called **akvavit** (*agvaveet*) – the water of life – is a spirit made from potatoes and often flavored with caraway. There are various kinds, including the popular dark and bitter **Gammel Dansk** (*gahmel dansk*), or "Old Danish," but if you want to try the classic **snaps**, ask for **Rød Ålborg** (*rurth olbor*), or "Red Ålborg." The Danish word for "cheers" is **skål** (*skawl*). This literally means "bowl" and was what the Vikings would shout to each other whenever the need for mead came over them.

## USEFUL WORDS AND PHRASES

| beer | øl(let) | *url* |
|---|---|---|
| bottle | en flaske | *flasker* |
| bowl | en skål | *skawl* |
| cake | en kage | *kah-yer* |
| check | regning(en) | *rining* |
| chef | kok(ken) | *kok* |
| coffee | kaffe(n) | *kaffer* |
| cup | en kop | *kop* |
| fork | en gaffel | *gaffel* |
| glass | et glas | *glas* |
| knife | en kniv | *kneeoo* |
| menu | menu(en) | *menew* |
| milk | mælk(en) | *melk* |
| napkin | en serviet | *sairveeyet* |
| plate | en tallerken | *tahlairken* |
| receipt | en kvittering | *kvittairing* |
| sandwich | et stykke smørrebrød | *sturgger smurrerbrurth* |
| snack | en snack | *snak* |
| soup | suppe(n) | *sawbber* |
| spoon | en ske | *skay* |
| sugar | sukker(et) | *sawgor* |
| table | et bord | *bor* |
| tea | te(en) | *tay* |
| teaspoon | en teske | *tayskay* |
| tip | drikkepenge(ne) | *dregger-peng-er* |
| waiter | en tjener | *chaynor* |
| waitress | en servitrice | *sairveetreeser* |

| **water** | vand(et) | *van* |
| **wine** | vin(en) | *veen* |
| **wine list** | vinkort(et) | *veenkort* |

**A table for one/two, please**
Et bord til en person/to, tak
*it bor til ayn pairsohn/toh tak*

**May I see the menu/wine list?**
Må jeg se menuen/vinkortet?
*maw yi say meneween/veenkordet*

**Is there a highchair/baby changing room?**
Er der en høj stol/et puslerum?
*air dair in hoy stohl/it puwsler-rum*

**What would you recommend?**
Hvad kan De anbefale?
*va ka dee anbefahler*

**Do you do children's portions?**
Har I børneportioner?
*har ee burnerpawshohnor*

**Do you have a vegetarian menu?**
Har I en vegetarisk menu?
*har ee in veggetarisk menew*

**I'd like …**
Må jeg bede om …
*may yi bay om*

**Just a cup of coffee, please**
Kun en kop kaffe, tak
*kawn in kop kaffer tak*

**Waiter/waitress!**
Tjener/frøken!
*ch<u>ay</u>nor/fr<u>ur</u>ggen*

**May we have the check, please?**
Må vi bede om regningen, tak?
*maw vee bay om rī ningen-eng tak*

**I only want a snack**
Jeg skal bare have en snack
*yi ska bar ha in snak*

**Is there a fixed-price menu?**
Er der en fast menu?
*air dair in fast men<u>ew</u>*

**I didn't order this**
Jeg bad ikke om dette
*yi bath <u>igg</u>er om d<u>e</u>dder*

**May we have some more …?**
Må vi bede om lidt mere …?
*maw vee bay om lit mair*

**The meal was very good, thank you**
Måltidet var udmærket, tak
*m<u>o</u>lteethet var <u>oo</u>thmair-get tak*

---

**YOU MAY HEAR**

**Velbekomme!**
Enjoy your meal

---

# MENU GUIDE

**agerhøne** partridge
**agurk** cucumber
**akvavit** aquavit, a potato-based spirit
**and** duck
**ansjos** anchovy
**appelsin-** orange…
**appelsinfromage** orange mousse
**artiskokke** artichokes
**asier** pickled cucumber chunks
**asparges** asparagus
**bagt(e)** baked
**bajerske pølser** hot dogs
**benløse fugle** beef (or veal) olives
**bladselleri** celery
**blodpølse** black pudding
**blomkål** cauliflower
**blomme-** plum…
**blåmuslinger** mussels
**boller** meat and flour dumplings; buns
**bouillon** broth
**brasede kartofler** sautéed potatoes
**brisler** sweetbread
**brombær-** blackberry…
**brændende kærlighed** mashed
  potatoes with bacon and onions
**brød** bread
**butterdej** puff pastry
**bækforel** trout
**bøf** beef
**bønner** beans
**bønnespirer** bean sprouts
**børnemenu** children's menu
**champignons** mushrooms
**chokoladeis** chocolate ice cream
**citron** lemon
**citronfromage** lemon mousse
**citronvand** lemonade
**crepinetter** pork rissoles

**dagens ret** dish of the day
**dampet, dampkogt** steamed
**dansk bøf** ground beef steak
**dansk vand** mineral water
**dild** dill
**dildsild** dill herring
**dildsmør** dill butter
**drueagurk** pickle
**druer** grapes
**engelsk bøf** steak and onions
**farseret** stuffed
**fasan** pheasant
**fedt** dripping
**fersken, ferskner** peach(es)
**ferskrøget laks** smoked salmon
**figner** figs
**fisk** fish
**fiskeboller** fish ball or dumpling
**fiskefrikadeller** fish rissoles
**fjerkræ** poultry
**flæsk** belly of pork
**flæskekarbonade** ground pork steak
**fløde** cream
**flødeost** cream cheese
**fløderand** vanilla mousse
**flødeskum** whipped cream
**flødestuvet** creamed
**forel** trout
**forloren hare** meat loaf
**forretter** appetizers
**fransk bøf** steak with parsley butter
**franskbrød** white bread
**franske kartofler** potato chips
**frikadeller** pork patties
**frisk(e)** fresh(ly)
**friteret, friturestegt** deep-fried
**frokostretter** lunch dishes
**frugt(er)** fruit

**frugttærte** fruit tart or flan
**fyldt(e)** filled, stuffed
**gaffelbidder** bite-sized pieces of marinated herring fillet
**gammeldags, gammaldaws** traditional
**gammelost** very strong cheese
**gemyse** vegetables
**gravad laks** marinated salmon
**grillstegt** broiled
**grovbrød** whole-kernel rye bread
**gryderet** casserole
**græskar** pickled pumpkin or squash
**grøn salat** green salad, tossed salad
**grøn(t)sager** vegetables
**grønkål** curly kale
**grønlandske rejer** Greenland shrimp
**grønne bønner** green beans
**grønærter** green peas; creamed peas
**gule ærter med flæsk** yellow split-pea soup with belly of pork
**gulerødder** carrots
**gås** goose
**gåsesteg** roasted goose
**hachis** ground beef in gravy
**hakket, hakkede** chopped
**hamburgerryg** smoked pork loin
**haresteg** roasted hare
**hasselnødder** hazelnuts
**havregrød** porridge
**hellefisk** flounder
**helleflynder** halibut
**hindbær-** raspberry...
**hjemmebag(t)** home-baked (pastries)
**hjemmelavet** homemade
**hjerter** heart
**hornfisk** garfish
**hovedretter** main courses
**hummer-** lobster...
**hummerhaler** lobster tails
**husets** of the house
**hvide bønner** broad beans

**hvide kartofler** boiled potatoes
**hvidkål** white cabbage
**hvidkålsrulle** stuffed cabbage
**hvidkålssuppe** cabbage soup
**hvidløg** garlic
**højreb** saddle of beef
**høns** chicken
**hønsefrikassé** creamy chicken stew
**håndmadder plain** open-faced sandwiches
**hårdkogt æg** hard-boiled egg
**is** ice cream
**jomfruhummer** Norwegian crayfish
**jordbær-** strawberry...
**jordbærsyltetøj** strawberry jam
**julienne** with thin vegetable strips
**kaffe** coffee
**kage(r)** cake(s)
**kalkun** turkey
**kalv(ekød)** veal
**kalvelever** veal liver
**kalvesteg** roasted veal
**kande** pot
**kanel** cinnamon
**kanin** rabbit
**karamelrand** caramel custard
**karbonade** ground pork steak
**karse** cress
**kartoffel, kartofler** potato(es)
**kartoffelmos** mashed potatoes
**kartoffelsalat** potato salad
**kastanie-** chestnut...
**kiks** crackers, cookies
**kirsebær-** cherry...
**klipfisk** salt cod
**knækbrød** crispbread
**kogt(e)** boiled
**kold(t)** cold
**kompot** stewed fruit
**kotelet** chop
**kransekage** marzipan cake

**krydder-** savory, spicy
**kryddersild** spicy red marinated herring
**krydderurter** herbs
**krydret** spiced
**kylling** chicken
**kyllingelever** chicken liver
**kyllingelår** chicken leg
**kærnemælk** buttermilk
**kød** meat
**kødboller** meatballs, meat dumplings
**kødgratin** meat soufflé
**kødpølse** sliced pork sausage
**kødretter** meat dishes
**kål** cabbage
**labskovs** meat and potato stew
**lage** marinade
**lagkage** gâteau
**laks** salmon
**lam** lamb
**lammekoteletter** lamb chops
**lammekølle** leg of lamb
**lammeryg** saddle of lamb
**lammesteg** roasted lamb
**lever** liver
**leverpostej** pâté
**løg** onions
**løgsovs** onion sauce
**løse ris** boiled rice
**majs** corn
**makrel** mackerel
**marineret, marinerede** marinated
**medisterpølse** fried pork sausage
**melboller** flour dumplings (in broth)
**millionbøf** ground beef in gravy
**mineralvand** carbonated mineral water
**morgencomplet, morgenmad** breakfast
**muslinger** mussels
**mørbrad** fillet
**nudler** noodles
**nyrer** kidneys
**nødder** nuts

**oksefilet** fillet of beef
**oksehalesuppe** oxtail soup
**oksehøjreb** saddle of beef
**oksemørbrad** roasted sirloin
**oksesteg** roasted beef
**oksetyksteg** roasted beef
**olie** oil
**ost** cheese
**osteanretning** cheese board
**pandekager** pancakes
**paneret** coated with breadcrumbs
**peber** pepper
**peberbøf** peppered steak
**peberrod** horseradish
**pighvar** turbot
**pikant** savory, spicy, herb-flavored
**platte** cold buffet served at table
**pocheret, pocherede** poached
**porrer** leeks
**portvin** port
**purløg** chives
**pære-** pear...
**pølse(r)** sausage(s)
**radiser** radishes
**ragout** stew
**rasp** breadcrumbs
**rejer** shrimp
**ret(ter)** dish(es), course(s)
**revelsben** spare ribs
**reven(t), revne** grated
**ribbensteg** roast spare ribs
**ribsgelé** redcurrant jelly
**ris** rice
**ristet franskbrød** toast
**ristet, ristede** fried, toasted
**rogn** fish roe
**rosenkål** Brussels sprouts
**rosiner** raisins
**roulade** sponge roll; rolled-up stuffed
    slice of meat; rolled-up joint of meat
**rugbrød** rye bread

**rullepølse** sliced streaky pork sausage
**rødbeder** beets
**rødspætte** plaice
**røget** smoked
**røget makrel** smoked mackerel
**røget sild** smoked herring
**røræg** scrambled egg
**rå** raw
**råcreme** cold vanilla cream sauce
**saft** juice
**salathoved** lettuce
**selleri** celery
**sennep** mustard
**sild** herring
**sildesalat** marinated herring salad
**skaldyr** shellfish
**skinke** ham
**skipperlabskovs** meat and potato stew
**smør** butter
**smørrebrød** open sandwiches
**småkager** cookies
**solbær-** blackcurrant…
**sovs** sauce, gravy
**spegepølse** salami
**spegesild** marinated herring
**spejlæg** fried egg
**spinat-** spinach…
**spisekort** menu
**sprængt** boiled
**steg** roasted (joint)
**stegt(e)** fried, roasted
**stikkelsbær-** gooseberry…
**sukker** sugar
**suppe(r)** soup(s)
**surkål** sauerkraut
**surt** pickles
**svampe** mushrooms
**sveske-** prune…
**svine-** pork…
**svinekam** roast pork
**svinekød** pork

**svær** pork crackling
**sylte** brawn
**syltet, syltede** preserved, pickled
**syltetøj** jam
**sød(t), søde** sweet
**sød-og-sur** sweet-and-sour
**sødlig** medium-sweet
**søtunge** sole
**te, the** tea
**torsk** cod
**trøfler** truffles
**tunge** tongue, sole
**tyttebær-** cranberry…
**tærte** tart(s)
**urter** herbs
**vaffel, vafler** waffle(s)
**vagtel** quail
**valnødde-** walnut
**vand** water
**vanillecreme** custard
**vegetarretter** vegetarian dishes
**vildt** game
**vildtsovs** redcurrant sauce
**vin(e)** wine(s)
**vinbjergsnegle** snails
**vindruer** grapes
**wienerbrød** flaky Danish pastry
**wienerschnitzel** pork or veal escalope
**ymer** milk curd, junket
**æble-** apple…
**æblemost** apple juice
**æbleskiver** warm doughnuts
**æg** egg(s)
**æggekage** omelette (with bacon)
**ærter** peas
**øl** beer
**øllebrød** beer-and-bread soup
**ørred** trout
**østers** oysters
**ål** eel
**ål i gelé** jellied eel

# DUTCH

## CONTENTS

INTRODUCTION 62

USEFUL PHRASES 63

DAYS, MONTHS, SEASONS 69

NUMBERS 70

TIME 71

COMMUNICATIONS 73

HOTELS 76

SHOPPING 80

EATING OUT 81

MENU GUIDE 84

# INTRODUCTION

## Pronunciation

When reading the imitated pronunciation, stress the part that is underlined. Pronounce each syllable as if it formed part of an English word, and you will be understood sufficiently well. Remember the points below, and your pronunciation will be even closer to the correct Dutch.

| | |
|---|---|
| *CH* | represents the guttural sound of "ch" as in Scottish "loch" (*don't* pronounce this as "lock") |
| *ey* | should be as in "day" |
| *oo* | as in "book" |
| *OO* | is like the French sound "du," or similar to the "eau" in "beauty" |
| *ow* | as in "cow," *not* as in "low" |

In vocabulary lists, where a Dutch word is pronounced the same as in English, then the English word is given, in quotation marks, for the pronounciation guide.

# USEFUL PHRASES

**Yes/No**
Ja/Nee
*ya/ney*

**Thank you**
Dank u wel
*dank oo vel*

**No, thank you**
Nee, dank u
*ney, dank oo*

**Please**
Alstublieft
*alstoobl__eeft__*

**I don't understand**
Ik begrijp het niet
*ick bec__Hreyp__ et neet*

**Do you speak English/French/German?**
Spreekt u Engels/Frans/Duits?
*spreykt oo __e__ngels/frans/dowts*

**I can't speak Dutch**
Ik spreek geen Nederlands
*ick spreyk c__H__eyn n__e__derlands*

**Please speak more slowly**
Wilt u alstublieft wat langzamer spreken
*vilt oo alstoobl__eeft__ vatt l__a__ngzahmer spr__ey__keh*

**Please write it down for me**
Wilt u het alstublieft voor mij opschrijven
*vilt OO et alstoobleeft foor mey opscHreyfeh*

**Good morning/good afternoon/good night**
Goedemorgen/goedemiddag/goedenavond
*CHoodemorcHen/CHoodemiddacH/CHoodenahfont*

**Goodbye**
Tot ziens
*tot zeens*

**How are you?**
Hoe gaat het met u?
*hoo CHaht et met OO*

**Excuse me, please**
Neem me niet kwalijk, alstublieft
*neym mey neet kvalek alstoobleeft*

**Sorry!**
Sorry!
*sorry*

**I'm really sorry**
Het spijt me echt
*et speyt mey ecHt*

**Can you help me?**
Kunt u mij helpen?
*kuhnt OO mey helpeh*

**I've lost my passport/money/room key/traveler's checks**
Ik heb mÿn paspoort/geld/kamer sleutel/reischeques verloren
*Ick hep meyn paspohrtCHeld/kahmeh slurrtel/reys sjecks verlohreh*

**Can you tell me ...?**
Kunt u mij vertellen ...?
*kuhnt oo mey fertelleh*

**May I have ...?**
Mag ik ... hebben?
*mahCH ick ... hebbeh*

**I would like ...**
Ik zou graag ...
*ick zow CHrahCH*

**Is there a ... here?**
Is er hier een ...?
*iss er here en*

**Where can I get ...?**
Waar kan ik ... krijgen?
*vahr kan ick ... kreyCHeh*

**Where is the US embassy?**
Waar is de Amerikaanse ambassade?
*vahr iss de Ameyrikahnseh ambassahde*

**How much is it?**
Hoeveel is het?
*hooveyl iss et*

**Do you take credit cards?**
Accepteert u credit cards?
*acksepteert oo 'credit cards'*

**Can I pay by check?**
Kan ik met een cheque betalen?
*kan ick met en sheck betahleh*

**Where are the restrooms?**
Waar zijn de toiletten?
*vahr zeyn de tvaletteh*

**What time is it?**
Hoe laat is het?
*hoo laht iss et*

**I must go now**
Ik moet nu gaan
*ick moot noo CHahn*

**Go away!**
Ga weg!
*CHa veCH*

**Cheers!**
Proost!
*prohst*

**Is there wheelchair access?**
Waar is de ingang voor rolstoelen?
*vahr iss de <u>in</u>chang voor rolstoohleh*

**Are there facilities for the disabled?**
Zÿn er gehandicapte faciliteiten?
*zeyn er <u>CH</u>ehandikapt fahcilit<u>ey</u>teh*

**Are guide dogs allowed?**
Mogen blindengeleide honden naar binnen?
*mooCHeh blihndeh<u>CH</u>eleydeh hondeh nahr binnen?*

## THINGS YOU'LL SEE OR HEAR

| | |
|---|---|
| aan de voorkant | at the front |
| aanbellen | ring |
| aankomst | arrival |
| achter | at the back |
| attentie | attention |
| a.u.b. | please |
| beneden | at the bottom, downstairs |
| betalen | pay |
| bezet | occupied |
| binnengaan | enter |
| boven | at the top, above, upstairs |
| controle | inspection |
| dames | women |
| defect | out of order |
| dicht | shut |
| douane | customs |
| duwen | push |
| geen, geen een | none, not any |
| geopend | open |
| gereserveerd | reserved |
| gesloten | closed |
| gevaar | danger |
| gratis | free |
| heren | men |
| ingang | entry |
| kapot | out of order |
| kassa | cash register, cash desk |
| kinderen | children |
| kloppen | knock |
| langzaam | slow |
| let op de opstap/ afstap | watch your step (literally step up or down) |
| links | left |
| niet roken a.u.b. | no smoking |

| niet ... | do not ... |
|---|---|
| omkeren | to turn |
| onder | under |
| open | open |
| openingstijden | opening hours |
| paspoort | passport |
| prijs | price |
| rechts | right |
| snel | fast |
| stad | town, city |
| stop | stop |
| straat | street |
| strafbaar | punishable |
| tarief | charges, price list |
| tijd | time |
| toegang | access |
| tot | until |
| trekken | pull |
| uitgang | exit |
| vanuit, van | from, of |
| verboden | prohibited |
| verhuren | to rent |
| verkopen | to sell |
| vertrek | departure |
| voetgangers | pedestrians |
| volwassenen | adults |
| voorzichtig | be careful |

# DAYS, MONTHS, SEASONS

| | | |
|---|---|---|
| **Sunday** | zondag | *z*o*ndacH* |
| **Monday** | maandag | *m*a*hndacH* |
| **Tuesday** | dinsdag | *d*i*nsdacH* |
| **Wednesday** | woensdag | *v*oo*nsdacH* |
| **Thursday** | donderdag | *d*o*nderdacH* |
| **Friday** | vrijdag | *fr*e*ydacH* |
| **Saturday** | zaterdag | *z*a*hterdacH* |
| | | |
| **January** | januari | *yan*oo*a*ry |
| **February** | februari | *febr*oo*a*ry |
| **March** | maart | *m*a*hrt* |
| **April** | april | *ahpr*i*l* |
| **May** | mei | *mey* |
| **June** | juni | *y*oo*ni* |
| **July** | juli | *y*oo*li* |
| **August** | augustus | *owch*u*stus* |
| **September** | september | *sept*e*mber* |
| **October** | oktober | *okt*o*ber* |
| **November** | november | *nov*e*mber* |
| **December** | december | *deys*e*mber* |
| | | |
| **Spring** | lente | *l*e*nteh* |
| **Summer** | zomer | *z*o*hmer* |
| **Fall** | herfst | *h*e*rfst* |
| **Winter** | winter | *v*i*nter* |
| | | |
| **Christmas** | Kerstmis | *k*e*rstmiss* |
| **Christmas Eve** | Kerstnacht | *kerstn*a*cHt* |
| **Good Friday** | Goede Vrijdag | *cH*oo*deh freydacH* |
| **Easter** | Pasen | *p*a*hseh* |
| | | |
| **New Year** | Nieuwjaar | *n*ee*wyahr* |
| **New Year's Eve** | Oudejaarsavond | *owdehyahrs*a*hfont* |

# NUMBERS

| | | | |
|---|---|---|---|
| 0 | nul *nool* | 5 | vijf *feyf* |
| 1 | een *eyn* | 6 | zes *zess* |
| 2 | twee *tvey* | 7 | zeven *zeyveh* |
| 3 | drie *dree* | 8 | acht *aCHt* |
| 4 | vier *feer* | 9 | negen *neyCHeh* |

| | |
|---|---|
| 10 | tien *teen* |
| 11 | elf *elf* |
| 12 | twaalf *tvahlf* |
| 13 | dertien *derteen* |
| 14 | veertien *feyrteen* |
| 15 | vijftien *feyfteen* |
| 16 | zestien *zessteen* |
| 17 | zeventien *zeyvehteen* |
| 18 | achttien *aCHteen* |
| 19 | negentien *neyCHenteen* |
| 20 | twintig *tvinticH* |
| 21 | eenentwintig *eynentvinticH* |
| 22 | tweeëntwintig *tveyentvinticH* |
| 30 | dertig *derticH* |
| 40 | veertig *feyrticH* |
| 50 | vijftig *feyfticH* |
| 60 | zestig *zessticH* |
| 70 | zeventig *zeyventicH* |
| 80 | tachtig *tacHticH* |
| 90 | negentig *neyCHenticH* |
| 100 | honderd *hondert* |
| 110 | honderd tien *hondert-teen* |
| 200 | tweehonderd *tvey hondert* |
| 1000 | duizend *dowzend* |
| 1,000,000 | een miljoen *eyn milyoon* |

# TIME

| today | vandaag | *fandahcH* |
|---|---|---|
| yesterday | gisteren | *cHistereh* |
| tomorrow | morgen | *morcHeh* |
| this week | deze week | *deyzeh veyk* |
| last week | vorige week | *foricHeh veyk* |
| next week | volgende week | *folcHende veyk* |
| this morning | vanmorgen | *fanmorcHeh* |
| this afternoon | vanmiddag | *fanmiddacH* |
| this evening | vanavond | *fanahfont* |
| tonight | vanavond, vannacht | *fanahfont, fannacHt* |
| last night | gisteravond | *cHisterafont* |
| tomorrow morning | morgenochtend | *morcHeh-ocHtent* |
| tomorrow night | morgenavond | *morcHeh-ahfont* |
| in three days | over drie dagen | *ofer dree dahcHeh* |
| three days ago | drie dagen geleden | *dree dacHeh cHeleydeh* |
| late | laat | *laht* |
| early | vroeg | *froocH* |
| soon | gauw | *cHow* |
| later on | later | *lahter* |
| at the moment | op het moment | *op et moment* |
| second | een seconde | *sekondeh* |
| minute | een minuut | *minoot* |
| ten minutes | tien minuten | *teen minooteh* |
| quarter of an hour | een kwartier | *kvarteer* |
| half an hour | een half uur | *hulf oor* |
| three quarters of an hour | drie kwartier | *dree kvarteer* |
| hour | een uur | *oor* |
| day | een dag | *dacH* |
| week | een week | *veyk* |
| month | een maand | *mahnt* |
| year | een jaar | *yahr* |

## TELLING TIME

Telling the time has similarities with English. Minutes past the hour being **over** and minutes before being **voor**. Thus 6.10 is **tien over zes**, literally "ten beyond six" and 5.50 is **tien voor zes**, "ten before six." The half hour is different; it is always related to the following hour rather than the previous one, so 5.30 is **half zes**, literally "half (before) six."

You will also hear people refer to the time in relation to the half hour. 5.20 can be either **twintig over vijf** "twenty past five" or **tien voor half zes** "ten to half past five." Similarly, 5.40 can be either **twintig voor zes** "twenty to six" or **tien over half zes** "ten past half past five." The quarter hour is always **kwart voor** "quarter to" or **kwart over** "quarter past." The twenty-four hour clock is used in all public transport timetables.

| one o'clock | een uur | *eyn oor* |
|---|---|---|
| ten past one | tien over een | *teen ofer eyn* |
| quarter past one | kwart over een | *kvahrt ofer eyn* |
| twenty past one | twintig over een | *tvintich ofer eyn* |
| half past one | half twee | *hulf tvey* |
| twenty to two | twintig voor twee | *tvintich foor tvey* |
| quarter to two | kwart voor twee | *kvahrt foor tvey* |
| ten to two | tien voor twee | *teen foor tvey* |
| two o'clock | twee uur | *tvey oor* |
| 13:00 (1 pm) | dertien uur | *derteen oor* |
| 16:30/4:30 pm | zestien uur dertig | *zessteen oor dertich* |
| 20:10/8:10 pm | twintig uur tien | *tvintich oor teen* |
| at half past five | om half zes | *om half zess* |
| at seven o'clock | om zeven uur | *om zeyveh oor* |
| noon | twaalf uur's middags | *tvahlf oor smiddachs* |
| midnight | middernacht | *middernacht* |

# COMMUNICATIONS

### USEFUL WORDS AND PHRASES

| | | |
|---|---|---|
| **code** | het netnummer | *netnummer* |
| **dial tone** | de kiestoon | *keestone* |
| **email address** | het email adres | *email ahdres* |
| **emergency** | spoedgeval | *spootcHefal* |
| **directory assistance** | inlichtingen | *inlicHtingeh* |
| **extension** | het toestel | *toostell* |
| **fax machine** | de fax machine | *fax mahsjeneh* |
| **mobile phone** | de mobiele telefoon | *mobeyleh telephone* |
| **number** | het nummer | *noomer* |
| **operator** | de telefoniste | *telefone-ist* |
| **payphone** | de telefooncel | *telephonecell* |
| **collect call** | het collect call | *'collect call'* |
| **telephone** | de telefoon | *telephone* |
| **website** | de Web site | *'web site'* |
| **wrong number** | verkeerd nummer | *ferkeyrt noomer* |

**Where is the nearest phone booth?**
Waar is de dichtstbijzijnde telefooncel?
*vahr iss dey dicHtsbeyzeyndeh telephonecell*

**I would like a number in …**
Ik wil graag een nummer hebben van …
*ick vill CHrahcH en noomeh hebbeh fan*

**I would like to speak to …**
Kan ik … spreken?
*kan ick … spreykeh*

**My number is …**
Mijn nummer is …
*meyn noomeh iss*

**Could you leave him a message?**
Kunt u een boodschap voor hem achterlaten?
*kuhnt oo en bohdscHap foor hem aCHterlahteh*

**I'll call back later**
Ik bel straks wel terug
*ick bell straks vell terruCH*

**What's your fax number/email address?**
Wat is uw fax nummer/email adres?
*vhat iss oo fax nummer/email ahdres*

**May I send an email/fax from here?**
Kan ik hiervandaan een fax/email sturen?
*kan ich heervandahn en fax/email stooren*

---

THINGS YOU'LL HEAR

**Daar spreekt u mee**
Speaking

**Het spijt me, hij is er niet**
Sorry, he's not in

**Met wie spreek ik?**
Who's calling?

**Kan hij u terugbellen?**
Can he call you back?

**Met wie wilt u spreken?**
Whom do you want to speak to?

**U bent verkeerd verbonden**
You've got the wrong number

**Hij is om … terug**
He'll be back at …

---

## THINGS YOU'LL SEE

| | |
|---|---|
| antwoord apparaat | answering machine |
| brand | fire |
| brandweer | fire department |
| defect | out of order |
| email adres | email address |
| fotokopieer apparaat | photocopier |
| gesprek | call, conversation |
| gouden gids | Yellow Pages |
| haak | hook |
| in het buitenland | abroad |
| inwerpen | insert |
| interlokaal gesprek | long-distance call |
| kiesschijf | the dial (on the telephone) |
| lokaal gesprek | local call |
| lokaal | local |
| maak het kort! | be brief! |
| munt, geldstuk | coin(s) |
| mobiele telefoon | mobile telephone |
| opnemen | lift (the receiver) |
| storingsdienst | repair service |
| tarief | charges |
| telefoniste | operator |
| telefoon | telephone |
| telefoonboek | phone book |
| telefooncel | telephone booth |
| telefoon kaart | phonecard |
| telefoonnummer | number |
| tik | unit |
| wachten | wait |

# HOTELS

## Useful Words and Phrases

| balcony | het balkon | *balkon* |
|---|---|---|
| bathroom | de badkamer | *batkahmeh* |
| bed | het bed | *bet* |
| bedroom | de slaapkamer | *slahpkahmeh* |
| breakfast | het ontbijt | *ontbeyt* |
| check | de rekening | *reykening* |
| dining room | de eetkamer | *eytkahmeh* |
| double room | de tweepersoonskamer | *tveypersohnskahmeh* |
| elevator | de lift | *lift* |
| full board | volpension | *follpenshon* |
| half board | halfpension | *halfpenshon* |
| hotel | het hotel | *hotel* |
| key | de sleutel | *slurrtel* |
| lobby | de foyer | *foyeh* |
| lounge | de conversatiezaal | *konversasiesahl* |
| lunch | de lunch | *'lunch'* |
| manager | de manager, de chef | *manager, shef* |
| reception | de receptie | *resepsie* |
| receptionist | | |
|   (*female*) | de receptioniste | *resepshonisteh* |
|   (*male*) | de receptionist | *resepshonist* |
| restaurant | het restaurant | *restorant* |
| restroom | het toilet | *tvalet* |
| room | de kamer | *kahmeh* |
| room service | de roomservice | *roomservis* |
| shower | de douche | *doosh* |
| single room | de eenpersoonskamer | *eynpersohnskahmeh* |
| twin room | een kamer met twee eenpersoonsbedden | *kahmeh met tvey eynpersohnsbeddeh* |

**Do you have any vacancies?**
Hebt u een kamer vrij?
*hept OO en k<u>a</u>hmeh frey*

**I have a reservation**
Ik heb een kamer besproken
*ick hep en k<u>a</u>hmeh besprohkeh*

**I'd like a single room**
Ik wil graag een eenpersoonskamer
*ick vill CHraCH en <u>ey</u>npersohnsk<u>a</u>hmeh*

**We'd like a double room**
Wij willen graag een tweepersoonskamer
*vey v<u>i</u>lleh CHraCH en tv<u>ey</u>persohnsk<u>a</u>hmeh*

**I'd like a room with a bathroom/balcony**
Ik wil graag een kamer met bad/balkon
*ick vill CHraCH en k<u>a</u>hmeh met bat/balk<u>o</u>n*

**Is there satellite/cable TV in the rooms?**
Hebben de kamers satelliet/kabel TV?
*heppeh de k<u>a</u>hmehs sah<u>tee</u>leet/k<u>a</u>hbel tch veh*

**I'd like a room for one night/three nights**
Ik wil graag een kamer voor een nacht/drie nachten
*ick vill CHraCH en k<u>a</u>hmeh foor eyn naCHt/dree n<u>a</u>CHteh*

**What is the charge per night?**
Hoeveel is het per nacht?
*hoov<u>ey</u>l iss et per naCHt*

**I don't know yet how long I'll stay**
Ik weet nog niet hoelang ik blijf
*ick vate noCH neet hool<u>a</u>ng ick bleyf*

**When is breakfast/dinner?**
Hoe laat is het ontbijt/diner?
*hoo laht iss et ontbeyt/deeney*

**Would you have my luggage brought up?**
Wilt u mijn bagage naar boven laten brengen?
*vilt oo meyn bacHage nahr bohfeh lahteh brengeh*

**Please call me at … o'clock**
Roep me alstublieft om … uur
*roop mey alstoobleeft om … oor*

**May I have breakfast in my room?**
Kan ik in mijn kamer ontbijten?
*kan ick in meyn kahmeh ontbeyteh*

**I'll be back at … o'clock**
Ik ben om … uur terug
*ick ben om … oor terrucH*

**My room number is …**
Mijn kamernummer is …
*meyn kahmehnoomer iss*

**I'm leaving tomorrow**
Ik vertrek morgen
*ick fer-treck morcHeh*

**May I have my check, please?**
Kan ik afrekenen, alstublieft?
*kan ick afreykeneh, alstoobleeft*

**Can you get me a taxi?**
Kunt u voor mij een taxi bestellen?
*kuhnt oo foor mey en taxi bestelleh*

## THINGS YOU'LL SEE

| | |
|---|---|
| **bad** | bath |
| **bagage** | luggage |
| **begane grond** | first floor |
| **diner** | dinner |
| **douche** | shower |
| **duwen** | push |
| **kamer** | room |
| **kamers vrij** | vacancies |
| **kinderen** | children |
| **logies met ontbijt** | bed and breakfast |
| **nacht** | night |
| **nooduitgang** | emergency exit |
| **overnachting** | overnight stay |
| **reservering** | reservation |
| **toeslag** | supplement |
| **trekken** | pull |
| **verdieping** | floor, story, |
| **vol, volgeboekt** | no vacancies |

## THINGS YOU'LL HEAR

**Alle tweepersoonskamers zijn bezet**
We have no double rooms left

**Het spijt me, we zitten vol**
I'm sorry, we're full

**Verlaat uw kamer alstublieft om ...**
Please vacate the room by ...

**Wilt u alstublieft vooruit betalen**
Please pay in advance

# SHOPPING

**Where is the ...department?**
Waar is de ...-afdeling?
*vahr iss deh ...-afdeyling*

**Do you have ...?**
Hebt u ...?
*hept OO*

**How much is this?**
Hoeveel kost dit?
*hooveyl kost dit*

**Do you have any more of these?**
Hebt u er hier nog meer van?
*hept OO er here noCH meyr fan*

**Where do I pay?**
Waar moet ik afrekenen?
*vahr moot ick afreykeneh*

**Do you have something less expensive?**
Hebt u iets goedkopers?
*hept OO eets CHoodkopers*

**May I have a receipt?**
Hebt u een kassabon voor me?
*hept OO en kassabon foor meh*

**May I have a refund?**
Kan ik mijn geld terugkrijgen?
*kan ick meyn CHeld terruCH-kreyCHeh*

**I'm just looking**
Ik kijk alleen wat rond
*ick keyk alleyn vatt rond*

# EATING OUT

There is a wide selection of good-quality restaurants in Holland, to suit all tastes and price brackets. The most common types are traditional Dutch, French, Italian, Chinese, and Indonesian.

You can also eat in a cafeteria (but don't confuse this with the American variety!); it is a combined bar, café, and restaurant with service provided at the counter or – for a little extra – at the table. There is usually a good variety of set menus at reasonable prices.

Another establishment whose name could be confusing to those used to the American interpretation is the café-bar or eetcafé. Like the cafeteria, it sells all kinds of food and drink, and is well worth trying if all you want is a quick snack. Full meals are often available.

## USEFUL WORDS AND PHRASES

| | | |
|---|---|---|
| beer | het bier | 'beer' |
| bottle | de fles | fless |
| bowl | de schaal | scHahl |
| cake | het gebak | cHebak |
| check | de rekening | reykening |
| chef | de chef-kok | sheff-kok |
| coffee | de koffie | koffee |
| cup | het kopje | kop-ye |
| fork | de vork | 'fork' |
| glass | het glas | cHlass |
| knife | het mes | mess |
| menu | het menu | menoo |
| milk | de melk | melk |
| plate | het bord | bort |
| recipe | het recept | resept |
| receipt | het bonnetje | bonneht-ye |
| sandwich | de boterham | bohterham |
| napkin | het servet | serfett |

| snack | het hapje | *hap-ye* |
|---|---|---|
| soup | de soep | *'soup'* |
| spoon | de lepel | *leypel* |
| sugar | de suiker | *sowker* |
| table | de tafel | *tahfell* |
| tea | de thee | *tey* |
| teaspoon | de theelepel | *teyleypel* |
| tip | de fooi | *fohy* |
| waiter | de kelner/ober | *kelner* |
| waitress | de serveerster | *serveyrsteh* |
| water | het water | *vahter* |
| wine | de wijn | *veyn* |

**A table for one/two, please**
Een tafel voor een persoon voor/twee personen, alstublieft
*en tahfell foor eyn persohn/tvey persohneh, alstoobleeft*

**May we see the menu/wine list?**
kunnen we de kaart/de wijnkaart krijgen?
*kuhneh vey deh kahrt/deh veynkahrt kreyCHeh*

**Do you do children's portions?**
Heeft u een kindermenu?
*heyft oo en kindermenoo*

**What would you recommend?**
Wat beveelt u aan?
*vaht behfehlt oo ahn*

**I'd like …**
Ik wil graag …
*ick vill CHrahCH*

**Just a cup of coffee, please**
Alleen een kopje koffie, alstublieft
*alleyn en kop-ye koffee, alstoobleeft*

**Waiter!**
Ober!
*ober*

**May we have the check, please?**
Kunnen we afrekenen, alstublieft?
*kuhnen vey afreykeneh, alstoobleeft*

**I only want a snack**
Ik wil alleen maar een hapje eten
*ick vill alleyn mahr en hap-ye eyteh*

**Is there a fixed-price menu?**
Hebt u een menu van de dag?
*hept oo en menoo fan deh dacH*

**Do you have a vegetarian menu?**
Heeft u een vegetarisch menu?
*heyft oo en vecHetaris menoo*

**I'm allergic to nuts/shellfish**
Ik ben allergisch voor noten/schaaldieren
*ick ben allecHees foor nohten s-chahldeereh*

**I didn't order this**
Ik heb dit niet besteld
*ick hep dit neet bestelt*

**May we have some more …?**
Kunnen we nog wat … krijgen?
*kuhneh vey nocH vatt … kreycheh*

**The meal was very good, thank you**
De maaltijd was erg lekker, dank u
*deh mahlteyt vass ercH lekker, dank oo*

# MENU GUIDE

aardappelen potatoes
aardappelpuree mashed potatoes
aardbeien strawberries
abrikozenjam apricot jam
abrikozenvlaai apricot flan
amandelen almonds
ananas pineapple
andijvie endive
ansjovissen anchovies
appelcompote stewed apples
appelflap apple turnover
appelmoes apple sauce
appelsap apple juice
appeltaart applecake
artisjok artichoke
asperges asparagus
aubergine eggplant
augurken pickles
azijn vinegar
baars bass
bak-en braadvet cooking fat
balkenbrij white pudding
banaan banana
banketletter roll of puff pastry with
   almond paste filling
basilicum basil
bearnaise saus sauce hollandaise
bediening service
belegen kaas strong cheese
beschuit type of rusk
bessenjenever blackcurrant liqueur
biefstuk beef steak
biefstuk van de haas fillet steak
bier van het vat draft beer
bieslook chives
bieten beets
bijgerecht side dish
bitterballen deep fried meatballs

blauw rare
bloedworst black pudding
bloemkool cauliflower
boerenjongens brandy with raisins
boerenkaas farmhouse cheese
boerenkool Scotch kale
boerenmeisjes apricots in brandy
boerenmetworst coarse sausage
boerenomelet omelette with ham and
   potatoes
bokking (gerookte) red herring (smoked)
bokking (verse) bloater
bonensla bean salad
bosbessen bilberries
boterham met ... ... sandwich
boterham met kaas cheese sandwich
boterhamworst sliced sausage
boterletter roll of puff pastry with
   almond paste filling
bouillon consommé
braadschotel casserole
brandewijn brandy
brood bread
broodje roll
broodje kaas cheese roll
bruine bonen dried brown beans
bruine bonensoep brown bean soup
bruine suiker brown sugar
casselerrib pickled smoked rib of pork
cassis blackcurrant cordial
champignon mushroom
champignonsoep mushroom soup
Chinese kool Chinese cabbage
chocoladepasta chocolate spread
chocoladevla chocolate custard
chocomel tinned or bottled chocolate
   drink
citroen lemon

**citroenthee** lemon tea

**compote** stewed fruit

**croquetje, kroket** croquette

**dame blanche** ice cream with chocolate sauce

**doorbakken, doorbraden** well done

**doperwten** garden peas

**droog** dry

**druiven (blauwe)** grapes (black)

**druiven (witte)** grapes (white)

**Duitse biefstuk** ground beef and onion steaks served on onion rings

**Edammer** Edam cheese

**eieren** eggs

**eierkoeken** flat round sponge cakes

**erwtensoep (met spek/worst)** pea soup (with bacon/sausage)

**fazant** pheasant

**fijngehakt** finely ground

**forel** trout

**frambozen** raspberries

**frikandel** rissole

**garnalencocktail** shrimp cocktail

**gebakje** small cake

**gebakken** fried

**gebakken kip** fried chicken

**gebakken mosselen** fried mussels

**gebakken paling** fried eel

**gebakken spierling** fried smelt

**gebonden** thickened

**gebonden soep** thickened soup

**gebraden** roasted

**gebraden eend** roasted duck

**gebraden fazant** roasted pheasant

**gebraden gehakt** roasted meatloaf

**gebraden konijn** roasted rabbit

**gedistilleerde dranken** spirits

**gehakt** ground meat

**gehaktbal** ground beef and pork rissole

**gekookt** boiled

**gekookte kip** boiled chicken

**gekookte mosselen** boiled mussels

**gekruid** seasoned with herbs or spices

**gemarineerd** marinated

**gemarineerd rundvlees** marinated beef

**gember (poeder)** ginger (ground)

**gemberkoek** gingerbread

**gepocheerde eieren** poached eggs

**gerecht** dish, course

**gerookt** smoked

**gerookte paling** smoked eel

**gerookte zalm** smoked salmon

**geroosterd** broiled

**geroosterd brood** toast

**gestoofd** stewed

**gestoofd konijn** stewed rabbit

**gestoofde paling** stewed eel

**gevulde koek** pastry with almond filling

**Goudse kaas** Gouda cheese

**groene haring** lightly salted herring, first of the season

**groene/rode paprika** green/red pepper

**groenten** vegetables

**groentesoep** vegetable soup

**gulasch, goulash** goulash

**haas** hare

**hachée** finely chopped meat

**halfvolle melk** skimmed milk

**halvarine** half butter and half margarine

**ham** ham (smoked or salted)

**hamlappen** belly of pork

**haring** herring

**heilbot** halibut

**hertevlees** venison

**hete bliksem** potatoes and apples mashed together

**hollandse biefstuk** thick slice of frying steak

**hom** soft roe

**honing** honey

**honingkoek** type of gingerbread

**hutspot (met klapstuk)** mashed potatoes with carrots, onions, and breast or rib of beef
**huzarensalade** potato salad with beets, pickle, salmon, sardines, etc
**ijs** ice cream
**jachtschotel** shepherd's pie
**janhagel** kind of cookie
**jenever** Dutch gin
**jeneverbessen** juniper berries
**jonge kaas** new cheese
**jonge klare** young Dutch gin
**kaas** cheese
**kaassoesjes** cheese puff
**kabeljauw** cod
**kadetje** soft roll
**kalfslever** calf's liver
**kalfsniertjes** calf's kidneys
**kalfsoester** escalope of veal
**kalfsschnitzel** veal schnitzel
**kalfstong** calf's tongue
**kalfsvlees** veal
**kalkoen** turkey
**karbonade** chop
**karnemelk** buttermilk
**karper** carp
**kasserole** casserole
**kastanjes** chestnuts
**kerriesoep** curry soup
**kersen** cherries
**kersenvlaai** cherry flan
**kervilsoep** chervil soup
**kikkerbilletjes** frogs' legs
**kippesoep** chicken soup
**knäckebrod** crispbread
**knakworst** hot dog
**knoflook** garlic
**koekjes** cookies
**koffietafel** cold buffet lunch (usually bread, cold meats, and cheese)
**kogelbiefstuk** thick end of rump

**komijnekaas** cheese with cumin seeds
**komkommer** cucumber
**koninginnesoep** cream of chicken soup
**kool** cabbage
**koolraap** rutabaga
**korst** crust
**kotelet** cutlet
**kreeft** lobster
**kreeftesoep** lobster soup
**krenten** currants
**krentenbrood** currant loaf
**kroepoek** shrimp crackers
**kropsla** cabbage lettuce
**kruiden** herbs
**kruidenboter** herb butter
**kruisbessen** gooseberries
**kuit** hard roe
**kwark** soft white cheese
**kwarktaart** cheesecake
**kwast** lemon drink
**lamskotelet** lamb cutlet, lamb chop
**lamsragout** lamb stew
**landwijn** simple wine, vin ordinaire
**laurierblad** bayleaf
**lekkerbekjes** deep-fried whiting fillets
**leverworst** liver sausage
**Limburgse vlaai** open fruit flan
**limonade** lemonade
**linzen** lentils
**loempia** spring roll (Indonesian)
**magere kaas** skimmed-milk cheese
**magere melk** skimmed milk
**makreel** mackerel
**marsepein** marzipan
**melk** milk
**mierik** horseradish
**moesappelen** cooking apples
**mosselen** mussels
**mosselensoep** mussel soup
**mosterd** mustard
**munt** mint

**nagerecht** dessert
**nasi goreng** Indonesian fried rice dish with meats and vegetables
**nieren** kidneys
**nieuwe haring** salted herring
**nootmuskaat** nutmeg
**oesters** oysters
**oliebol** doughnut
**olijfolie** olive oil
**olijven** olives
**omelet** omelette
**ontbijtkoek** type of gingerbread
**ontbijtspek** (lean, smoked) bacon
**ossestaart** oxtail
**ossestaartsoep** oxtail soup
**oude kaas** strong cheese
**paling** eel
**palingworst** type of sausage
**paneermeel** breadcrumbs
**pannekoek** pancake
**patates frites** french fries
**patrijs** partridge
**peper** pepper
**perenmoes** puréed pears
**perziken** peaches
**peterselie** parsley
**piccalilly** pickles
**pikant** piquant
**pils** type of lager
**pindakaas** peanut butter
**pocheren** to poach
**pommes frites** french fries
**pompelmoes** grapefruit
**pompelmoessap** grapefruit juice
**pompoen** pumpkin
**prei** leek
**preisoep** leek soup
**pruimedant** type of prune
**pruimen** plums
**pruimenjam** plum jam
**rabarber** rhubarb

**radijs** radish
**ree/reebok** roe/roebuck
**reebout** leg of venison
**regenboogforel** rainbow trout
**rijst** rice
**rijstebrij** rice pudding
**rijstevlaai** rice tart
**rivierkreeft** crayfish
**riviervis** freshwater fish
**rode kool** red cabbage
**rode wijn** red wine
**roerei** scrambled eggs
**roggebrood** ryebread
**rookworst** smoked sausage
**room** cream
**roomboter** dairy butter
**roomijs** ice cream
**rosbief** roasted beef
**rozijnen** currants
**rundervlees** beef
**Russisch ei** egg salad
**sardientjes** sardines
**saucijzenbroodje** sausage roll
**saus** sauce
**savooiekool** savoy cabbage
**schartong** lemon sole
**schelvis** haddock
**schnitzel** veal cutlet
**schol** plaice
**schuimpje** meringue
**selderij** celery
**sinaasappel** orange
**sinaasappelsap** orange juice
**slaatje** salad
**slagroom** whipped cream
**slakken** snails
**slaolie** salad oil
**slasaus** salad cream
**slavinken** ground pork rolled in bacon
**smeerkaas** cheese spread

**snijbonen** string beans
**snoekbaars** perch
**soep van de dag** soup of the day
**spa water** mineral water
**specerijen** spices
**speculaas** spiced cookie
**spek** bacon, usually rather fatty
**sperziebonen** French beans
**spiegelei** fried egg
**spiering** smelt
**spijskaart** menu
**spinazie** spinach
**spirituosa** spirits
**spruiten, spruitjes** Brussels sprouts
**stokbrood** French loaf
**stokvis** stockfish
**stoofperen** stewing pears
**stroopwafel** waffle with syrup filling
**taart** cake
**tarwebrood** wheaten bread
**tomatensoep** tomato soup
**tong** sole
**tongrolletjes** rolled fillets of sole
**tonijn** tuna
**tosti/toastie** toasted sandwich
**tuinbonen** broad beans
**uien** onions
**uiensoep** onion soup
**uitgebreide koffietafel** buffet lunch
  with soup and dessert
**vanillevla** custard sauce
**varkensbiefstuk** pork fillet
**varkenshaas** pork fillet
**varkensoester** pork escalope
**varkenspoot** leg of pork
**varkensrib pickled** smoked rib of
  pork
**varkensrollade** rib, tailend (rolled)
**varkensvlees** pork
**venkel** fennel
**vermout** vermouth

**verse haring** fresh herring
**verse oesters** fresh oysters
**verse worst** sausage
**vet** fat
**vis** fish
**vissoep** fish soup
**vleet** skate
**vlierbessen** elderberries
**volkorenbrood** wholemeal bread
**voorgerecht** starter
**voorn** roach
**vruchten** fruit
**vruchtensap** fruit juice
**vruchtensla** fruit salad
**wafel** waffle, wafer
**walnoot** walnut
**waterkers** watercress
**wijn** wine
**wijting** whiting
**witte bonen** dried white beans
**wittebrood** white bread
**wittekool** white cabbage
**witte wijn** white wine
**wortel** carrot
**zalm** salmon
**zalmslaatje** salmon salad
**zeepaling** sea-eel
**zeetong** Dover sole
**zilveruitjes** pickled silverskin onions
**zoet** sweet
**zoetwatervis** freshwater fish
**zoet-zuur** sweet-sour
**zout** salt
**zoute haring** salted herring
**zoutjes** salty/savory meatballs
**zult** brawn
**zure haring** pickled herring
**zwarte bessen** blackcurrants
**zwarte bessenjam** blackcurrant jam
**zwarte kersenjam** black cherry jam
**zwezerik** sweetbread

# FINNISH

## CONTENTS

| | |
|---|---|
| INTRODUCTION | 90 |
| USEFUL PHRASES | 91 |
| DAYS, MONTHS, SEASONS | 97 |
| NUMBERS | 98 |
| TIME | 99 |
| COMMUNICATIONS | 101 |
| HOTELS | 104 |
| SHOPPING | 108 |
| EATING OUT | 109 |
| MENU GUIDE | 113 |

# INTRODUCTION

## PRONUNCIATION

When reading the imitated pronunciation, the first syllable of each word is underlined and should be stressed. Try to pronounce each syllable clearly. The intonation is flat without extremes. The following sounds need special attention:

| Letter | Approximate Pron. | Symbol | Example |
|--------|-------------------|--------|---------|
| *Consonants* | | | |
| h | as in "hot" whatever its position in the word | h | lahti _lah_hti |
| j | like "y" as in "you" | y | ja *yah* |
| r | always rolled | r | raha _rah_hah |
| s | "s" as in "set" | s | sillä _sil_la |
| ng | pronounced as in "singer" | ng | sangen _sahn_gayn |
| *Vowels* | | | |
| a/aa | like "a" as in "car" | ah | matala _mah_tahlah |
| e | like "ay" as in "lay" | ay | kolme _koal_may |
| i | like "i" as in "pin" | i | takki _tah_kki |
| ii | "ee" as in "see" | ee | siitä _see_ta |
| o/oo | "a" sound between "aw" in "law" and "oa" in "coat" | oa | olla _oal_lah |
| u/uu | like "oo" as in "pool" | oo | hupsu _hoop_soo |
| y/yy | like "u" in French "sur" or "ü" in German "über" | ew | yksi _ewk_si |
| ä/ää | like "a" as in "hat" | a | äkkiä _ak_kia |
| ö/öö | like "ur" as in "fur," but without any "r" sound | ur | tyttö _tewt_tur |

When a double consonant appears in the original Finnish word, try to make sure that the letter is clearly pronounced twice.

## FINNISH ALPHABETICAL ORDER

In the lists of *Things You'll See* and in the Menu Guide we have followed Finnish alphabetical order. The following letters are listed after z: å, ä, ö.

# USEFUL PHRASES

### Yes, No, OK, etc.

**Yes/No**
Kyllä/Ei
_kew_lla/_ay_

**OK**
Selvä
_say_lva

**That's fine**
Hyvä on
_hew_va on

**That's right**
Aivan niin
_ah_vahn neen

### Greetings, Introductions

**How do you do, pleased to meet you**
Päivää, hauska tutustua
_pah_vah _haoo_skah _too_toostooah

**Good morning**
Huomenta
_hooa_mentah

**Good evening/good night**
Iltaa/Hyvää yötä
_el_taah/_hewaah ewur_tah

**Goodbye**
Näkemiin
_na_kaymeen

**How are you?**
Mitä kuuluu?
_mitta koo_loo

**My name is**
Nimeni on
_nim_mayni on

**What's your name?**
Mikä teidän nimenne on?
_mik_ka _tay_dan _nim_maynnay on

_(familiar form)_
Mikä sinun nimesi on?
_mik_ka _sen_noon _nim_maysi on

**This is …**
Tämä on …
_tam_ma on

**Hello/Hi!**
Terve/ Hei!
_tay_rvay/hey

## PLEASE, THANK YOU, APOLOGIES

**Thank you/No, thank you**
Kiitos/Ei kiitos
_kee_toss/ay _kee_toss

**Please**
Olkaa/Ole hyvä
_oal_kaa/_oal_ay _hew_vah

**Excuse me!/Sorry!**
Anteeksi!
_ahn_tayksi

## WHERE, HOW, ASKING

**Excuse me, please**
Anteeksi
_ahn_tayksi

**Can you tell me …?**
Voitteko sanoa minulle …?
_voat_teaykoa _sah_noah _min_noollay

**May I have …?**
Voinko saada …?
_voan_koa _saa_dah

**Would you like a …?**
Haluaisitteko …?
_hahloo_ahsittekoa

**Would you like to …?**
Haluaisitteko …?
_hahloo_ahsittekoa

**What's that?**
Mitä se on?
_mit_ta say on

**How much is it?**
Paljonko se on?
_pahl_yoankoa say on

**Where is the …?**
Missä on …?
_mis_sa on

**Is there wheelchair access?**
Voiko sinne mennä rullatuolissa oleva henkilö?
_voa_koa _sin_nay _mayn_nah _rool_laot_ooo_alissah _oal_ayvah _hayn_kiloe

**Are guide dogs allowed?**
Onko opaskoirilla pääsy sinne?
_oan_koa _oap_ahs_koa_rillah _paa_sew _sin_nay

ABOUT ONESELF

**I'm from …**
Olen … sta/lta
_oal_ayn … stah/ltah

**I'm … years old**
Olen … vuotta vanha
_oal_ayn … _vooat_tah _vaon_hah

93

I'm a …
Olen …
*oalayn*

**I'm married/single/divorced**
Olen naimisissa/naimaton/eronnut
*oalayn naoimisissah/naoimahtoan/ayroannoot*

**I have … sisters/brothers/children**
Minulla on … sisaria/veljiä/lapsia
*minnoollah on … sissahrriah/vayllyeea/lapseea*

### HELP, PROBLEMS

**Can you help me?**
Voitteko auttaa minua?
*voattaykoa ahoottaa minnooah*

**I don't understand**
En ymmärrä
*ayn ewmmarrah*

**Does anyone here speak English?**
Puhuuko joku täällä englantia?
*poohookoa yokoo taalla aynglahntiah*

**I can't speak Finnish**
En puhu suomea
*ayn poohoo sooamayah*

**I don't know**
En tiedä
*ayn tiayda*

**Please speak more slowly**
Puhukaa hitaammin olkaa hyvä?
*poohookaa hihtaammin oalkaa hewva*

**Please write it down for me**
Voisitteko kirjoittaa sen minulle?
*voasittaykoa keeryoattaa sayn minnoollay*

**I've lost my way**
Olen eksynyt
*oalayn eksewnewt*

**Go away!**
Menkää pois!
*maynkaa poais*

## LIKES, DISLIKES, SOCIALIZING

**I like/love …**
Pidän/Rakastan …
*pidan/rahkahstahn*

**I don't like …**
En pidä …
*ayn pida*

**I hate…**
Vihaan …
*veehaan*

**Do you like …?**
Pidätkö …?
*peedatkur*

**It's delicious/awful!**
Se on herkullista/kauheaa!
*say on hayrkoollistah/kaoohayah*

**I don't drink/smoke**
En juo/polta
*ayn yooah/poaltah*

**Do you mind if I smoke?**
Pahastutteko jos poltan?
*paohaostoottaykoa yoas poaltahn*

**What would you like to drink?**
Mitä haluaisitte juoda?
*mitta haolooasittay yooahdah*

**I would like a …**
Haluaisin …
*hahlooahsin*

**Nothing for me, thanks**
Kiitos, ei mitään minulle
*keetoss, ay mittaan minnoollay*

**Cheers!** *(toast)*
Kippis/Skål!
*kippiss/skoal*

---

### THINGS YOU'LL HEAR

| | |
|---|---|
| anteeksi | excuse me |
| anteeksi? | excuse me? |
| ei kestä | don't mention it |
| hei/terve | hello |
| henkilöllisyystodistus, olkaa hyvä | identification papers, please |
| hyvä | fine |
| hyvää matkaa! | have a good trip! |
| hyvästi | goodbye |
| mitä sanoitte? | what did you say? |
| näkemiin | see you later |
| niinkö? | is that right? |
| olkaa hyvä | here you are |
| ottakaa itse | help yourself |
| selvä | right! OK! |
| tulkaa sisään | come in |
| varo! | look out! |

---

# DAYS, MONTHS, SEASONS

| | | |
|---|---|---|
| Sunday | sunnuntai | _soonnoontah_ |
| Monday | maanantai | _maanahntah_ |
| Tuesday | tiistai | _teestah_ |
| Wednesday | keskiviikko | _kayskiveekkoa_ |
| Thursday | torstai | _toarstah_ |
| Friday | perjantai | _payryahntah_ |
| Saturday | lauantai | _lahoontah_ |
| | | |
| January | tammikuu | _tahmmikkoo_ |
| February | helmikuu | _haylmikoo_ |
| March | maaliskuu | _maalisskoo_ |
| April | huhtikuu | _hoohtikkoo_ |
| May | toukokuu | _toaookoakoo_ |
| June | kesäkuu | _kayssakoo_ |
| July | heinäkuu | _haynakoo_ |
| August | elokuu | _ayloakoo_ |
| September | syyskuu | _sewskoo_ |
| October | lokakuu | _loakahkoo_ |
| November | marraskuu | _mahrrahskoo_ |
| December | joulukuu | _yoaoolookoo_ |
| | | |
| Spring | kevät | _kayvat_ |
| Summer | kesä | _kayssa_ |
| Fall | syksy | _sewksew_ |
| Winter | talvi | _tahlvi_ |
| | | |
| Christmas | joulu | _yoaooloo_ |
| Christmas Eve | jouluaatto | _yoaooloo-aahttoa_ |
| Good Friday | pitkäperjantai | _pitkapayryahntah_ |
| Easter | pääsiäinen | _paassiaynen_ |
| New Year | uusi vuosi | _ooossi vooassi_ |
| New Year's Eve | uuden vuoden aatto | _ooodayn vooaden aahttoa_ |
| Pentecost | helluntai | _haylloontah_ |

# NUMBERS

| | | | |
|---|---|---|---|
| 0 | nolla _noallah_ | 6 | kuusi _koossi_ |
| 1 | yksi _ewksi_ | 7 | seitsemän _saytsayman_ |
| 2 | kaksi _kahksi_ | 8 | kahdeksan _kahdayksahn_ |
| 3 | kolme _koalmay_ | 9 | yhdeksän _ewhdayksan_ |
| 4 | neljä _naylya_ | 10 | kymmenen _kewmmaynayn_ |
| 5 | viisi _veessi_ | | |

11 yksitoista _ewksitoastah_
12 kaksitoista _kahksitoastah_
13 kolmetoista _koalmaytoastah_
14 neljätoista _naylyatoastah_
15 viisitoista _veessitoastah_
16 kuusitoista _koossitoastah_
17 seitsemäntoista _saytsaymantoastah_
18 kahdeksantoista _kahdayksahntoastah_
19 yhdeksäntoista _ewhdayksantoastah_

20 kaksikymmentä _kahksikewmmaynta_
21 kaksikymmentäyksi _kahksikewmmayntawksi_
22 kaksikymmentäkaksi _kahksikewmmayntakahksi_
30 kolmekymmentä _koalmaykewmmaynta_
40 neljäkymmentä _naylyakewmmaynta_
50 viisikymmentä _veessikewmmaynta_
60 kuusikymmentä _koossikewmmaynta_
70 seitsemänkymmentä _saytsaymankewmmaynta_
80 kahdeksankymmentä _kahdayksahnkewmmaynta_
90 yhdeksänkymmentä _ewhdayksankewmmaynta_
100 sata _sahtah_
110 satakymmenen _sahtahkewmmaynayn_
200 kaksisataa _kahksisahtaah_
1,000 tuhat _toohaht_
10,000 kymmenentuhatta _kewmmaynayntoohattah_
20,000 kaksikymmentätuhatta _kahksikewmmayntatoohattah_
100,000 satatuhatta _sahtahtoohattah_
1,000,000 miljoona _milyoanah_

# TIME

| today | tänään | _tanan_ |
| yesterday | eilen | _aylayn_ |
| tomorrow | huomenna | _hooaomaynnah_ |
| this week | tällä viikolla | _talla veekoallah_ |
| last week | viime viikolla | _veemay veekoallah_ |
| next week | ensi viikolla | _aynsi veekoallah_ |
| this morning | tänä aamuna | _tanna aahmoonnah_ |
| this afternoon | tänä iltapäivänä | _tanna iltahpayvana_ |
| this evening/ | tänä iltana/ | _tanna iltahnnah/_ |
| tonight | yönä | _ewurna_ |
| in three days | kolmen päivän kuluttua | _koalmayn payvan kooloottooah_ |
| three days ago | kolme päivää sitten | _koalmay payvaa sittayn_ |
| late | myöhään | _mewrhaan_ |
| early | aikaisin | _ahikahisin_ |
| soon | pian | _peeahn_ |
| later on | myöhemmin | _myerhammin_ |
| at the moment | tällä hetkellä | _talla haytkaylla_ |
| second | sekunti | _saykoontti_ |
| minute | minuutti | _minnootti_ |
| ten minutes | kymmenen minuuttia | _kewmmaynayn minnoottiah_ |
| quarter of an hour | neljännes tuntia | _nayljannays toontiah_ |
| half an hour | puoli tuntia | _pooahli toontiah_ |
| hour | tunti | _toonti_ |
| day | päivä | _paiva_ |
| every day | joka päivä | _yoakah paiva_ |
| all day | koko päivän | _koakoa paivan_ |
| week | viikko | _veekkoa_ |
| two weeks | kaksi viikkoa | _kahksi veekkoah_ |
| month | kuukausi | _kookahoosi_ |
| year | vuosi | _vooahsi_ |

## TELLING TIME

The 24-hour clock is always used in the written form in
timetables and for appointments, and also verbally in enquiry
offices and if talking about the times of television and radio
programs. However, in most other situations, people will use
the 12-hour clock.

"What time is it?" is **Mitä kello on?**. "O'clock" is translated
as **kello**. "(It's) one (o'clock)" is (**Kello on**) **yksi**; "(It's) four
(o'clock)" is (**Kello on**) **neljä** and so on. Note that the half
hour (**puoli**) refers forward to the next hour, so "half past five"
is **puoli kuusi**, literally "half (to) six."

To express minutes after the hour, state the number of
minutes followed by **yli** (past) and the hour. For example, "ten
past five" is **kymmentä yli viisi**. For minutes to the hour use
**vaille**, which means "toward." For example, "twenty to eleven"
is **kaksikymmentä vaille yksitoista**.

"Quarter" is **neljännes**, so "quarter past three" is **neljännestä
yli kolme**, and "quarter to eight" is **neljännestä vaille
kahdeksan**.

| | | |
|---|---|---|
| **one o'clock** | kello yksi | _kaylloa_ _ewk_si |
| **ten past one** | kymmentä yli yksi | _kewm_maynta _ewli_ _ewk_si |
| **quarter past one** | neljännestä yli yksi | _nayl_yannaysta _ewli_ _ewk_si |
| **twenty past two** | kaksikymmentä yli kaksi | _kahk_si_kewm_maynta _ewli_ _kahk_si |
| **1:30** | yksi kolmekymmentä | _ewk_si _koal_may_kewm_maynta |
| **twenty to two** | kaksikymmentä vaille kaksi | _kahk_si_kewm_maynta _vahillay_ _kahk_si |
| **quarter to two** | neljännestä vaille kaksi | _nayl_yannaysta _vahillay_ _kahk_si |
| **two o'clock** | kello kaksi | _kaylloa_ _kahk_si |
| **midday** | keskipäivä | _kayskipaiva_ |
| **midnight** | keskiyö | _kayskiewur_ |

# COMMUNICATIONS

## Useful Words and Phrases

| | | |
|---|---|---|
| **code** | koodi | _koaoa_di |
| **collect call** | vastapuhelu | _vahstahpoo_hayloo |
| **dial tone** | soittoääni | _soattoaah_ni |
| **directory assistance** | tiedusteluja | _tiay_doostaylooyah |
| **email address** | sähköpostiosoite | _sahkoepoastiossoatay_ |
| **emergency** | hätätilanne | _hatatillah_nnay |
| **extension** | posti, alanumero | _poasti, ahlahnoo_mayroa |
| **fax machine** | faksi | _fahk_si |
| **internet** | internet | _internet_ |
| **mobile phone** | kännykkä | _kannewk_ka |
| **number** | numero | _noom_mayroa |
| **operator** | operaattori | _oapay_raattoari |
| **phonecard** | puhelinkortti | _poohaylinkoart_ti |
| **telephone** | puhelin | _poohay_lin |
| **telephone booth** | puhelinkioski | _poohaylinkioas_ki |
| **website** | web-sivusto | web-_sivoostoa_ |
| **wrong number** | väärä numero | _vaa_ra _noo_mmayroa |

**Where is the nearest phone booth?**
Missä on lähin puhelinkioski?
_missa on lahin poohaylinkioaski_

**I would like a number in …**
Haluaisin numeron … ssa/lla
_hahlooahsin noommayroan … ssah/llah_

**I would like to speak to …**
Haluaisin puhua … kanssa
_hahlooahsin puuhooah … kahnssah_

**My number is …**
Numeroni on …
_noommayroani on_

**Could you leave him/her a message?**
Voisitteko jättää hänelle sanoman?
_voy_sittaykoa _jatta_ _ha_nayllay _sah_noamahn

**I'll call back later**
Soitan myöhemmin uudestaan
_soa_tahn _mewur_haymmin _oo_daystaan

**What's your fax number/email address?**
Mikä on teidän faksinumero/sähköpostiosoite?
_mikka_ on _tay_dan _fahk_si_noom_mayroh/_sah_koe_poas_ti_oa_soytay

**May I send an email/fax from here?**
Voinko lähettää täältä sähköpostia?
_voyn_koa _la_hayttaa _taa_lta _sah_koe_poas_tiah

---

## EMERGENCIES

| accident | onnettomuus | _oann_aytto_amoos_ |
|---|---|---|
| ambulance | ambulanssi | _ahm_boolahnssi |
| breakdown | epäkunto | _ay_pak_koon_toah |
| burglary | murtovarkaus | _moor_toa_vahr_kahoos |
| crash | yhteenajo | _ewh_tayn_ah_yoa |
| emergency | hätätilanne | _hata_ti_llahnnay |
| fire | tulipalo | _tooll_ipahloa |
| fire department | palokunta | _pah_loak_koon_tah |
| police | poliisi | _poa_leessi |
| police station | poliisiasema | _poh_leessi_ah_saymah |

**Help!**
Apua!
_ahpooah_

**Stop!**
Pysähdy!/Pysähdyttäkää!
_pewr_sahdew/_pewr_sahdewttakaa

**Get an ambulance!**
Kutsukaa ambulanssi!
_koot_sookaa _ahm_boolahnssi

**Hurry up!**
Kiirehtikää!
_keer_ayhtikaa

**My address is …**
Osoitteeni on …
_oas_oattayni on

**My passport/car has been stolen**
Passini/ autoni on varastettu
_pah_ssihni/_aoo_toani on _vah_rahstayttoo

# HOTELS

## Useful Words and Phrases

| | | |
|---|---|---|
| balcony | parveke | *pahr*vaykay |
| bathroom | kylpyhuone | *kewlpewhooa*nay |
| bed | vuode | *vooa*day |
| bed & breakfast | huone aamiaisella | *hooa*nay *aa*miahssayllah |
| breakfast | aamiainen | *aa*miahinayn |
| car park | parkkipaikka | *pahrkkipa*hikkah |
| check | lasku | *lahs*koo |
| dining room | ruokasali | *rooa*kah*sah*li |
| dinner | päivällinen | *pa*ivallinnayn |
| double room | kahden hengen huone | *kah*dayn *hayn*gayn *hooa*nay |
| elevator | hissi | *his*si |
| full board | täysihoito | *tawurs*i*hoah*toa |
| guesthouse | täysihoitola | *tawurs*i*hoah*toalah |
| half board | puolihoito | *pooa*li*hoa*toa |
| hotel | hotelli | *hoa*taylli |
| key | avain | *ah*vahin |
| lunch | lounas | *loaoo*nahss |
| maid | siivooja | *see*voahyah |
| manager | johtaja | *yohh*tahyah |
| receipt | kuitti | *koo*itti |
| reception | vastaanotto | *vahs*taan*notto*a |
| receptionist | vastaanottoapulainen | *vahs*taamn*otto*a-poollahinayn |
| restroom | toiletti | *toa*laytti |
| room | huone | *hooa*nay |
| room service | huonepalvelu | *hooa*nay*pahl*vayloo |
| shower | suihku | *sooihk*oo |
| single room | yhden hengen huone | *ewh*dayn *hayn*gayn *hooa*nay |
| twin room | kaksi eri vuodetta | *kahk*si *ay*ri *vooa*dayttah |

**Do you have any vacancies?**
Onko teillä vapaita huoneita?
_oan_koa _tay_lla _vah_paotah _hooa_naytah

**I have a reservation**
Minulla on varaus
_min_noollah on _vah_rahoos

**I'd like a single room**
Haluaisin yhden hengen huoneen
_hah_looahsin _ewh_dayn _hayn_gayn _hooa_nayn

**I'd like a room with a bathroom/balcony**
Haluaisin huoneen jossa on kylpyhuone/parveke
_hah_looahsin _hooa_nayn _yoas_sah on  _kewl_pew_hooa_nay/_pahr_vaykay

**Is there satellite/cable TV in the rooms?**
Onko huoneissa satelliitti/kaapeli-teeveetä?
_oan_koa _hooa_nayssah _saht_aylleetti/_kaah_paylli-_tay_vayta

**I'd like a room for one night/three nights**
Haluaisin huoneen yhdeksi/kolmeksi yöksi
_hah_looahsin _hooa_nayn _ewh_dayksi/_koal_mayksi _ewurk_si

**What is the charge per night?**
Mitä maksaa yksi yö?
_mit_ta _mahk_saah _ewk_si ewur

**When is breakfast/dinner?**
Koska on aamiainen/päivällinen?
_koas_kah on _aa_miahnayn/ _pai_vallinnayn

**Please wake/call me at one o'clock**
Herättäkää minut kello yksi
_hay_rattakaa _min_noot _kayll_oa _ewk_si

**May I have breakfast in my room?**
Voinko saada aamiaisen huoneeseeni?
_voan_koa _saa_dah _aa_miahssayn _hooa_naysayni

**My room number is …**
Huoneeni numero on …
*hooanayni noommayroa on*

**There is no toilet paper in the bathroom**
Kylpyhuoneessa ei ole toilettipaperia
*kewlpewhooanayssah ay oalay toalayttipahpayriah*

**The window won't open**
Ikkuna ei avaudu
*ikkoonah ay ahvaoodoo*

**There isn't any hot water**
Ei ole kuumaa vettä
*ay oalay koomaa vaytta*

**I'm leaving tomorrow**
Lähden huomenna
*lahhdayn hooamaynnah*

**When do I have to vacate the room?**
Koska minun on luovutettava huone?
*koaskah minnoon on looavootayttahvah hooanay*

**May I have the check, please?**
Saisinko laskuni?
*saosinkoa lahskooni*

**I'll pay by credit card**
maksan luottokortilla
*mahksahn looattoakoartillah*

**I'll pay cash**
Maksan käteisellä
*mahksahn kataysaylla*

**Can you get me a taxi?**
Voitteko hankkia minulle taksin?
*voattaykoa hahnkkiah minnoollay tahksin*

## THINGS YOU'LL SEE

| | |
|---|---|
| **aamiainen** | breakfast |
| **hissi** | elevator |
| **hätäuloskäytävä** | emergency exit |
| **kylpyhuone** | bathroom |
| **lasku** | check |
| **lounas** | lunch |
| **portaat** | stairs |
| **pääsy kielletty** | no admission |
| **sisäänkäynti** | entrance |
| **suihku** | shower |
| **työnnä** | push |
| **täynnä** | no vacancies |
| **vedä** | pull |

## THINGS YOU'LL HEAR

**Valitan, mutta hotelli täynnä**
I'm sorry, we're full

**Ei ole enää kahden/yhden hengen huoneita jäljellä**
There are no double/single rooms left

**Kuinka moneksi yöksi?**
For how many nights?

**Kuinka maksatte?**
How will you be paying?

**Voitteko maksaa etukäteen**
Please pay in advance

**Huone on luovutettava puoleen päivään mennessä**
You must vacate the room by noon

# SHOPPING

**Excuse me, where is/are …?**
Anteeksi, missä on …?
_ahn_tayhksi, _mi_ssa on

**Do you have …?**
Onko teillä…?
_oan_koa _tayl_la …

**How much is this?**
Paljonko tämä maksaa?
_pahl_yoankoa _ta_ma _mahk_saa

**Where do I pay?**
Missä voin maksaa?
_mi_ssa voan _mahk_saa

**Do you take credit cards?**
Hyväksyttekö luottokortteja?
_hew_vaksewttaykur _looat_toa_koart_tayjah

**May I have a receipt?**
Voinko saada kuitin?
_voan_koa _saa_dah _kooi_tin

**Do you have anything less expensive?**
Onko teillä mitään halvempaa?
_oan_koa _tayl_la _mit_tan _hahl_vaympaa

**May I have a refund?**
Voinko saada hyvityksen?
_voan_koa _saa_dah _hew_vitewksayn

**That's fine. I'll take it**
Se on hyvä. Otan sen
say on _hew_va. _oat_ahn sayn

**It isn't what I wanted**
Se ei ole mitä haluan
say ay _oal_ay _mit_ta _hah_looahn

# EATING OUT

It is not difficult to eat well and fairly inexpensively in Finland. Menus are often displayed on the window or door of an eating establishment, so you can readily fit your choice of restaurant to your budget. It is not customary to leave a tip for the waiter or waitress, but if you are especially pleased with the service, you may leave some small change or something more substantial. Note that the same tipping guidelines apply to taxi drivers, barbers, and hairdressers.

Every town has a number of cafés, often called **kahvila** or **baari**, where, at lunchtime, you can order an open sandwich, consisting of white or rye bread with a cheese, ham, or egg topping, plus a salad garnish, various pasties filled with minced meat, chopped salmon, rice and eggs, etc. Do not forget to taste the delicious pastries, such as the Finnish equivalent of Danish pastries, which are called **viineri** ("Viennese").

There is a variety of small restaurants with a selection of traditional dishes or snacks. Meatballs are a typical dish, and also a variety of frankfurter sausages, sold in street kiosks at night. Other popular dishes are pea soup and cabbage rolls. As well as salmon from the northern rivers – often served as **raavi lohi** or **gravad lax**, a Scandinavian speciality – freshwater fish such as **kuha** and **siika** (resembling hake or haddock in flavour) are plentiful. Smoked or grilled Baltic herring can also be recommended, not forgetting salted herring, which is an unmissable classic. If your visit falls in August, you can join in crayfish parties downing a few chilled vodkas to accompany it!

Beer, lager, and vodka are popular, but a wide selection of wines is also available. Finns, like other Scandinavians, are great coffee drinkers, and coffee is often served very strong with a dash of cream, which the more health-conscious Finns now sometimes leave out.

Traditional sweets consist mostly of berries, either the wild varieties or cultivated ones. Finnish ice cream and chocolates are highly recommended.

## Useful Words and Phrases

| | | |
|---|---|---|
| appetizer | alkuruoka | _ahlkoorooakah_ |
| beer | olut | _oaloot_ |
| bread | leipä/ä | _laypa/a_ |
| butter | voi/ta | _voa/tah_ |
| cake | leivos | _layvoas_ |
| check | lasku | _lahskoo_ |
| child's portion | lasten annos | _lahstayn ahnnoss_ |
| coffee | kahvi/a | _kahhvi/ah_ |
| cup | kuppi | _kooppi_ |
| dessert | jälkiruoka | _jalkkirooakkah_ |
| fork | haarukka | _haahrookkah_ |
| glass | lasi | _lahsi_ |
| knife | veitsi | _vaytsi_ |
| main course | pääruoka | _pahrooakah_ |
| menu | menu/ruokalista | _maynoo/rooakahlistah_ |
| milk | maito/a | _mahto/ah_ |
| napkin | servietti | _sayrviaytti_ |
| pepper | pippuri/a | _pippoori/ah_ |
| plate | lautanen | _laootahnayn_ |
| receipt | kuitti | _kooitti_ |
| salt | suola/a | _sooalah/ah_ |
| sandwich | voileipä | _voalaypa_ |
| snack | välipala | _valippahlah_ |
| soup | keitto/a | _kaytto/ah_ |
| spoon | lusikka | _loosikkah_ |
| sugar | sokeri/a | _soakayri/ah_ |
| table | pöytä | _purewta_ |
| tea | tee/tä | _tayh/ta_ |
| teaspoon | teelusikka | _tayhloosikkah_ |
| tip | juomaraha | _yooamahrahhah_ |
| waiter | tarjoilija | _tahryoaliyah_ |
| waitress | tarjoilijatar | _tahryoaliyahtahr_ |
| water | vesi/vettä | _vaysi/vaytta_ |
| wine | viini/ä | _veeni/a_ |
| wine list | viinilista | _veenilistah_ |

**A table for one, please**
Pöytä yhdelle, kiitos
_purewta ewhdayllay keetoss_

**A table for two/three, please**
Pöytä kahdelle/kolmelle, kiitos
_purewta kahdayllay/koalmayllay, keetoss_

**Is there a highchair?**
Onko teillä lastentuolia?
_pankoa taylla lahstayn tooaliah_

**May we see the menu/wine list?**
Saammeko nähdä ruoka/viinilistan
_saammaykoa nahda rooakah/veenilistahn_

**What would you recommend?**
Mitä suosittelisitte?
_mitta sooasittaylissittay_

**I'd like …**
Saisinko …
_sahsinkoah_

**Just a cup of coffee/tea, please**
Vain kuppi kahvia, kiitos
_vahin kooppi kahhviah, keetoss_

**I only want a snack**
Haluaisin vain välipalan
_hahlooahsin vahin vallipahlahn_

**Is there a fixed-price menu?**
Onko teillä päivänannos?
_pankoa taylla pavan ahnnoss_

**A carafe of house red, please**
Pullo talon viiniä, kiitos
_poolloa tahloan veenia keetoss_

**Do you have any vegetarian dishes?**
Onko teillä kasvisruokia?
_oan_koa _taylla_ _kahs_vis_roo_akiah

**May we have some water?**
Voisimmeko saada vettä?
_voa_simmekoa _saa_dah _vaytta_

**Can you warm this bottle/baby food for me?**
Voisitteko lämmittää tämän pullon/vauvanruoan minulle?
_voa_sittekoa _lammittaa_ _taman_ _poolloan/_vahoo_vahn_roo_han _minnoollay

**Waiter/waitress!**
Tarjoija/Neiti!
_tahr_yoaliyah/_nayh_ti

**We didn't order this**
Tämä ei ole sitä mitä tilasimme
_tama_ ay _oalay_ _sitta_ _mitta_ _tillahsimmay

**May we have some more …?**
Saammeko hieman lisää …?
_saam_mekoa _hayamahn_ _lissaa

**May I have another knife/fork?**
Voinko saada toisen veitsen/haarukan?
_voan_koa _saadah_ _toahsayn_ _vayt_sayn/_haah_rookkahn

**May we have the check, please?**
Saammeko laskun, kiitos?
_saam_maykoa _lahsk_oon _kee_toss

**May I have a receipt, please?**
Voisinko saada kuitin?
_voa_sinkoa _saadah_ _koo_itin

**The meal was very good, thank you**
Ateria oli oikein hyvä, kiitos
_ah_tayriah _oa_li _oa_kayn _hew_va _kee_toss

# MENU GUIDE

**aamiainen** breakfast
**alkuruoka** appetizer
**ananas** pineapple
**anjovis** anchovies
**ankka** duck
**ankkapasteijaa** duck pâté
**aprikoosi** apricot
**artisokka** artichoke
**avokaado** avocado
**baari** café
**banaani** banana
**beef stroganoff** beef casserole
**blinis** buckwheat pancakes served with freshwater cod roe
**bortsch** beet soup served with sour cream
**crêpes Suzette** pancakes flambéed with orange sauce
**etanoita** snail
**fasaania** pheasant
**gratinoitu** baked in a milk, cream, and cheese sauce
**gravad lax** semi-raw salmon
**grillattu** broiled
**haarukka** fork
**hanhi** goose
**hapoton kivennäisvesi** still mineral water
**haudukas** braised
**hedelmäsalaatti** fruit salad
**herneitä** peas
**hillo** jam
**hirvenlihaa** venison
**hummeri** lobster
**hummerikeitto** lobster soup
**huoneen lämpötilassa** room temperature
**hyvin kuiva/brut** very dry

**häränkieltä** ox tongue
**iso katkarapu** shrimp
**jauhelihaa** ground beef
**jukurttia** yogurt
**juomaraha** tip; gratuity
**juussi** juice
**juustoa** cheese
**juustotarjotin** cheese board
**jälkiruoka** dessert
**jälkiruoka-astia** dessert dish
**jäätelöä** ice cream
**kaakao** hot chocolate
**kaali** cabbage
**kahvi/a** coffee
**kahvi (musta)** coffee (black)
**kahvi ja kerma** white coffee with cream
**kahviaamiainen** continental breakfast
**kahvila** café
**kakku** cake
**kala- ja äyriäisruokaa** seafood
**kalaa** fish
**kalakeitto** fish soup
**kaljaa** home-brewed non-alcoholic beer
**kalkkuna** turkey
**kanaa kermakastikkeessa** chicken in cream sauce
**kanaa riisin kanssa** chicken with rice
**kanaa sieni- ja valkoviinikastikkeessa** chicken with mushrooms and wine
**kananmaksapasteijaa** chicken liver pâté
**kania** rabbit
**karhunpaisti** bear steak
**katkarapucocktail** shrimp cocktail
**katkarapuja** shrimp
**kaurapuuro** oatmeal porridge
**kebab** kabob
**keitetty** boiled
**keitetty muna** boiled egg

keitto/a soup
kermajuustoa cream cheese
kermakastikkeessa in cream sauce
kermavaahto whipped cream
keskikypsä medium
kevyt light
kiisseli gelatin fruit dessert made of
    wild berries
kinkku ham
kirsikka cherry
kreippi grapefruit
kuha white freshwater fish
kuitti receipt
kuiva dry
kuivattu luumu prune
kukkakaali cauliflower
kuoriaisia shellfish
kuorrutettu ja paistettu meriantura
    sole dipped in flour and fried in
    butter
kuppi cup
kurkku cucumber
kyljys chop
kylkipaisti rib steak
kypsäksi/hyvin paistettu well done
kypsytetty rasvassa deep-fried
lakkalikööri cloudberry liqueur
lammas/ta lamb/mutton
lammaspata vihanneksilla mutton
    stew with vegetables
lampaanniska rack of lamb
lampaanreisi leg of lamb
lasi glass
lasku check
lasten annos child's portion
lautanen plate
leikkeleitä ham and patés; cold,
    sliced meats
leipä/ä bread
leivos cake
lihaa meat

lihaliemi broth
lihapata beef casserole
lihapullia meatball
likööri liqueur
limonaatia lemonade
lintua poultry
lohi salmon
lounas lunch
lusikka spoon
luumu plum
maito/a milk
maitokahvi white coffee
makaroonia noodles
makea dessert
makkara salami-type sausage, cold
    meats
mansikoita strawberry
manteli almond
marsipaani marzipan
meriantura viini- ja sienikastikkeessa
    sole in white wine and
    mushrooms
mersimarjalikööri arctic bramble
    liqueur
minttuteetä mint tea
munakas omelette
munakokkeli scrambled eggs
munkki doughnut
munuainen kidney
murot cereal
mustaherukka blackcurrant
mustikkapiirakka blueberry tart
mätiä roe
nakki(makkara) hot dog
näkkileipää crispbread
naudanliha beef
ohukainen pancake
olut beer/ale
omeletti omelette
omena apple
omenapiiras apple pie

osteri oyster
paistettu kana roasted chicken
paistettu muna fried egg
paistettu omena baked apple
paisti joint
paistinperunat fried potatoes
palapaisti stew
papuja beans
parsa asparagus
persikka peach
peruna potato
perunamuhennos mashed potatoes
perunoiden ja vihannesten kanssa
  with potatoes and vegetables
pihvi ja ranskalaiset steak and fries
pihvi steak
piimä sour milk
piiras tart, pie
pilsneri lager beer
pinaattia leaf spinach
piparkakku ginger snap
piparminttu peppermint
pippuria pepper
polarlikööri cranberry liqueur
poreileva kivennäisvesi carbonated
  mineral water
porkkana carrot
poronliha reindeer
porsaankyljys pork chop
porsasta pork
pulla coffee bread
punakaali red cabbage
punakampela plaice
punapaprika red pepper
punaviiniä red wine
puolikypsä rare
purjosipuli leek
puuro porridge
päivällinen dinner
päivän ruoka dish of the day
päivän ruokalista menu of the day

pääruoka main course
päärynä pear
pöytä table
raastettu grated
raavilohi semi-raw salmon
ranskalaiset french fries
rapu crayfish
retiisi radish
riisi rice
roquefort blue cheese
roseeviiniä rosé wine
ruis rye
ruispuuro rye porridge
ruokalista menu
rypäle grap
saksanpähkinä walnut
salaatti salad, lettuce
sekasalaatti mixed salad
sekavihannekset with assorted
  vegetables
servietti napkin
sieni mushroom
siideri cider
siika freshwater white fish
silakka Baltic herring (often broiled or
  smoked)
silli salted herring (in various
  sauces)
sillisalaatti root vegetable salad with
  salted herring
simpukoita valkoviinissä mussels in
  white wine
sinappia mustard
sipsit potato chips
sipuli onion
sipulikeitto French onion soup
sipulikeitto leivänkuutioiden kanssa
  baked onion soup
sitruuna lemon
sitruunateetä lemon tea
smörgåsbord cold table/starters

**sokeri/a** sugar
**sorsa** duck
**suola** salt
**suolakurkku** pickles
**sämpylä** round roll
**taimen** trout
**talon viiniä** table wine
**tarjoilija** waiter
**tarjoilijatar** waitress
**taskurapu** crab
**tee/tä** tea
**teelusikka** teaspoon
**teetä maidon kanssa** tea with milk
**tomaatti** tomato
**tomaattikeitto** tomato soup
**tonnikala** tuna
**tummaa** dark
**tuore appelsiinimehu** freshly squeezed
    orange juice
**turistiruokalista** tourist menu
**turska** cod
**tynnyriolut** draft beer
**vadelmia** raspberry
**välipala** snack
**valkoista** white
**valkokastike** white sauce
**valkosipuli/a** garlic
**valkoviiniä** white wine

**vaniljakastike** vanilla custard
**vartaassa paistettu** roasted on a spit
**vasikanmaksaa** veal liver
**vasikka** veal
**veitsi** knife
**veriohukkaat** black pudding pancakes
**vesi/vettä** water
**vesihaudutettu muna** poached egg
**vihanneksia** vegetables
**vihanneskeitto** soup with chopped
    vegetables
**vihreä paprika** green pepper
**vihreä salaatti** green salad
**viiliä** curds (local yogurt)
**viineri** Danish pastry
**viini/ä** wine
**viinikastike** wine sauce
**viinikastikkeessa** in red wine sauce
**viinilista** wine list
**vin** wine
**vispikerma** whipped cream
**vohveli** wafer, waffle
**voi/ta** butter
**voileipä** sandwich
**voileipäpöytä** cold table/appetizers
**vuohenjuusto** goat's cheese
**vuosikerta viini** vintage wine
**Wienershcnitzel** breaded escalope

# FRENCH

## CONTENTS

INTRODUCTION                   118
USEFUL PHRASES                 119
DAYS, MONTHS, SEASONS          125
NUMBERS                        126
TIME                           127
COMMUNICATIONS                 129
EMERGENCIES                    131
HOTELS                         132
SHOPPING                       136
EATING OUT                     137
MENU GUIDE                     141

# INTRODUCTION

### PRONUNCIATION

When reading the imitated pronunciation, the same value should be given to all syllables, since there is hardly any stress in French words. Pronounce each syllable as if it formed part of an English word and you will be understood. Remember the points below, and your pronunciation will be even closer to the correct French.

*an*  represents the nasal sound as in **vin**, **un** and **main** – similar to saying "an" without sounding the "n"

*g*  is pronounced hard as in "get"

*i*  pronounced as "eye"

*j*  like the "s" sound in "leisure"

*on*  represents the nasal sound as in **bon**, **en**, and **temps** – similar to saying "on" without sounding the "n"

*oo*  is how we imitate the French "u" (say "seen" with your lips rounded as if you were about to whistle, and the result will be close enough)

### USE OF THE FRENCH WORD "ON"

Phrases involving "I" or "we" and impersonal phrases have sometimes been translated with the French word "on." For example: **Can I camp here?** Est-ce qu'on peut camper ici? Literally, "on" means "one," but is not a formal word like it is in English.

### GENDERS AND ARTICLES

French has two genders for nouns – masculine and feminine. We generally give the definite article ("the") – **le** for masculine nouns, **la** for feminine nouns, and **les** for plural nouns. Where the indefinite article ("a, an") is more appropriate, we have used **un** for masculine and **une** for feminine nouns or the words for "some," **du** (masculine), **de la** (feminine), and **des** (plural).

# USEFUL PHRASES

### Yes, No, OK etc

**Yes/no**
Oui/non
*wee/non*

**OK**
D'accord
*dakkor*

**That's fine**
C'est bien
*seh byan*

**That's right**
C'est exact
*set exakt*

### Greetings, Introductions

**How do you do, pleased to meet you**
Enchanté (de faire votre connaissance)
*onshontay duh fair vottr konnessonss*

**Good morning**
Bonjour
*bonjoor*

**Good evening/Good night**
Bonsoir
*bonswahr*

**Goodbye**
Au revoir
*oh-rvwahr*

**How are you?**
Comment allez-vous?
*kommont allay voo*

*(familiar form)*
Comment ça va?
*kommon sa va*

**My name is …**
Je m'appelle …
*juh mappell*

**What's your name?**
Comment vous appelez-vous?
*komm<u>on</u> vooz appellay voo*

*(familiar form)*
Comment tu t'appelles?
*komm<u>on</u> <u>too</u> tappell*

**This is …**
Voici …
*vwah-see*

**Hello/Hi!**
Bonjour/Salut!
*b<u>on</u>joor/sal<u>oo</u>*

PLEASE, THANK YOU, APOLOGIES

**Thank you/No, thank you**
Merci/Non, merci
*mairsee/n<u>on</u> mairsee*

**Please**
S'il vous plaît
*seel voo pleh*

**Excuse me!/Sorry!**
Pardon!
*pard<u>on</u>*

WHERE, HOW, ASKING

**Excuse me, please**
Pardon
*pard<u>on</u>*

**Can you tell me …?**
Pouvez-vous me dire …?
*poovay voo muh deer*

**May I have …?**
Est-ce que je pourrais avoir …?
*esskuh juh poorray avwah*

**Would you like a …?**
Est-ce que vous voulez un/une …?
*esskuh voo voolay <u>an</u>/<u>oo</u>n*

**Would you like to …?**
Est-ce que vous voulez …?
*esskuh voo voolay*

**Is there … here?**
Est-ce qu'il y a … ici?
*esskeel-ya … ee-see*

**What's that?**
Qu'est-ce que c'est?
*kesskuh seh*

**How much is it?**
Combien ça coûte?
*k<u>on</u>by<u>an</u> sa koot*

**Where is the …?**
Où est le/la …?
*oo eh luh/la*

**Is there wheelchair access?**
Y a-t-il un accès pour les personnes à mobilité réduite?
*eeahteel onaksay poor lay payrson ah mobeelitay raydooeet*

**Are guide dogs allowed?**
Les chiens guide sont-ils admis?
*lay sheean geed sontel admee?*

**ABOUT ONESELF**

**I'm from …**
Je viens de …
*juh vy<u>an</u> duh*

**I'm ... years old**
J'ai ... ans
*jay ... on*

**I'm a ...**
Je suis ...
*juh swee*

**I'm married/single/divorced**
Je suis marié/célibataire/divorcé
*juh swee maree-ay/sayleebatair/deevorssay*

**I have ... sisters/brothers/children**
J'ai ... soeurs/frères/enfants
*jay ... suhr/frair/onfon*

## HELP, PROBLEMS

**Can you help me?**
Pouvez-vous m'aider?
*poovay voo mayday*

**I don't understand**
Je ne comprends pas
*juh nuh konpron pa*

**Does anyone here speak English?**
Est-ce qu'il y a quelqu'un ici qui parle anglais?
*esskeel-ya kellkan ee-see kee parl ongleh*

**I can't speak French**
Je ne parle pas français
*juh nuh parl pa fronseh*

**I don't know**
Je ne sais pas
*juh nuh seh pa*

**Please speak more slowly**
Pouvez-vous parler plus lentement, s'il vous plaît?
*poovay voo parlay ploo lontmon seel voo pleh*

**Please write it down for me**
Pouvez-vous me l'écrire, s'il vous plaît?
*poovay voo muh laykreer seel voo pleh*

**I've lost my way**
Je me suis perdu
*juh me swee pairdoo*

**Go away!**
Allez-vous-en!
*allay vooz on*

## LIKES, DISLIKES, SOCIALIZING

**I like/love …**
J'aime/j'adore …
*jem/jador*

**I don't like …**
Je n'aime pas …
*juh nem pa*

**I hate …**
Je déteste …
*juh daytest*

**Do you like …?**
Aimez-vous …?
*aymay voo*

**It's delicious/awful!**
C'est délicieux/horrible!
*seh dayleess-yuh/orreeb-l*

**I don't drink/smoke**
Je ne bois pas/ne fume pas
*juh nuh bwah pa/nuh foom pa*

**Do you mind if I smoke?**
Cela ne vous ennuie pas que je fume?
*suhla nuh vooz onwee pa kuh juh foom*

**What would you like to drink?**
Qu'est-ce que vous voulez boire?
*kesskuh voo voolay bwahr*

**I would like a …**
Je voudrais un/une …
*juh voodreh <u>an</u>/<u>oon</u>*

**Nothing for me, thanks**
Rien pour moi, merci
*ry<u>an</u> poor mwah mairsee*

**Cheers!** *(toast)*
Santé!
*s<u>on</u>tay*

---

### THINGS YOU'LL HEAR

| | |
|---|---|
| à bientôt | see you later |
| attention! | look out! |
| au revoir | goodbye |
| bien | fine |
| bon! | right! OK! |
| bonjour | hello |
| bon voyage! | have a good trip! |
| entrez | come in |
| excusez-moi | excuse me |
| je vous en prie | don't mention it |
| papiers, s'il vous plaît | identification papers, please |
| pardon!/pardon? | excuse me? |
| qu'est-ce que vous avez dit? | what did you say? |
| servez-vous | help yourself |
| voici | here you are |
| vraiment? | is that right? |

# DAYS, MONTHS, SEASONS

| Sunday | dimanche | *deemonsh* |
| Monday | lundi | *landee* |
| Tuesday | mardi | *mardee* |
| Wednesday | mercredi | *mairkruhdee* |
| Thursday | jeudi | *juhdee* |
| Friday | vendredi | *vondruhdee* |
| Saturday | samedi | *sammdee* |
| | | |
| January | janvier | *jonvee-ay* |
| February | février | *fayvree-ay* |
| March | mars | *marss* |
| April | avril | *ahvreel* |
| May | mai | *meh* |
| June | juin | *jwan* |
| July | juillet | *jwee-ay* |
| August | août | *oo* |
| September | septembre | *septonbr* |
| October | octobre | *oktobr* |
| November | novembre | *novonbr* |
| December | décembre | *dayssonbr* |
| | | |
| Spring | le printemps | *pranton* |
| Summer | l'été | *laytay* |
| Fall | l'automne | *lohton* |
| Winter | l'hiver | *leevair* |
| | | |
| Christmas | Noël | *noh-el* |
| Christmas Eve | la veille de Noël | *vay duh noh-el* |
| Good Friday | Vendredi saint | *vondredee san* |
| Easter | Pâques | *pak* |
| New Year | le Nouvel An | *noovel on* |
| New Year's Eve | la veille du Jour de l'an | *vay doo joor duh lon* |
| Pentecost | la Pentecôte | *pontkoht* |

# NUMBERS

| | | | | |
|---|---|---|---|---|
| 0 | zéro *zayro* | | 10 | dix *deess* |
| 1 | un, une *an, oon* | | 11 | onze *onz* |
| 2 | deux *duh* | | 12 | douze *dooz* |
| 3 | trois *trwah* | | 13 | treize *trez* |
| 4 | quatre *kattr* | | 14 | quatorze *kattorz* |
| 5 | cinq *sank* | | 15 | quinze *kanz* |
| 6 | six *seess* | | 16 | seize *sez* |
| 7 | sept *set* | | 17 | dix-sept *deess-set* |
| 8 | huit *weet* | | 18 | dix-huit *deess-weet* |
| 9 | neuf *nuhf* | | 19 | dix-neuf *deess-nuhf* |

| | |
|---|---|
| 20 | vingt *van* |
| 21 | vingt et un *vantay an* |
| 22 | vingt-deux *van duh* |
| 30 | trente *tront* |
| 40 | quarante *karront* |
| 50 | cinquante *sankont* |
| 60 | soixante *swassont* |
| 70 | soixante-dix *swassont-deess* |
| 80 | quatre-vingts *kattruhvan* |
| 90 | quatre-vingt-dix *kattruh-vandeess* |
| 100 | cent *son* |
| 110 | cent-dix *sondeess* |
| 200 | deux cents *duh-son* |
| 1,000 | mille *meel* |
| 10,000 | dix mille *deess meel* |
| 20,000 | vingt mille *van meel* |
| 100,000 | cent mille *son meel* |
| 1,000,000 | un million *meel-ion* |

## TIME

| today | aujourd'hui | *ohjoord-wee* |
|---|---|---|
| yesterday | hier | *yair* |
| tomorrow | demain | *duhma__n__* |
| this week | cette semaine | *set suhmen* |
| last week | la semaine dernière | *suhmen dairnee-air* |
| next week | la semaine prochaine | *suhmen proshen* |
| this morning | ce matin | *suh matta__n__* |
| this afternoon | cet après-midi | *set apreh-meedee* |
| this evening/ tonight | ce soir | *suh swahr* |
| in three days | dans trois jours | *do__n__ trwah joor* |
| three days ago | il y a trois jours | *eelya trwah joor* |
| late | tard | *tar* |
| early | tôt | *toh* |
| soon | bientôt | *bya__n__toh* |
| later on | plus tard | *pl__oo__ tar* |
| at the moment | pour le moment, maintenant | *poor luh mom__on__, mantn__on__* |
| second | une seconde | *suhg__on__d* |
| minute | une minute | *meen__oo__t* |
| ten minutes | dix minutes | *dee meen__oo__t* |
| quarter of an hour | un quart d'heure | *kar dur* |
| half an hour | une demi-heure | *duhmee ur* |
| three quarters of an hour | trois quarts d'heure | *trwah kar dur* |
| hour | une heure | *ur* |
| day | un jour | *joor* |
| every day | chaque jour | *shak joor* |
| all day | toute la journée | *toot la joornay* |
| week | une semaine | *suhmen* |
| two weeks | quinze jours, deux semaines | *ka__nz__ joor, duh suhmen* |
| month | un mois | *mwah* |
| year | une année, un an | *annay, __on__* |

127

## TELLING TIME

The 24-hour clock is always used in the written form in timetables and for appointments, and also verbally in enquiry offices and if talking about the times of television and radio programs. However, in most other situations, people will use the 12-hour clock.

"What time is it?" is **quelle heure est-il?**. "O'clock" is translated as **heure(s)**, meaning "hour(s)." "(It's) one o'clock" is **(il est) une heure**; "(it's) four o'clock" is **(il est) quatre heures** and so on. To denote the half hour use **et demie**, so "5:30" is **cinq heures et demie**.

To express minutes after the hour, state the hour followed by the number of minutes. For example, "ten past five" is **cinq heures dix**. For minutes to the hour use **moins**, which means "less." For example, "twenty to eleven" is **onze heures moins vingt**.

"Quarter" is **quart**, so "quarter past three" is **trois heures et quart**, and "quarter to eight" is **huit heures moins le quart**. The word "at" in phrases such as "at quarter past two" can be translated as **à**: **à deux heures et quart**.

| | | |
|---|---|---|
| **am** | du matin | _doo matan_ |
| **pm** (*afternoon*) | de l'après-midi | duh lapreh-meedee |
| (*evening*) | du soir | _doo swahr_ |
| **one o'clock** | une heure | _oon ur_ |
| **ten past one** | une heure dix | _oon ur deess_ |
| **quarter past one** | une heure et quart | _oon ur ay kar_ |
| **twenty past two** | deux heures vingt | duhz ur _van_ |
| **1:30** | une heure et demie | _oon ur ay duhmee_ |
| **twenty to two** | deux heures moins vingt | duhz ur mw_an_ _van_ |
| **quarter to two** | deux heures moins le quart | duhz ur mw_an_ luh kar |
| **two o'clock** | deux heures | duhz ur |
| **midday** | midi | meedee |
| **midnight** | minuit | meenwee |

# COMMUNICATIONS

## USEFUL WORDS AND PHRASES

| call(*verb*) | appeler | *applay* |
|---|---|---|
| code | l'indicatif | *andeekateef* |
| collect call | une communication en PCV | *kommooneekass-ion on pay say vay* |
| dial tone | la tonalité | *tonaleetay* |
| email address | l'adresse électronique | *adrays aylayktroneek* |
| directory assistance | les renseignements | *ronsen-yuhmon* |
| fax machine | le fax | *fax* |
| internet | l'internet | *internet* |
| mobile phone | le téléphone portable | *taylayfon portabul* |
| number | le numéro | *noomayroh* |
| operator | l'opérateur | *opayratur* |
| (*female*) | l'opératrice | *opay-ratreess* |
| phonecard | la télécarte | *taylaykart* |
| telephone | le téléphone | *taylayfon* |
| telephone booth | une cabine | *kabeen* |
| website | le site web | *site web* |
| wrong number | un faux numéro | *foh noomayroh* |

**Where is the nearest phone booth?**
Où se trouve la cabine téléphonique la plus proche?
*oo suh troov la kabeen taylay-foneek la ploo prosh*

**I would like a number in …**
Je voudrais un numéro à …
*juh voodreh an noomayroh ah*

**I would like to speak to …**
Je voudrais parler à …
*juh voodreh parlay ah*

**My number is …**
Mon numéro est le …
*mon noomayroh eh luh*

**Could you leave him/her a message?**
Pouvez-vous lui laisser un message?
*poovay voo lwee lessay <u>an</u> muhssaj*

**I'll call back later**
Je rappellerai plus tard
*juh rappelray pl<u>oo</u> tar*

**What's your fax number/email address?**
Quel est votre numéro de fax/adresse électronique?
*kaylay votr noomayro duh faks/adrays aylayktroneek*

**May I send an email/fax from here?**
Puis-je envoyer un message électronique/fax d'ici?
*pooeej ronvwahiay an maysahj aylayktroneek /faks deesee?*

---

### THINGS YOU'LL HEAR

**A qui désirez-vous parler?**
Whom would you like to speak to?

**Vous avez un faux numéro**
You've got the wrong number

**C'est de la part de qui?**
May I ask who's calling?

**Lui-même/elle-même**
Speaking

**Ne quittez pas**
Hold the line

**Pourriez-vous rappeler plus tard?**
Could you call back later?

**Désolé, il/elle n'est pas là**
Sorry, he/she is not in

---

# EMERGENCIES

## Useful Words and Phrases

| | | |
|---|---|---|
| **accident** | un accident | *ak-seedon* |
| **ambulance** | une ambulance | *onboolonss* |
| **breakdown** | une panne | *pan* |
| **burglary** | un cambriolage | *konbri-olaj* |
| **crash** | un accident | *ak-seedon* |
| **emergency** | l'urgence | *oorjonss* |
| **fire** | le feu | *fuh* |
| **fire department** | les pompiers | *ponp-yay* |
| **police** | la police | *poleess* |
| **police station** | le poste de police | *posst duh poleess* |

**Help!**
A l'aide!
*ah led*

**Stop!**
Arrêtez!
*arretay*

**Get an ambulance!**
Appelez une ambulance!
*applay oon onboolonss*

**Hurry up!**
Faites vite!
*fet veet*

**My address is …**
Mon adresse est …
*mon adress eh*

**My passport/car has been stolen**
On a volé mon passeport/ma voiture
*on ah volay mon passpor/ma vwahtoor*

# HOTELS

**USEFUL WORDS AND PHRASES**

| | | |
|---|---|---|
| balcony | un balcon | *balkon* |
| bathroom | la salle de bain | *sal duh ban* |
| bed | le lit | *lee* |
| bed & breakfast | chambre d'hôte | *shonbr doht* |
| bedroom | la chambre | *shonbr* |
| breakfast | le petit déjeuner | *puhtee day-juhnay* |
| car park | le parking | *par-keeng* |
| check | la note | *not* |
| dining room | la salle à manger | *sal ah monjay* |
| dinner | le dîner | *deenay* |
| double bed | un grand lit | *gran lee* |
| double room | une chambre pour deux personnes | *shonbr poor duh pairson* |
| elevator | l'ascenseur | *assonssur* |
| full board | la pension complète | *ponss-ion konplet* |
| guesthouse | une pension de famille | *ponss-ion duh famee* |
| half board | la demi-pension | *duhmee ponss-ion* |
| hotel | un hôtel | *oh-tell* |
| key | la clé, la clef | *klay* |
| lunch | le déjeuner | *day-juhnay* |
| maid | la femme de chambre | *fam duh shonbr* |
| manager | le directeur | *deerektur* |
| receipt | le reçu | *ruh-soo* |
| reception | la réception | *raysseps-ion* |
| receptionist | le/la réceptionniste | *raysseps-ioneest* |
| restroom | les toilettes | *twallet* |
| room | la chambre | *shonbr* |
| room service | le service en chambre | *sairveess on shonbr* |
| shower | la douche | *doosh* |
| single bed | un lit d'une personne | *lee doon pairson* |
| single room | une chambre pour une personne | *shonbr poor oon pairson* |
| twin room | une chambre à deux lits | *shonbr ah duh lee* |

**Do you have any vacancies?**
Avez-vous des chambres de libres?
*avay voo day shonbr duh leebr*

**I have a reservation**
J'ai réservé
*jay rayzairvay*

**I'd like a single room**
Je voudrais une chambre pour une personne
*juh voodreh oon shonbr poor oon pairson*

**I'd like a room with a bathroom/balcony**
Je voudrais une chambre avec salle de bain/balcon
*juh voodreh oon shonbr avek sal duh ban/balkon*

**Is there satellite/cable TV in the rooms?**
Les chambres ont-elles la télé par satellite/cablée?
*Lay shoombr ontayl la taylay pahr satayleet/kablay*

**I'd like a room for one night/three nights**
Je voudrais une chambre pour une nuit/trois nuits
*juh voodreh oon shonbr poor oon nwee/trwah nwee*

**What is the charge per night?**
Quel est le prix pour une nuit?
*kell eh luh pree poor oon nwee*

**When is breakfast/dinner?**
A quelle heure servez-vous le petit déjeuner/le dîner?
*ah kell ur sairvay voo luh puhtee day-juhnay/luh deenay*

**Please wake/call me at … o'clock**
Réveillez-moi à … heures, s'il vous plaît
*rayvay-yay mwah ah … ur seel voo pleh*

**May I have breakfast in my room?**
Pouvez-vous me servir le petit déjeuner dans la chambre?
*poovay voo meh sairveer luh puhtee day-juhnay don la shonbr*

**My room number is …**
Le numéro de ma chambre est le …
*luh noomayroh duh ma shonbr eh luh*

**There is no toilet paper in the bathroom**
Il n'y a pas de papier toilette dans la salle de bain
*eel nya pa duh papee-ay twalet don la sal duh ban*

**The window won't open**
Pas moyen d'ouvrir la fenêtre
*pa mwi-an doovreer la fuhn-ettr*

**There isn't any hot water**
Il n'y a pas d'eau chaude
*eel nya pa doh shohd*

**I'm leaving tomorrow**
Je pars demain
*juh par duhman*

**When do I have to vacate the room?**
A quelle heure dois-je libérer la chambre?
*ah kell ur dwah juh leebayray la shonbr*

**May I have the check, please?**
Pouvez-vous préparer ma note, s'il vous plaît?
*poovay voo prayparay ma not seel voo pleh*

**I'll pay by credit card**
Je payerai avec une carte de crédit
*juh pay-uhray avek oon kart duh kraydee*

**I'll pay cash**
Je payerai comptant
*juh pay-uhray konton*

**Can you get me a taxi?**
Pouvez-vous m'appeler un taxi?
*poovay voo mapplay an taxee*

## THINGS YOU'LL SEE

| | |
|---|---|
| addition | check |
| ascenseur | elevator |
| complet | no vacancies |
| déjeuner | lunch |
| douche | shower |
| entrée | entrance |
| entrée interdite | no admission |
| escalier | stairs |
| petit déjeuner | breakfast |
| poussez | push |
| privé | private |
| salle de bain | bathroom |
| sortie de secours | emergency exit |
| tirez | pull |

## THINGS YOU'LL HEAR

**Je suis désolé, mais nous sommes complets**
I'm sorry, we're full

**Nous n'avons plus de chambres pour deux personnes/
une personne**
There are no double/single rooms left

**Pour combien de nuits?**
For how many nights?

**Comment payez-vous?**
How will you be paying?

**Veuillez payer d'avance**
Please pay in advance

**La chambre doit être libérée à midi**
You must vacate the room by noon

# SHOPPING

**Excuse me, where is/are …?**
Pardon, pouvez-vous me dire où se trouve …?
*pard<u>on</u> poovay voo muh deer oo suh troov*

**Do you have …?**
Avez-vous …?
*avay voo*

**How much is this?**
Ça coûte combien?
*sa koot k<u>on</u>by<u>an</u>*

**Where do I pay?**
Où faut-il payer?
*oo foh-teel pay-ay*

**Do you take credit cards?**
Acceptez-vous les cartes de crédit?
*ak-septay voo lay kart duh kraydee*

**May I have a receipt?**
Puis-je avoir un reçu?
*pwee<u>j</u> avwahr <u>an</u> ruhs<u>oo</u>*

**Do you have something less expensive?**
Avez-vous quelque chose de moins cher?
*avay voo kellkuh shohz duh mw<u>an</u> shair*

**May I have a refund?**
Pouvez-vous me rembourser?
*poovay voo muh r<u>on</u>boorsay*

**That's fine. I'll take it**
C'est bien. Je le prends
*seh by<u>an</u>. juh luh pr<u>on</u>*

**It isn't what I wanted**
Ce n'est pas ce que je voulais
*suh neh pa suh kuh juh vooleh*

# EATING OUT

It is not difficult to eat well and inexpensively in France. Since prices have to be displayed, by law, in the window of an eating establishment, you can readily fit your choice of restaurant to your budget. Although service is included in the check, it is customary to leave a tip for the waiter or waitress. In cafés, even if you have just popped in for coffee or a drink, it is traditional to leave the leftover coins from your change.

Every town has a number of cafés where, at lunchtime, you can order a simple sandwich, a **croque-monsieur** (a broiled ham and cheese sandwich which, with the addition of an egg, becomes a **croque-madame**), the **plat du jour** (dish of the day), **rillettes** (pork or goose meat ground very finely so that it can be spread on bread), pâté, or a platter of crudités or cold meats.

**Bistros** are small bars, often family-run, that also sometimes serve a selection of traditional dishes or snacks at lunchtime and in the evening. The **menu du jour** (today's menu) is usually good value. Regional specialities that you may encounter include: **crêpes** in Brittany; **choucroute** (sauerkraut with sausages and pieces of smoked ham) and onion tart in Alsace; **ratatouille** in Provence; and **bouillabaisse** (fish soup) and **salade niçoise** (mixed salad containing olives, anchovies, tuna, tomatoes, and other vegetables) around the Mediterranean coast. House wine is available in carafes, but if you prefer your wine by the bottle, you will find a few listed on the menu.

**Brasseries** are often large and noisy – not the place to go for an intimate dinner – and offer beer on tap as well as wine. They stay open late, and snacks and full meals are usually available at any time.

French cafés and bars always sell coffee. If you ask for **un café** or **un expresso**, you'll get a small, black coffee. **Un crème** is a small coffee with milk and **un grand crème** is a large coffee with milk. You can also ask for **un café léger** (weak coffee) or **un café bien serré** (very strong coffee).

## USEFUL WORDS AND PHRASES

| | | |
|---|---|---|
| beer | de la bière | *bee-air* |
| bread | du pain | *pan* |
| butter | du beurre | *bur* |
| cake | du gâteau | *gattoh* |
| check | l'addition | *addeess-ion* |
| child's portion | une portion enfant | *porss-ion onfon* |
| coffee | du café | *kaffay* |
| cup | une tasse | *tass* |
| dessert | un dessert | *daissair* |
| fork | une fourchette | *foorshet* |
| glass | un verre | *vair* |
| knife | un couteau | *kootoh* |
| main course | le plat principal | *pla pranseepal* |
| menu | le menu | *muhnoo* |
| milk | du lait | *leh* |
| napkin | une serviette | *sairvee-et* |
| pepper | du poivre | *pwahvr* |
| plate | une assiette | *assee-et* |
| receipt | le reçu | *ruhssoo* |
| salt | du sel | *sel* |
| sandwich | un sandwich | *sondweech* |
| snack | un snack | *'snack'* |
| soup | de la soupe | *soop* |
| spoon | une cuillère | *kwee-air* |
| starter | une entrée | *ontray* |
| sugar | du sucre | *sookr* |
| table | une table | *tabb-l* |
| tea | du thé | *tay* |
| teaspoon | une cuillère à café | *kwee-air ah kaffay* |
| tip | un pourboire | *poorbwahr* |
| waiter | un serveur | *sairvur* |
| waitress | une serveuse | *sairvuhz* |
| water | de l'eau | *oh* |
| wine | du vin | *van* |
| wine list | la carte des vins | *kart day van* |

**A table for one, please**
Une table pour une personne, s'il vous plaît
<u>oo</u>n tabb-l poor <u>oo</u>n pairson seel voo pleh

**A table for two/three, please**
Une table pour deux/trois personnes, s'il vous plaît
<u>oo</u>n tabb-l poor duh/trwah pairson seel voo pleh

**Is there a highchair?**
Auriez-vous une chaise haute?
oriayvoo oon shayz oht

**May we see the menu/wine list?**
Le menu/la carte des vins, s'il vous plaît
luh muhn<u>oo</u>/la kart day v<u>an</u> seel voo pleh

**What would you recommend?**
Que recommandez-vous?
kuh ruhkomm<u>on</u>day voo

**I'd like …**
J'aimerais …
jemmereh

**Just a cup of coffee/tea, please**
Un café/thé seulement
<u>an</u> kaffay/tay suhlm<u>on</u>

**I only want a snack**
Je voudrais juste manger un snack
juh voodreh <u>joo</u>st m<u>on</u>jay <u>an</u> snack

**Is there a fixed-price menu?**
Est-ce qu'il y a un menu du jour?
esskeel-ya <u>an</u> muhn<u>oo</u> d<u>oo</u> joor

**A carafe of house red, please**
Une carafe de vin rouge maison, s'il vous plaît
<u>oo</u>n karaff duh v<u>an</u> rooj mezz<u>on</u> seel voo pleh

**Do you have any vegetarian dishes?**
Est-ce que vous servez des plats végétariens?
*esskuh voo sairvay day pla vayjaytary<u>an</u>*

**Could we have some water?**
Est-ce que nous pourrions avoir de l'eau?
*esskuh noo pooree-<u>on</u> avwahr duh loh*

**Can you warm this bottle/baby food for me?**
Pourriez-vous réchauffer ce biberon/petit pot pour moi?
*pooreeay voo rayshohfay suh beebuhron/puhteepoh poor mwah*

**Waiter/waitress!**
Garçon/Mademoiselle!
*garss<u>on</u>/madmwazel*

**We didn't order this**
Ce n'est pas ce que nous avons commandé
*sneh pa suh kuh nooz av<u>on</u> komm<u>on</u>day*

**May we have some more …?**
Est-ce qu'on peut avoir plus de …?
*essk<u>on</u> puh avwahr pl<u>oo</u> duh*

**May I have another knife/fork?**
Est-ce que je peux avoir un autre couteau/une autre fourchette?
*esskuh juh puh avwahr <u>an</u> oht-r kootoh/<u>oon</u> oht-r foorshet*

**May we have the check, please?**
L'addition, s'il vous plaît
*laddeess-i<u>on</u> seel voo pleh*

**May I have a receipt, please?**
Est-ce que je peux avoir un reçu, s'il vous plaît?
*esskuh juh puh avwahr <u>an</u> ruhss<u>oo</u> seel voo pleh*

**The meal was very good, thank you**
C'était très bon, merci
*sayteh treh b<u>on</u> mairsee*

# MENU GUIDE

**à la broche** roasted on a spit
**à la jardinière** with assorted vegetables
**à la normande** in cream sauce
**à point** medium
**abricot** apricot
**agneau** lamb
**ail** garlic
**ailloli** garlic mayonnaise
**amande** almond
**ananas** pineapple
**anchois** anchovies
**andouillette** spicy sausage
**artichaut** artichoke
**asperge** asparagus
**au gratin** baked in a milk, cream, and
    cheese sauce
**avocat** avocado
**banane** banana
**bavaroise** light mousse
**béarnaise** with béarnaise sauce (thick
    sauce made with eggs and butter)
**béchamel** white sauce, béchamel sauce
**beurre** butter
**beurre noir** dark melted butter
**bien cuit** well done
**bière** beer
**bière à la pression** draft beer
**bière blonde** lager
**bifteck** steak
**bisque de homard** lobster soup
**blanquette de veau** veal stew
**bleu** rare
**bœuf** beef
**bœuf braisé** braised beef
**bœuf en daube** beef casserole
**bouillabaisse** fish soup from the Midi
**bouilli** boiled
**bouillon** broth

**boulette** meatball
**bouquet rose** shrimp
**bourride** fish soup
**braisé** braised
**brioche** round roll
**brochette** kabob
**brut** very dry
**cabillaud** cod
**café** coffee (black)
**café au lait** white coffee
**café complet** continental breakfast
**café crème** white coffee
**calamar/calmar** squid
**calvados** apple brandy
**canard** duck
**caneton** duckling
**carbonnade** beef cooked in beer
**carotte** carrot
**carré d'agneau** rack of lamb
**carrelet** plaice
**carte** menu
**carte des vins** wine list
**casse-croûte** snacks
**cassis** blackcurrant
**cassoulet** bean, pork, and duck casserole
**cerise** cherry
**chambré** at room temperature
**champignon** mushroom
**chantilly** whipped cream
**charcuterie** sausages, ham, and pâtés;
    pork products
**charlotte** dessert consisting of layers of
    fruits, cream, and finger cookies
**chausson aux pommes** apple turnover
**cheval** horse
**chèvre** goat's cheese
**chevreuil** venison
**chocolat chaud** hot chocolate

chou cabbage
chou à la crème cream puff
chou-fleur cauliflower
chou rouge red cabbage
cidre cider
citron lemon
citron pressé fresh lemon juice
cocktail de crevettes shrimp cocktail
cœur heart
colin hake
compote stewed fruit, compote
concombre cucumber
confit preserved in fat
confiture jam
consommé clear soup
coq au vin chicken in red wine
côte de porc pork chop
côtelette chop
coupe dessert dish
crabe crab
crème cream; creamy sauce or dessert;
  white coffee
crème à la vanille vanilla custard
crème anglaise custard
crème chantilly whipped cream
crème pâtissière rich creamy custard
crêpe pancake
crêpes Suzette pancakes flambéed with
  orange sauce
crevette grise shrimp
crevette rose prawn
croque-madame broiled cheese and ham
  sandwich with a fried egg
croque-monsieur broiled cheese and
  ham sandwich
crudités selection of salads, chopped
  raw vegetables
crustacés shellfish
déjeuner lunch
digestif liqueur
dinde turkey

dîner dinner
doux sweet
eau minérale gazeuse/plate carbonated/
  still mineral water
entrecôte rib steak
entrée starter
entremets dessert
épinards en branches leaf spinach
escalope de veau milanaise veal
  escalope with tomato sauce
escalope panée breaded escalope
escargot snail
estouffade de bœuf beef casserole
faisan pheasant
farci stuffed
flageolets kidney beans
flan custard tart
foie de veau veal liver
foie gras goose or duck liver preserve
foies de volaille chicken livers
fonds d'artichaut artichoke hearts
fondue savoyarde cheese fondue
fraise strawberry
framboise raspberry
frit deep-fried
frites french fries
fromage cheese
fromage blanc cream cheese
fromage de chèvre goat's cheese
fruits de mer seafood
galette round, flat cake or savory
  wholemeal crèpe
garni with potatoes and vegetables
gâteau cake
gaufre wafer, waffle
gigot d'agneau leg of lamb
glace ice cream
grand cru vintage wine
gratin baked cheese dish
gratin dauphinois sliced potatoes
  baked in milk, cream, and cheese

**gratinée** baked onion soup
**grillé** broiled
**hachis parmentier** shepherd's pie
**haricots** beans
**homard** lobster
**hors-d'œuvre** appetizer
**huître** oyster
**jambon** ham
**julienne** soup with chopped vegetables
**jus** juice
**lait** milk
**langue de bœuf** ox tongue
**lapin** rabbit
**léger** light
**légume** vegetable
**lièvre** hare
**limonade** lemonade
**marchand de vin** in red wine sauce
**marron** chestnut
**massepain** marzipan
**menthe** peppermint
**menthe à l'eau** mint cordial
**menu du jour** today's menu
**menu gastronomique** gourmet menu
**menu touristique** tourist menu
**millefeuille** custard slice
**morue** cod
**mouclade** mussels in creamy sauce with
    saffron, turmeric, and white wine
**moules marinière** mussels in white
    wine
**mousseux** sparkling; carbonated
**moutarde** mustard
**mouton** mutton
**nature** plain
**navarin** mutton stew with vegetables
**noisette** hazelnut
**noix** walnut
**nouilles** noodles
**œuf à la coque** boiled egg
**œuf poché** poached egg

**œufs à la neige** floating islands
    (poached egg whites on top of custard)
**œufs brouillés** scrambled eggs
**œuf sur le plat** fried egg
**oie** goose
**oignon** onion
**omelette** omelette
**omelette paysanne** omelette with
    potatoes and bacon
**orange pressée** fresh orange juice
**pain** bread
**pain au chocolat** chocolate puff pastry
**palette de porc** shoulder of pork
**pamplemousse** grapefruit
**pastis** anise-flavored alcoholic drink
**pâté de canard** duck pâté
**pâté de foie de volaille** chicken liver
    pâté
**pâtes** pasta
**pêche** peach
**petit déjeuner** breakfast
**petit pain** roll
**petit pois** peas
**petits fours** small fancy pastries
**petit suisse** light, white cream cheese
**pistache** pistachio
**plat du jour** dish of the day
**plateau de fromages** cheese board
**poire** pear
**poire belle Hélène** pear in chocolate
    sauce
**poireau** leek
**poisson** fish
**poivre** pepper
**poivron** red or green pepper
**pomme** apple
**pomme bonne femme** baked apple
**pomme de terre** potato
**pommes Dauphine** potato fritters
**pommes de terre sautées** fried potatoes
**pommes frites** french fries

**porc** pork
**potage** soup
**potage printanier** vegetable soup
**pot-au-feu** beef and vegetable stew
**potée** vegetable and meat stew
**poule au pot** chicken and vegetable stew
**poule au riz** chicken with rice
**poulet chasseur** chicken with mushrooms and white wine
**poulet rôti** roasted chicken
**provençale** with tomatoes, garlic, and herbs
**prune** plum
**pruneau** prune
**purée** mashed potatoes
**purée de marrons** chestnut purée
**radis** radish
**ragoût** stew
**raisin** grape
**râpé** grated
**riz** rice
**rognon** kidney
**roquefort** blue cheese
**rôti** joint
**rouille** sauce accompanying **bouillabaisse**
**saint-honoré** cream puff cake
**salade** salad, lettuce
**salade composée** mixed salad
**salade verte** green salad
**sanglier** wild boar
**sauce aurore** white sauce with tomato
**sauce béarnaise** thick sauce with eggs and butter
**sauce blanche** white sauce
**sauce matelote** wine sauce
**sauce suprême** creamy sauce
**sauce vinot** wine sauce
**saucisse** sausage
**saucisson** salami-type sausage

**saumon** salmon
**saumon fumé** smoked salmon
**sec** dry
**sel** salt
**sirop** cordial
**sole bonne femme** sole in white wine and mushrooms
**sole meunière** sole dipped in flour and fried in butter
**soupe à l'oignon** French onion soup
**soupe aux tomates** tomato soup
**soupe de poisson** fish soup
**steak frites** steak and french fries
**steak haché** ground meat, ground beef
**sucre** sugar
**suprême de volaille** chicken in cream sauce
**tarte** tart, pie
**tarte frangipane** almond cream tart
**tarte Tatin** baked apple dish
**terrine** pâté
**thé** tea
**thé à la menthe** mint tea
**thé au lait** tea with milk
**thé citron** lemon tea
**thon** tuna
**tomate** tomato
**tourte** covered pie
**truite** trout
**veau** veal
**velouté de tomate** cream of tomato soup
**viande** meat
**vin** wine
**vin blanc** white wine
**vin de pays** local wine
**vin de table** table wine
**vin rosé** rosé wine
**vin rouge** red wine
**volaille** poultry
**yaourt** yogurt

# GERMAN

## CONTENTS

INTRODUCTION 146
USEFUL PHRASES 147
DAYS, MONTHS, SEASONS 153
NUMBERS 154
TIME 155
COMMUNICATIONS 157
EMERGENCIES 159
HOTELS 160
SHOPPING 164
EATING OUT 165
MENU GUIDE 169

# INTRODUCTION

## Pronunciation

When reading the imitated pronunciation, stress the part that is underlined. Pronounce each syllable as if it formed part of an English word, and you will be understood sufficiently well. Remember the points below, and your pronunciation will be even closer to the correct German.

*g*    is pronounced hard as in "get."

KH    represents the guttural German "ch" and should sound like the Scottish "loch" (which *isn't* "lock").

*oo*    represents the long German "u"; make this an English "oo" as in "food" (*not* short as in "foot").

*oo*    represents the shorter German "u," as in English "took," "book."

*(v)*    is how we imitate the German "ü," which sounds like the "ee" in "seen" if you pronounce it with rounded lips (or like the French "u").

*ow*    should sound like the "ow" in "cow" (*not* as in "low").

## "You" and "I"

In most cases we have given the polite form for "you" – which is **Sie** (*zee*). The familiar form **du** (*doo*) can also be used, but normally only if you are talking to someone you know well and would regard as a personal friend.

Questions involving "I" have sometimes been translated with **man**, for example "Can I ...?" **Kann man ...?**. Literally **man** means "one" but is not a formal word as it is in English.

# USEFUL PHRASES

## Yes, No, OK etc

**Yes/No**
Ja/Nein
*ya/nine*

**OK**
Okay
*okay*

**That's fine**
In Ordnung
*in ortnoong*

**That's right**
Stimmt
*shtimmt*

## Greetings, Introductions

**How do you do, pleased to meet you**
Guten Tag, freut mich
*gooten tahk froyt mich*

**Good morning/good afternoon/good evening**
Guten Morgen/Guten Tag/Guten Abend
*gooten morgen/gooten tahk/gooten ahbent*

**Good night** (*going to bed*)
Gute Nacht
*gootuh naкнt*

(*leaving late at night*)
Auf Wiedersehen
*owf veeder-zayn*

**Goodbye**
Auf Wiedersehen
*owf veeder-zayn*

**How are you?**
Wie geht es Ihnen?
*vee gayt ess eenen*

(*familiar form*)
Wie geht es dir?
*vee gayt ess deer*

**My name is …**
Ich heiße …
*ish hice-uh*

**What's your name?**                 *(familiar form)*
Wie heißen Sie?                        Wie heißt du?
*vee hice-en zee*                      *vee hice-t doo*

**This is …**
Das ist …
*dass ist*

**Hello/Hi**
Hallo
*hallo*

### Please, Thank You, Apologies

**Thank you/No, thank you**
Danke/Nein, danke
*dankuh/nine dankuh*

**Please**
Bitte
*bittuh*

**Excuse me!**
Entschuldigung!
*ent-shooldigoong*

### Where, How, Asking

**Excuse me, please**
Entschuldigen Sie bitte
*ent-shooldigen zee bittuh*

**Can you tell me …?**
Können Sie mir sagen …?
*kurnen zee meer zahgen*

**May I have …?**
Kann ich … haben?
*kan ish … hahben*

**Would you like a …?**
Möchten Sie einen/eine/ein …?
*murshten zee ine-en/ine-uh/ine*

**Would you like to …?**
Möchten Sie …?
*murshten zee*

**Is there … here?**
Gibt es hier …?
*geept ess heer*

**What's that?**
Was ist das?
*vass ist dass*

**How much is it?**
Was kostet das?
*vass kostet dass*

**Where is the …?**
Wo ist der/die/das …?
*vo ist dair/dee/dass*

**Is there wheelchair access?**
Kann man dort mit einem Rollstuhl hinein?
*kan man dohrt mit ine-nem rollstuhl hin-ine*

**Are guide dogs allowed?**
Sind Blindenhunde erlaubt?
*zint blindenhoonduh airlowpt*

**ABOUT ONESELF**

**I'm from …**
Ich bin aus …
*ish bin owss*

**I'm … years old**
Ich bin … Jahre alt
*ish bin … yaruh allt*

**I'm a …**
Ich bin …
*ish bin*

**I'm married/single/divorced**
Ich bin verheiratet/single/geschieden
*ish bin fairhyrahtet/single/gusheeden*

**I have … sisters/brothers/children**
Ich habe … Schwestern/Brüder/Kinder
*ish hahbuh … shvestern/brooder/kinder*

## HELP, PROBLEMS

**Can you help me?**
Können Sie mir helfen?
*kurnen zee meer helfen*

**I don't understand**
Ich verstehe nicht
*ish fairshtayuh nisht*

**Do you speak English/French?**
Sprechen Sie Englisch/Französisch?
*shprechen zee eng-lish/frantsur-zish*

**Does anyone here speak English?**
Spricht hier jemand Englisch?
*shprisht heer yaymant eng-lish*

**I can't speak German**
Ich spreche kein Deutsch
*ish shpreshuh kine doytsh*

**I don't know**
Ich weiß nicht
*ish vice nisht*

**Please speak more slowly**
Sprechen Sie bitte etwas langsamer
*shpreshen zee bittuh etvass langzahmer*

**Please write it down for me**
Könnten Sie es mir bitte aufschreiben?
*kurnten zee ess meer bittuh owf-shryben*

**I've lost my way**
Ich habe mich verlaufen
*ish hahbuh mish fairlowfen*

(driving)
Ich habe mich verfahren
*ish hahbuh mish fairfaren*

LIKES, DISLIKES, SOCIALIZING

**I like …**
Ich möchte … gern
*ish murshtuh … gairn*

**I love …**
Ich liebe …
*ish leebuh*

**I don't like …**
Ich möchte … nicht gern
*ish murshtuh … nisht gairn*

**Do you like …?**
Möchten Sie …?
*murshten zee*

**It's delicious/awful!**
Es ist köstlich/furchtbar!
*ess ist kurstlish/foorshtbar*

**I don't drink/smoke**
Ich trinke/rauche nicht
*ish trinkuh/rowкнuh nisht*

**Do you mind if I smoke?**
Haben Sie etwas dagegen, wenn ich rauche?
*hahben zee etvass dagaygen ven ish rowкнuh*

**What would you like (to drink)?**
Was möchten Sie (trinken)?
*vass murshten zee (trinken)*

**I would like a …**
Ich möchte gern einen/eine/ein …
*ish murshtuh gairn ine-en/ine-uh/ine*

**Nothing for me, thanks**
Nichts für mich, danke
*nishts foor mish dankuh*

**Cheers!**
Prost!
*prohst*

---

### THINGS YOU'LL HEAR

| | |
|---|---|
| Achtung! | attention, look out! |
| bedienen Sie sich | help yourself |
| bis später | see you later |
| bitte? | excuse me? |
| bitte (schön/sehr) | here you are, you're welcome |
| danke gleichfalls | the same to you |
| Entschuldigung | excuse me |
| gut | good |
| gute Reise | have a good trip |
| ich verstehe nicht | I don't understand |
| ich weiß nicht | I don't know |
| timmt | that's right |
| Verzeihung | excuse me |
| vielen Dank | thank you very much |
| wie bitte? | what did you say? |
| wie geht es Ihnen? | how are you? |
| wie geht's? | how are things? |
| wirklich? | is that so? |
| | really? |

# DAYS, MONTHS, SEASONS

| Sunday | Sonntag | _zo_ntahk |
| Monday | Montag | _mo_hntahk |
| Tuesday | Dienstag | _dee_nstahk |
| Wednesday | Mittwoch | _mi_tvoкн |
| Thursday | Donnerstag | _do_nnerstahk |
| Friday | Freitag | _fry_tahk |
| Saturday | Samstag, | _za_mstahk, |
| | Sonnabend | _zo_nnahbent |

| January | Januar | _ya_nooar |
| February | Februar | _fay_brooar |
| March | März | mairts |
| April | April | april |
| May | Mai | my |
| June | Juni | _yoo_nee |
| July | Juli | _yoo_lee |
| August | August | ow_goo_st |
| September | September | zept_e_mber |
| October | Oktober | okt_o_ber |
| November | November | nov_e_mber |
| December | Dezember | dayts_e_mber |

| Spring | Frühling | _frœ_ling |
| Summer | Sommer | _zo_mmer |
| Fall | Herbst | hairpst |
| Winter | Winter | _vi_nter |

| Christmas | Weihnachten | _vy_naкнten |
| Christmas Eve | Heiligabend | _hy_lish-_ah_bent |
| New Year | Neujahr | n_oy_-yar |
| New Year's Eve | Silvester | zilv_e_ster |
| Easter | Ostern | _oh_stern |
| Good Friday | Karfreitag | karfr_y_tahk |
| Pentecost | Pfingsten | pf_i_ngsten |

# NUMBERS

| | | | |
|---|---|---|---|
| 0 | null *nool* | 10 | zehn *tsayn* |
| 1 | eins *ine-ss* | 11 | elf *elf* |
| 2 | zwei *tsvy* | 12 | zwölf *tsvurlf* |
| 3 | drei *dry* | 13 | dreizehn *dry-tsayn* |
| 4 | vier *feer* | 14 | vierzehn *veer-tsayn* |
| 5 | fünf *fOOnf* | 15 | fünfzehn *fOOnf-tsayn* |
| 6 | sechs *zex* | 16 | sechzehn *zesh-tsayn* |
| 7 | sieben *zeeben* | 17 | siebzehn *zeep-tsayn* |
| 8 | acht *aKHt* | 18 | achtzehn *aKHt-tsayn* |
| 9 | neun *noyn* | 19 | neunzehn *noyn-tsayn* |

| | |
|---|---|
| 20 | zwanzig *tsvantsish* |
| 21 | einundzwanzig *ine-oont-tsvantsish* |
| 22 | zweiundzwanzig *tsvy-oont-tsvantsish* |
| 30 | dreißig *drysish* |
| 40 | vierzig *feertsish* |
| 50 | fünfzig *fOOnftsish* |
| 60 | sechzig *zeshtsish* |
| 70 | siebzig *zeeptsish* |
| 80 | achtzig *aKHtsish* |
| 90 | neunzig *noyntsish* |
| 100 | hundert *hoondert* |
| 110 | hundertzehn *hoondert-tsayn* |
| 200 | zweihundert *tsvy-hoondert* |
| 1,000 | tausend *towzent* |
| 10,000 | zehntausend *tsayn-towzent* |
| 100,000 | hunderttausend *hoondert-towzent* |
| 1,000,000 | eine Million *ine-uh mill-yohn* |

Ordinal numbers are formed by adding **-te**, or **-ste** if the number ends in **-ig**. For example, **fünfte** (*fOOnftuh*, "fifth"), **zwanzigste** (*tsvantsishstuh*, "twentieth"). Exceptions are: **erste** (*airstuh*, "first"), **dritte** (*drittuh*, "third"), and **siebte** (*zeeptuh*, "seventh").

# TIME

## TELLING TIME

To say the hour in German use the word **Uhr** (*oor*) preceded by the appropriate number, for example: **neun Uhr** (*noyn oor*) is "nine o'clock." The 24-hour clock is used much more commonly in Germany.

The word for "past" is **nach** (*nahкн*). So **zehn nach neun** (*tsayn nahкн noyn*) is "ten past nine." The word for "to" is **vor** (*for*). So **zehn vor neun** (*tsayn for noyn*) is "ten to nine." The word for "(a) quarter" is **viertel** (*feertel*). So **viertel nach/vor neun** (*feertel nahкн/for noyn*) is "(a) quarter past/to nine."

The important thing to remember when telling the time is that, when talking about the half hour, Germans count back from the next full hour, so that, for example, "half past nine" is said in German as "half ten." So **es ist halb zehn** (*ess ist halp tsayn*) means "it's half past nine." Think "half to" instead of "half past."

## USEFUL WORDS AND PHRASES

| today | heute | *hoytuh* |
|---|---|---|
| yesterday | gestern | *gestern* |
| tomorrow | morgen | *morgen* |
| this week | diese Woche | *deezuh voкнuh* |
| last week | letzte Woche | *letstuh voкнuh* |
| next week | nächste Woche | *naykstuh voкнuh* |
| this morning | heute morgen | *hoytuh morgen* |
| this afternoon | heute nachmittag | *hoytuh nahкнmit-tahk* |
| this evening | heute abend | *hoytuh ahbent* |
| tonight | heute abend | *hoytuh ahbent* |
| last night | | |
|   *(last evening)* | gestern Abend | *gestern ahbent* |
|   *(late at night)* | gestern Nacht | *gestern naкнt* |
| in three days | in drei Tagen | *in dry tahgen* |
| three days ago | vor drei Tagen | *for dry tahgen* |

| late | spät | *shpayt* |
|---|---|---|
| early | früh | *frö* |
| soon | bald | *balt* |
| later on | später | *shpayter* |
| at the moment | im Moment | *im moment* |
| second | die Sekunde | *zekoonduh* |
| minute | die Minute | *minootuh* |
| one minute | eine Minute | *ine-uh minootuh* |
| two minutes | zwei Minuten | *tsvy minooten* |
| quarter of an hour | eine Viertelstunde | *feertelshtoonduh* |
| half an hour | eine halbe Stunde | *halbuh shtoonduh* |
| three quarters of an hour | eine Dreiviertelstunde | *dryfeertel-shtoonduh* |
| hour | die Stunde | *shtoonduh* |
| day | der Tag | *tahk* |
| every day | jeden Tag | *yayden tahk* |
| all day | den ganzen Tag | *dayn gantsen tahk* |
| the next day | am nächsten Tag | *am nayksten tahk* |
| week | die Woche | *voкнuh* |
| two weeks | zwei Wochen | *tsvy voкнen* |
| month | der Monat | *mohnaht* |
| year | das Jahr | *yar* |
| what time is it? | wie spät ist es? | *vee shpayt ist ess* |
| am | morgens | *morgens* |
| pm | nachmittags | *nahкнmittahks* |
| (in the evening) | abends | *ahbents* |
| one o'clock | ein Uhr | *ine oor* |
| ten past one | zehn nach eins | *tsayn nahкн ine-ss* |
| quarter past one | viertel nach eins | *feertel nahкн ine-ss* |
| half past one | halb zwei | *halp tsvy* |
| twenty to two | zwanzig vor zwei | *tsvantsish for tsvy* |
| quarter to two | viertel vor zwei | *feertel for tsvy* |
| 13:00 | dreizehn Uhr | *dry-tsayn oor* |
| 16:30 | sechzehn Uhr dreißig | *zesh-tsayn oor drysish* |
| at half past five | um halb sechs | *oom halp zex* |

# COMMUNICATIONS

## USEFUL WORDS AND PHRASES

| | | |
|---|---|---|
| code | die Vorwahl | _fo_rvahl |
| collect call | das R-Gespräch | _ai_r-gushpraysh |
| dial tone | das Amtszeichen | _a_mts-tsyshen |
| directory assistance | die Auskunft | _ow_sskoonft |
| email address | die E-mail Adresse | ee-mail adressuh |
| extension | der Nebenanschluß | _na_yben-anshlooss |
| fax | das Fax | fax |
| internet | das Internet | 'internet' |
| mobile phone | das Mobiltelefon | mohbeeltelef_oh_n |
| payphone | das Münztelefon | m_oo_nts-telef_oh_n |
| phonecard | die Telefonkarte | telef_oh_n-kartuh |
| telephone | das Telefon | telef_oh_n |
| website | die Webseite | 'website' |
| wrong number | die falsche Nummer | _fa_lshuh n_oo_mmer |

**Where is the nearest phone booth?**
Wo ist die nächste Telefonzelle?
_vo ist dee na_ykstuh telef_oh_n-tselluh

**I would like a number in …**
Ich hätte gern eine Nummer in …
ish h_e_ttuh gairn _ine_-uh n_oo_mmer in

**I would like to speak to …**
Kann ich bitte … sprechen?
kan ish b_i_ttuh … shpr_e_shen

**Hello, this is … speaking**
Hallo, hier spricht …
h_a_llo heer shprisht

**Could you leave him/her a message?**
Können Sie ihm/ihr etwas ausrichten?
_k_urnen zee eem/eer _e_tvass _ow_ssrishten

**I'll call back later**
Ich rufe später zurück
*ish r<u>oo</u>fuh shp<u>ay</u>ter tsoor<u>oo</u>k*

**Sorry, (I've got the) wrong number**
Tut mir leid, ich habe mich verwählt
*toot meer lite ish h<u>ah</u>buh mish fairv<u>ay</u>lt*

**What's your fax number/email address?**
Wie ist ihre Faxnummer/E-mail Adresse?
*vee isst eeruh faxnummer/ee-mail adressuh*

**May I send an email/fax from here?**
Kann ich von hier eine E-mail/ein Fax senden?
*kan ish von hear ine-nuh ee-mail/ine fax senden*

---

**THINGS YOU'LL HEAR**

**Am Apparat**
Speaking

**Wen möchten Sie sprechen?**
Whom would you like to speak to?

**Sie sind falsch verbunden**
You've got the wrong number

**Wer spricht bitte?**
Who's speaking please?

**Welche Nummer haben Sie?**
What is your number?

**Tut mir leid, er ist nicht im Hause**
Sorry, he's not here

**Ich werde ihm/ihr sagen, daß Sie angerufen haben**
I'll tell him/her you called

**Bitte warten**
Please hold

# EMERGENCIES

## Useful Words and Phrases

| accident | der Unfall | _oo_nfal |
| ambulance | der Krankenwagen | kr_a_nken-vahgen |
| breakdown | die Panne | p_a_nnuh |
| burglary | der Einbruch | _ine_-brooкн |
| crash | der Zusammenstoß | tsooz_a_mmen-shtohss |
| emergency | der Notfall | n_oh_tfal |
| fire | das Feuer | f_o_yer |
| fire department | die Feuerwehr | f_o_yer-vayr |
| police | die Polizei | poli-ts_y_ |
| police station | die Polizeiwache | poli-ts_y_-vaкнuh |

**Help!**
Hilfe!
h_i_lfuh

**Stop!**
Halt!
halt

**Get an ambulance!**
Rufen Sie einen Krankenwagen!
r_oo_fen zee _ine_-en kr_a_nken-vahgen

**Hurry up!**
Beeilen Sie sich!
buh-_ile_-en zee zish

**My address is …**
Meine Adresse ist …
m_ine_-uh adr_e_ssuh ist

**My passport/car has been stolen**
Mein Paß/Auto ist gestohlen worden
mine pas/_owto_ ist gusht_oh_len vorden

# HOTELS

### Useful Words and Phrases

| | | |
|---|---|---|
| bath *(tub)* | die Badewanne | *bahduh-vannuh* |
| bathroom | das Bad | *baht* |
| bed | das Bett | *bet* |
| bed and breakfast | Übernachtung mit Frühstück | *ɷbernakhtoong mit frɷshtɷk* |
| bedroom | das (Schlaf)zimmer | *(shlahf)tsimmer* |
| breakfast | das Frühstück | *frɷshtɷk* |
| check | die Rechnung | *reshnoong* |
| dining room | der Speisesaal | *shpyzuh-zahl* |
| dinner *(evening)* | das Abendessen | *ahbentessen* |
| double bed | das Doppelbett | *doppelbet* |
| double room | das Doppelzimmer | *doppeltsimmer* |
| elevator | der Aufzug, der Lift | *owf-tsook, lift* |
| full board | Vollpension | *follpangz-yohn* |
| hotel | das Hotel | *hotel* |
| key | der Schlüssel | *shlɷssel* |
| lobby | das Foyer | *fwa-yay* |
| lounge | der Aufenthaltsraum | *owfenthaltsrowm* |
| lunch | das Mittagessen | *mittahkessen* |
| maid | das Zimmermädchen | *tsimmer-maydshen* |
| manager | der Geschäftsführer | *gushefts-fɷrer* |
| receipt | die Quittung | *kvittoong* |
| reception | der Empfang | *empfang* |
| receptionist | der Empfangschef | *empfangs-shef* |
| *(woman)* | die Empfangsdame | *empfangs-dahmuh* |
| restroom | die Toilette | *twalettuh* |
| room | das Zimmer | *tsimmer* |
| room service | der Zimmerservice | *tsimmer-'service'* |
| shower | die Dusche | *dooshuh* |
| single bed | das Einzelbett | *ine-tselbet* |
| single room | das Einzelzimmer | *ine-tsel-tsimmer* |
| sink | das Waschbecken | *vashbecken* **twin** |
| room | das Zweibettzimmer | *tsvybet-tsimmer* |

**Do you have any vacancies?**
Haben Sie Zimmer frei?
*hahben zee tsimmer fry*

**I have a reservation**
Ich habe ein Zimmer reserviert
*ish hahbuh ine tsimmer rezerveert*

**I'd like a single room**
Ich möchte ein Einzelzimmer
*ish murshtuh ine ine-tsel-tsimmer*

**I'd like a room with a bathroom/balcony**
Ich möchte ein Zimmer mit Bad/Balkon
*ish murshtuh ine tsimmer mit baht/balkong*

**Is there satellite/cable TV in the rooms?**
Gibt es Satelliten/Kabel fernsehen in den Zimmern?
*gipt as zateleeten/kahbel fairnzayhen in den tsimmen*

**I'd like a room for one night/three nights**
Ich möchte ein Zimmer für eine Nacht/drei Nächte
*ish murshtuh ine tsimmer fCOr ine-uh naKHt/dry neshtuh*

**What is the charge per night?**
Was kostet es pro Nacht?
*vass kostet ess pro naKHt*

**When is breakfast/dinner?**
Wann wird das Frühstück/Abendessen serviert?
*vann veert dass frCOhshtCOk/ahbentessen zairveert*

**Please wake/call me at … o'clock**
Bitte wecken Sie mich um … Uhr
*bittuh vecken zee mish oom … oor*

**May I have breakfast in my room?**
Können Sie mir das Frühstück auf mein Zimmer bringen?
*kurnen zee meer dass frCOshtCOk owf mine tsimmer bring-en*

**My room number is …**
Meine Zimmernummer ist …
*mine-uh tsimmer-noommer ist*

**There is no toilet paper in the bathroom**
Im Badezimmer ist kein Toilettenpapier
*im bahduh-tsimmer ist kine twaletten-papeer*

**The window won't open**
Das Fenster geht nicht auf
*dass fenster gayt nisht owf*

**There isn't any hot water**
Es gibt kein warmes Wasser
*ess geept kine varmess vasser*

**I'm leaving tomorrow**
Ich reise morgen ab
*ish ryzuh morgen ap*

**When do I have to vacate the room?**
Bis wann muß ich das Zimmer räumen?
*biss van mooss ish dass tsimmer roymen*

**May I have the check, please?**
Kann ich bitte die Rechnung haben?
*kan ish bittuh dee reshnoong hahben*

**I'll pay by credit card**
Ich zahle mit Kreditkarte
*ish tsahluh mit kredeetkartuh*

**I'll pay cash**
Ich zahle in bar
*ish tsahluh in bar*

**Can you get me a taxi?**
Können Sie mir ein Taxi bestellen?
*kurnen zee meer ine taxi bushtellen*

## THINGS YOU'LL SEE

| | |
|---|---|
| Aufzug | elevator |
| Bad | bath |
| belegt | no vacancies |
| drücken | push |
| Dusche | shower |
| Eingang | entrance |
| Empfang | reception |
| Frühstück | breakfast |
| kein Zutritt | no admission |
| Mittagessen | lunch |
| Notausgang | emergency exit |
| Parkplatz | car park |
| Rechnung | bill, check |
| Speisesaal | restaurant, dining room |
| ziehen | pull |

## THINGS YOU'LL HEAR

**Tut mir leid, wir sind voll belegt**
I'm sorry, we're full

**Es sind keine Einzelzimmer/Doppelzimmer mehr frei**
There are no single/double rooms left

**Für wie lange?**
For how long?

**Wie möchten Sie zahlen?**
How would you like to pay?

**Könnten Sie bitte im voraus bezahlen**
Could you please pay in advance

**Sie müssen das Zimmer bis zwölf Uhr räumen**
You must vacate the room by noon

## SHOPPING

**Excuse me, where is/are …?**
Entschuldigung, wo finde ich …?
*ent-sh**oo**ldigoong vo f**i**nduh ish*

**Do you have …?**
Haben Sie …?
*h**ah**ben zee*

**How much is this?**
Was kostet das?
*vass k**o**stet dass*

**Where do I pay?**
Wo ist die Kasse?
*vo ist dee k**a**ssuh*

**Do you take credit cards?**
Akzeptieren Sie Kreditkarten?
*aktsept**ee**ren zee kred**ee**tkarten*

**May I have a receipt?**
Kann ich eine Quittung bekommen?
*kan ish **ine**-uh kv**i**ttoong buk**o**mmen*

**Do you have something less expensive?**
Haben Sie etwas Billigeres?
*h**ah**ben zee **e**tvass b**i**lligeress*

**May I have a refund?**
Kann ich mein Geld zurückbekommen?
*kan ish mine gelt tsoor**ü**k-buk**o**mmen*

**That's fine. I'll take it**
In Ordnung. Ich nehme es
*in **o**rtnoong ish n**a**ymuh ess*

**It isn't what I wanted**
Es ist nicht das, was ich wollte
*ess ist nisht dass vass ish v**o**lltuh*

# EATING OUT

In Germany you'll find a wide range of places to eat, from the gourmet restaurant to the sausage and fries kiosk on the pavement. Fast food outlets, Chinese, Italian and Greek restaurants will be familiar. Not so perhaps the **Balkangrill**, serving spicy dishes from the Balkan countries.

If you want something typically German, you could do a lot worse than try a small **Gasthaus** (*gast-howss*), or inn. Some dishes vary from region to region, but one shared characteristic you'll find is that German portions are not skimpy. Germans tend to eat a lot of meat; vegetarians might have to make a special request.

Ask for a small beer (**ein kleines Bier**, *ine kline-ess beer*) and you'll normally get a glass of around 0.2 liters. A large beer (**ein großes Bier**, *ine grohss-ess beer*) will normally be 0.4 or 0.5 liters, although in Bavaria you may well get a liter, which is known as **eine Maß** (*ine-uh mahss*). German beer is usually **Pils**. In some areas you might try **Alt**, which is a darker beer. German wine is either **süß** (*süss*, "sweet"), **trocken** (*trocken*, "dry") or, if you like it dry and a little sharper, **herb** (*hairp*). If you'd like to try a local wine, ask for **einen Wein aus dieser Gegend** (*ine-en vine owss deezer gaygent*).

If you're having a drink in a pub or bar you don't pay when ordering. Instead, the barman or barmaid will keep a tally of what you've bought, often ticking it off on your beer mat. If you sit at a table, you can expect table service (for no extra charge). There are no restrictions on taking children into pubs.

## USEFUL WORDS AND PHRASES

| beer | das Bier | *beer* |
|------|----------|--------|
| bottle | die Flasche | *flashuh* |
| bread | das Brot | *broht* |
| butter | die Butter | *bootter* |
| café | das Café | *kaffay* |

| | | |
|---|---|---|
| **cake** | der Kuchen | _kooкнen_ |
| **check** | die Rechnung | _reshnoong_ |
| **carafe** | die Karaffe | _karaffuh_ |
| **children's portion** | der Kinderteller | _kinderteller_ |
| **coffee** | der Kaffee | _kaffay_ |
| **cup** | die Tasse | _tassuh_ |
| **dessert** | das Dessert | _dessair_ |
| **fork** | die Gabel | _gahbel_ |
| **glass** | das Glas | _glahss_ |
| **half-liter** | der halbe Liter | _halbuh leeter_ |
| **knife** | das Messer | _messer_ |
| **main course** | das Hauptgericht | _howpt-gurisht_ |
| **menu** | die Speisekarte | _shpyzuh-kartuh_ |
| **milk** | die Milch | _milsh_ |
| **napkin** | die Serviette | _zairvee-ettuh_ |
| **pepper** | der Pfeffer | _pfeffer_ |
| **plate** | der Teller | _teller_ |
| **receipt** | die Quittung | _kvittoong_ |
| **restaurant** | das Restaurant | _restorong_ |
| **salt** | das Salz | _zalts_ |
| **sandwich** | das belegte Brot | _bulayktuh broht_ |
| **snack** | der Imbiß | _imbiss_ |
| **soup** | die Suppe | _zooppuh_ |
| **spoon** | der Löffel | _lurfel_ |
| **appetizer** | die Vorspeise | _forshpyzuh_ |
| **sugar** | der Zucker | _tsooker_ |
| **table** | der Tisch | _tish_ |
| **tea** | der Tee | _tay_ |
| **teaspoon** | der Teelöffel | _taylurfel_ |
| **tip** | das Trinkgeld | _trinkgelt_ |
| **waiter** | der Ober | _ohber_ |
| **waitress** | die Bedienung | _budeenoong_ |
| **water** | das Wasser | _vasser_ |
| **wine** | der Wein | _vine_ |
| **wine list** | die Weinkarte | _vine-kartuh_ |

**A table for one/two/three, please**
Einen Tisch für eine Person/zwei/drei Personen, bitte
*ine-en tish foor ine-uh pairzohn/tsvy/dry pairzohnen bittuh*

**May I see the menu/wine list?**
Könnte ich bitte die Speisekarte/Weinkarte haben?
*kurntuh ish bittuh dee shpyzuh-kartuh/vine-kartuh hahben*

**What would you recommend?**
Was könnten Sie empfehlen?
*vass kurnten zee empfaylen*

**I'd like …**
Ich hätte gern …
*ish hettuh gairn*

**Just a cup of coffee, please**
Nur eine Tasse Kaffee, bitte
*noor ine-uh tassuh kaffay bittuh*

**I only want a snack**
Ich möchte nur eine Kleinigkeit
*ish murshtuh noor ine-uh kline-ishkite*

**Is there a fixed-price menu?**
Gibt es ein Tagesgericht?
*geept ess ine tahges-gurisht*

**A liter carafe of house red, please**
Einen Liter roten Tafelwein, bitte
*ine-en leeter rohten tahfel-vine bittuh*

**Do you have any vegetarian dishes?**
Haben Sie vegetarische Gerichte?
*hahben zee vegetarishuh gurishtuh*

**May we have some water, please?**
Könnten Sie uns ein Glas Wasser geben?
*kurnten zee oonss ine glas vasser gayben*

**Do you do children's portions?**
Gibt es auch Kinderteller?
*geept ess owkʜ kinderteller*

**Is there a highchair/baby changing room?**
Gibt es dort einen Hochstuhl/einen Wickelraum?
*gipt as dohrt ine-nen hoкʜshtuhl/ine-nen vikkelrowm*

**Can you warm this bottle/baby food for me?**
Können Sie diese Flasche/Babynahrung für mich aufwärmen?
*kurnnen zee deezuh flahshuh/baibee-nahrunk foor mish owf-vaɣrmer*

**Waiter/Waitress!**
Herr Ober!/Fräulein!
*hair ohber/froyline*

**We didn't order this**
Das haben wir nicht bestellt
*dass hahben veer nisht bushtellt*

**May we have some more …?**
Könnten wir noch etwas … haben?
*kurnten veer noкʜ etvass … hahben*

**May we have the check, please?**
Zahlen, bitte
*tsahlen bittuh*

**May I have a receipt, please?**
Könnte ich bitte eine Quittung bekommen?
*kurntuh ish bittuh ine-uh kvittoong bukommen*

**May we pay separately?**
Können wir getrennt bezahlen?
*kurnen veer gutrennt butsahlen*

**The meal was very good, thank you**
Es hat sehr gut geschmeckt, vielen Dank
*es hat zair goot gushmeckt feelen dank*

# MENU GUIDE

**Äpfel** apples
**Apfelkompott** stewed apples
**Apfelmus** apple purée
**Apfelsaft** apple juice
**Apfelsinen** oranges
**Apfelstrudel** apple strudel
**Apfeltasche** apple turnover
**Apfelwein** cider
**Aprikosen** apricots
**Artischocken** artichokes
**Auflauf** (baked) pudding or omelette
**Aufschnitt** sliced cold meats, cold cuts
**Austern** oysters
**Backpflaume** prune
**Baiser** meringue
**Balkansalat** cabbage and pepper salad
**Bananen** bananas
**Bandnudeln** ribbon noodles
**Bedienung** service
**Beilagen** side dishes
**Berliner** jam doughnut
**Bier** beer
**Birnen** pears
**Biskuit** sponge cake
**Biskuitrolle** Swiss roll
**Bismarckhering** filleted pickled herring
**Blätterteig** puff pastry
**blau** boiled
**Blaukraut** red cabbage
**Blumenkohl** cauliflower
**blutig** rare
**Blutwurst** black pudding
**Bockwurst** large hot dog
**Bohnen** beans
**Bouillon** clear soup
**Bouletten** meatballs
**Braten** roasted meat
**Bratensoße** gravy

**Bratkartoffeln** fried potatoes
**Bratwurst** broiled pork sausage
**Brot** bread
**Brötchen** roll
**Brühwurst** large hot dog
**Buttercremetorte** cream cake
**Buttermilch** buttermilk
**Champignons** mushrooms
**Dampfnudeln** sweet yeast dumpling
**Dicke Bohnen** fava beans
**Dillsoße** dill sauce
**durchgebraten** well-done
**durchwachsen** with fat
**durchwachsener Speck** fatty bacon
**Eier** eggs
**Eierauflauf** omelette
**Eierkuchen, Eierpfannkuchen** pancake
**Eierspeise** egg dish
**eingelegt** pickled
**Eintopf** stew
**Eintopfgericht** stew
**Eis** ice
**Eisbecher** sundae
**Eisbein** knuckles of pork
**englisch** rare
**Entenbraten** roasted duck
**Erbsen** peas
**Erdbeertorte** strawberry cake
**Essig** vinegar
**Falscher Hase** meat loaf
**Fenchel** fennel
**Fisch** fish
**Fischfrikadellen** fish cakes
**Fischstäbchen** fish sticks
**Fleischkäse** meat loaf
**Fleischklößchen** meatball(s)
**Fleischwurst** pork sausage
**Forelle** trout

**Frikadelle** rissole
**Frikassee** fricassee
**Fruchtsaft** fruit juice
**Gans** goose
**Gebäck** pastries, cakes
**gebacken** baked
**gebraten** roast
**gedünstet** steamed
**Geflügel** poultry
**gefüllt** stuffed
**gekocht** boiled
**gemischter Salat** mixed salad
**Gemüse** vegetable(s)
**gepökelt** salted, pickled
**geräuchert** smoked
**Geschnetzeltes** strips of meat in sauce
**Geselchtes** salted and smoked meat
**Getränke** beverages
**Gewürze** spices
**Gewürzgurken** pickles
**gratiniert** au gratin
**Grieß** semolina
**grüne Bohnen** green beans
**grüne Nudeln** green pasta
**Gulasch** goulash
**Gurkensalat** cucumber salad
**Hackfleisch** ground meat
**Hähnchen** chicken
**Hähnchenkeule** chicken leg
**Hammelfleisch** mutton
**Hartkäse** hard cheese
**Hauptspeisen** main courses
**Hausfrauenart, Hausmacher** homemade
**Hecht** pike
**Heidelbeeren** bilberries, blueberries
**Heilbutt** halibut
**Herz** heart
**Himbeeren** raspberries
**Himmel und Erde** potato and apple purée
 with black pudding or liver sausage
**Honig** honey

**Honigkuchen** honey cake
**Huhn** chicken
**Hühnersuppe** chicken soup
**Hummer** lobster
**Kabeljau** cod
**Kaffee** coffee
**Kalbfleisch** veal
**Kalbsbraten** roasted veal
**kaltes Büfett** cold buffet
**Kaninchen** rabbit
**Karotten** carrots
**Karpfen** carp
**Kartoffelknödel** potato dumplings
**Kartoffeln** potatoes
**Kartoffelpüree** potato purée
**Käse** cheese
**Käsekuchen** cheesecake
**Käseplatte** selection of cheeses
**Kasserolle** casserole
**Kassler** smoked and braised pork chop
**Kastanien** chestnuts
**Katenrauchwurst** smoked sausage
**Keule** leg, haunch
**Kirschen** cherries
**klare Brühe** clear soup
**Klöße** dumplings
**Knäckebrot** crispbread
**Knackwurst** hot dog
**Knoblauch** garlic
**Knochen** bone
**Knödel** dumplings
**Kohl** cabbage
**Konfitüre** jam
**Königskuchen** type of fruit cake
**Kopfsalat** lettuce
**Kotelett** chop
**Krabben** shrimp
**Kraftbrühe** beef consommé
**Kräuter** herbs
**Krautsalat** coleslaw
**Kroketten** croquettes

**Kuchen** cake
**Kürbis** pumpkin
**Labskaus** meat, fish, and potato stew
**Lachs** salmon
**Lachsforelle** sea trout
**Lamm** lamb
**Lauch** leek
**Leber** liver
**Leberkäse** baked pork and beef loaf
**Leipziger Allerlei** mixed vegetables
**Linseneintopf** lentil stew
**Linsensuppe** lentil soup
**Mandeln** almonds
**mariniert** marinaded, pickled
**Marmelade** jam
**Meeresfrüchte** seafood
**Meerrettich** horseradish
**Meerrettichsoße** horseradish sauce
**Melone** melon
**Miesmuscheln** mussels
**Milch** milk
**Milchmixgetränk** milk shake
**Milchreis** rice pudding
**Mineralwasser** carbonated mineral
  water
**Möhren, Mohrrüben** carrots
**Mus** purée
**Muscheln** mussels
**Muskat(nuß)** nutmeg
**Nachspeisen** desserts
**Nieren** kidneys
**Nüsse** nuts
**Obstsalat** fruit salad
**Ochsenschwanzsuppe** ox tail soup
**Öl** oil
**Oliven** olives
**Olivenöl** olive oil
**Omelett** omelette
**Orangen** oranges
**Orangensaft** orange juice
**Palatschinken** stuffed pancakes

**Paprika** peppers
**Paradiesäpfel** tomatoes
**Pastete** vol-au-vent
**Petersilie** parsley
**Pfannkuchen** pancake(s)
**Pfeffer** pepper
**Pfirsiche** peaches
**Pflaumen** plums
**Pflaumenkuchen** plum tart
**pikant** spicy
**Pilze** mushrooms
**Platte** selection
**pochiert** poached
**Pökelfleisch** salted meat
**Porree** leek
**Potthast** braised beef with sauce
**Poularde** young chicken
**Preiselbeeren** cranberries
**Prinzeßbohnen** unsliced string beans
**Pumpernickel** black rye bread
**Püree** (potato) purée
**püriert** puréed
**Puter** turkey
**Radieschen** radishes
**Rahm** (sour) cream
**Räucheraal** smoked eel
**Räucherhering** kipper, smoked herring
**Räucherlachs** smoked salmon
**Räucherspeck** smoked bacon
**Reibekuchen** potato waffles
**Reis** rice
**Reisauflauf** rice pudding
**Renke** whitefish
**Rettich** radish
**Rhabarber** rhubarb
**Rindfleisch** beef
**Risi-Pisi** rice and peas
**Rohkostplatte** selection of salads
**rosa** rare to medium
**Rosenkohl** Brussels sprouts
**Rosinen** raisins

**Rostbraten** roasted
**Rösti** fried potatoes and onions
**Röstkartoffeln** fried potatoes
**Rote Bete** beets
**rote Grütze** red fruit jelly
**Rotkohl, Rotkraut** red cabbage
**Rühreier** scrambled eggs
**Sahne** cream
**Salate** salads
**Salatsoße** salad dressing
**Salz** salt
**Salzburger Nockerln** sweet soufflés
**Salzkartoffeln** boiled potatoes
**sauer** sour
**Sauerbraten** marinaded pot roast
**Sauerkraut** white cabbage, finely chopped and pickled
**Sauerrahm** sour cream
**Schaschlik** (shish-)kabob
**Schellfisch** haddock
**Schinken** ham
**Schinkenröllchen** rolled ham
**Schinkenwurst** ham sausage
**Schlagsahne** whipped cream
**Schmorbraten** pot roast
**Scholle** plaice
**Schulterstück** slice of shoulder
**Schwarzbrot** brown rye bread
**Schwarzwälder Kirschtorte** Black Forest cherry gâteau
**Schweinefleisch** pork
**Schweinshaxe** knuckle of pork
**Seezunge** sole
**Semmel** bread roll
**Semmelknödel** bread dumplings
**Senf** mustard
**Spargel** asparagus
**Spätzle** homemade noodles
**Speck** fatty bacon
**Speisekarte** menu
**Spiegeleier** fried eggs

**Spinat** spinach
**Spitzkohl** white cabbage
**Sprudel(wasser)** mineral water
**Streuselkuchen** cake with crumble topping
**Suppen** soups
**süß** sweet
**süß-sauer** sweet-and-sour
**Tafelwasser** (uncarbonated) mineral water
**Tagesgericht** dish of the day
**Tageskarte** menu of the day
**Taube** pigeon
**Tee** tea
**Thunfisch** tuna
**Tintenfisch** squid
**Tomaten** tomatoes
**Törtchen** tart(s)
**Torte** gâteau
**Truthahn** turkey
**überbacken** au gratin
**verlorene Eier** poached eggs
**Vollkornbrot** dark whole grain bread
**Vorspeisen** hors d'oeuvres, appetizers
**Waffeln** waffles
**Weichkäse** soft cheese
**Weincreme** pudding with wine
**Weintrauben** grapes
**Weißbrot** white bread
**Weißwein** white wine
**Wild** game
**Windbeutel** cream puff
**Wirsing** savoy cabbage
**Wurst** sausage
**Würstchen** hot dog(s)
**Wurstplatte** selection of sausages
**Zitrone** lemon
**Zucker** sugar
**Zunge** tongue
**Zwiebeln** onions
**Zwischengerichte** entrées

# GREEK

## CONTENTS

INTRODUCTION                    174
USEFUL PHRASES                  176
DAYS, MONTHS, SEASONS           181
NUMBERS                         182
TIME                            183
COMMUNICATIONS                  185
HOTELS                          188
SHOPPING                        192
EATING OUT                      193
MENU GUIDE                      196

# INTRODUCTION

## Pronunciation

When reading the imitated pronunciation, stress the part that is underlined. Pronounce each syllable as if it formed part of an English word, and you will be understood sufficiently well. Remember the points below, and your pronunciation will be even closer to the correct Greek.

| | |
|---|---|
| *e* | is always short, as in "bed" |
| *i* | is always long, as in "Lolita" |
| | (So when you see the imitation *ine*, remember to make this two syllables "ee-ne." Similarly, *ne* and *me* should be kept short – *don't* say "nee" or "mee.") |
| *g* | should be a rolled, guttural sound at the back of the throat. |
| *h* | is a guttural "ch," as in the Scottish "loch" (*Don't* pronounce this as "lock.") |
| *oo* | long, as in "moon" |
| *th* | as in "then" or "the" (Notice this particularly, and *don't* confuse it with TH in small capitals.) |
| TH | as in "theater" or "thin" |

## The Greek Alphabet

To help you read signs or notices printed in capital letters (which are sometimes quite unlike their lower-case counterparts), the Greek alphabet is given below. Alongside each letter is its name and a guide to its pronunciation.

| *letter* | | *name* | *pronunciation* |
|---|---|---|---|
| A | α | alfa | *a* as in "father" |
| B | β | vita | *v* as in "victory" |
| Γ | γ | ghamma | before *a*, *o* and *u*, it is a guttural *gh*; before *e* and *i* sounds, it is like *y* in "yes" |

| Δ | δ | dhelta | *th* as in "then" |
|---|---|---|---|
| E | ε | epsilon | *e* as in "end" |
| Z | ζ | zita | *z* as in "zest" |
| H | η | ita | *i* as in "Maria" |
| Θ | θ | thita | *th* as in "theater" (TH in the imitated pronunciation system) |
| I | ι | yiota | before *a* and *o* sounds, like *y* in "yes"; otherwise like *i* in "Maria" |
| K | κ | kapa | like *k* in "king," but softer |
| Λ | λ | lamdha | *l* as in "love" |
| M | μ | mi | *m* as in "mother" |
| N | ν | ni | *n* as in "no" |
| Ξ | ξ | ksi | *x* as in "box," or *ks* as in "books" |
| O | o | omikron | *o* as in "orange" |
| Π | π | pi | like *p* in "Peter," but softer |
| P | ρ | ro | *r* as in "Rome," trilled or rolled |
| Σ | σ, ς | sighma | *s* as in "sing." The alternative small letter ς is used only at the end of a word |
| T | τ | taf | like *t* in "tea," but softer |
| Y | υ | ipsilon | *i* as in "Maria" |
| Φ | φ | fi | *f* as in "friend" |
| X | χ | hi | *ch* as in the Scottish "loch." But before *e* or *i* sounds, it is like *h* in "hue" |
| Ψ | ψ | psi | like *ps* in "lapse" |
| Ω | ω | omegha | *o* as in "orange" |

Note that the Greek question mark is a semicolon (;). Stress is indicated by an accent above the Greek letter and underscoring in the pronuciation.

## USEFUL PHRASES

**Yes/No**
Ναι/Όχι
*ne/ohi*

**Thank you**
Ευχαριστώ
*efharisto*

**No, thank you**
Όχι, ευχαριστώ
*ohi efharisto*

**Please**
Παρακαλώ
*parakalo*

**I don't understand**
Δεν καταλαβαίνω
*then katalaveno*

**Do you speak English/French/German?**
Μιλάτε Αγγλικά/Γαλλικά/Γερμανικά;
*milate Anglika/Galika/Yermanika*

**I can't speak Greek**
Δέν μιλάω Ελληνικά
*then milao elinika*

**Please speak more slowly**
Παρακαλώ, μιλάτε πιό αργά;
*parakalo, milate pio arga*

**Please write it down for me**
Μου το γράφετε, παρακαλώ;
*moo to grafete, parakalo*

**Good morning/good afternoon/good night**
Καλημέρα/καλησπέρα/καληνύχτα
*kalimera/kalispera/kalinihta*

**Goodbye**
Αντίο
*andio*

**How are you?**
Τι κάνεις;
*ti kanis*

**Excuse me, please**
Συγγνώμη, παρακαλώ
*ingnomi, parakalo*

**Sorry!**
Συγγνώμη!
*ingnomi*

**I'm really sorry**
Ειλικρινά, λυπάμαι
*ilikrina, lipame*

**Can you help me?**
Μπορείς να με βοηθήσεις;
*oris na me voiTHisis*

**Can you tell me ...?**
Μου λέτε ...;
*moo lete*

May I have ...?
Μπορώ να έχω ...;
*boro na eho*

I would like ...
Θα ήθελα ...
*тна iтнela*

Is there ... here?
Υπάρχει ... εδώ;
*iparhi ... etho*

Where are the toilets?
Που είναι οι τουαλέτες;
*poo ine i tooaletes*

Where can I get ...?
Που μπορώ να πάρω ...;
*poo boro na paro*

Is there wheelchair access?
Υπάρχει πρόσβαση για αναπηρικό καροτσάκι;
*iparhi prosvasi ya anapiriko karotsaki*

How much is it?
Πόσο κάνει;
*poso kani*

Do you take credit cards?
Δέχεστε πιστωτικές κάρτες;
*theheste pistotikes kartes*

May I pay by check?
Μπορώ να πληρώσω με επιταγή;
*boro na pliroso me epitayi*

**What time is it?**
Τι ώρα είναι;
_ti ora ine_

**I must go now**
Πρέπει να πηγαίνω τώρα
_prepi na piyeno tora_

**Cheers!**
Εις υγείαν!
_is iyian_

**Go away!**
Παράτα με!
_paratame_

---

## THINGS YOU'LL SEE OR HEAR

| | | |
|---|---|---|
| **ανακοίνωση** | _anakinosi_ | announcement |
| **ΑΝΑΧΩΡΗΣΕΙΣ/** | _anahorisis_ | departures |
| **αναχωρήσεις** | | |
| **ΑΝΟΙΚΤΑ/ανοικτά** | _anikta_ | open |
| **ΑΝΟΙΚΤΟΝ/ανοικτόν** | _anikton_ | open |
| **ΑΣΑΝΣΕΡ/ασανσέρ** | _asanser_ | elevator |
| **αντίο** | _andio_ | goodbye |
| **απαγορεύεται** | _apagorevete_ | no smoking |
| **το κάπνισμα** | _to kapnisma_ | |
| **αργά** | _arga_ | slow |
| **αριστερά** | _aristera_ | left |
| **ΑΦΙΞΕΙΣ/αφίξεις** | _afixis_ | arrivals |
| **βιβλιοθήκη** | _vivliothiki_ | library |
| **ΓΥΝΑΙΚΩΝ/γυναικών** | _yinekon_ | women |
| **ΔΕΝ ΛΕΙΤΟΥΡΓΕΙ/** | _then litooryi_ | out of order |
| **δεν λειτουργεί** | | |
| **δεξιά** | _thexia_ | right |

$\longrightarrow$

| | | |
|---|---|---|
| διάλειμμα | thi<u>a</u>lima | interval |
| ΕΙΣΟΔΟΣ/είσοδος | <u>i</u>sothos | entrance |
| έκθεση | <u>e</u>kTHesi | exhibition, show room |
| έλεγχος | <u>e</u>lenhos | inspection |
| ελεύθερος | el<u>e</u>fTHeros | free |
| ΕΞΟΔΟΣ/έξοδος | <u>e</u>xothos | exit |
| ευχαριστώ | efharist<u>o</u> | thank you |
| καλώς ήρθατε | kal<u>o</u>s <u>i</u>rτHate | welcome |
| ΚΑΠΝΙΖΟΝΤΕΣ/καπνίζοντες | kapn<u>i</u>zodes | smokers |
| ΚΑΤΗΛΗΜΜΕΝΟΣ/ κατηλημμένος | katilim<u>e</u>nos | occupied |
| ΚΙΝΔΥΝΟΣ/κίνδυνος | k<u>i</u>nthinos | danger |
| ΚΛΕΙΣΤΑ/κλειστά | klist<u>a</u> | closed |
| ΚΛΕΙΣΤΟΝ/κλειστόν | klist<u>o</u>n | closed |
| μέχρι | m<u>e</u>hri | until |
| μη | mi | do not |
| ναί | ne | yes |
| ορίστε; | or<u>i</u>ste? | can I help you? |
| όχι | <u>o</u>hi | no |
| παρακαλώ | parakal<u>o</u> | please; can I help you? |
| πεζοί | pez<u>i</u> | pedestrians |
| προσοχή παρακαλώ | prosoh<u>i</u> parakal<u>o</u> | attention, please |
| ΠΡΟΣΟΧΗ!/προσοχή! | prosoh<u>i</u> | caution! |
| ΣΥΡΑΤΕ/σύρατε | s<u>i</u>rate | pull |
| ΣΤΟΠ/στόπ | stop | stop |
| στρίψατε | str<u>i</u>psate | turn |
| ΣΧΟΛΕΙΟ/σχολείο | s-hol<u>i</u>o | school |
| ΤΑΜΕΙΟ/ταμείο | tam<u>i</u>o | cash register |
| ΤΕΛΩΝΕΙΟ/Τελωνείο | Telon<u>i</u>o | customs |
| ΤΟΥΡΙΣΤΙΚΗ ΑΣΤΥΝΟΜΙΑ/ Τουριστική Αστυνομία | Tooristik<u>i</u> Astinom<u>i</u>a | Tourist Police |
| χαίρετε | h<u>e</u>rete | hello |
| ωθήσατε | oτH<u>i</u>sate | push |
| ώρες λειτουργίας | <u>o</u>res litoory<u>i</u>as | opening hours |

# DAYS, MONTHS, SEASONS

| | | |
|---|---|---|
| Sunday | Κυριακή | *kiriaki* |
| Monday | Δευτέρα | *theftera* |
| Tuesday | Τρίτη | *triti* |
| Wednesday | Τετάρτη | *tetarti* |
| Thursday | Πέμπτη | *pembti* |
| Friday | Παρασκευή | *paraskevi* |
| Saturday | Σάββατο | *savato* |
| January | Ιανουάριος | *ianooarios* |
| February | Φεβρουάριος | *fevrooarios* |
| March | Μάρτιος | *martios* |
| April | Απρίλιος | *aprilios* |
| May | Μάιος | *maios* |
| June | Ιούνιος | *ioonios* |
| July | Ιούλιος | *ioolios* |
| August | Αύγουστος | *avgoostos* |
| September | Σεπτέμβριος | *septemvrios* |
| October | Οκτώβριος | *oktovrios* |
| November | Νοέμβριος | *noemvrios* |
| December | Δεκέμβριος | *thekemvrios* |
| Spring | άνοιξη | *anixi* |
| Summer | καλοκαίρι | *kalokeri* |
| Fall | φθινόπωρο | *fтнinoporo* |
| Winter | χειμώνας | *himonas* |
| Christmas | Χριστούγεννα | *hristooyena* |
| Christmas Eve | παραμονή | *paramoni* |
| | Χριστουγέννων | *hristooyenon* |
| Good Friday | Μεγάλη | *megali* |
| | Παρασκευή | *paraskevi* |
| Easter | Πάσχα | *pas-ha* |
| New Year | Πρωτοχρονιά | *protohronia* |
| New Year's Eve | Παραμονή | *paramoni* |
| | Πρωτοχρονιάς | *protohronias* |

# NUMBERS

0 μηδέν *mithen*
1 ένα *ena*
2 δύο *thio*
3 τρία *tria*
4 τέσσερα *tesera*

5 πέντε *pende*
6 έξι *exi*
7 επτά *epta*
8 οχτώ *ohto*
9 εννιά *enia*

10 δέκα *theka*
11 έντεκα *edeka*
12 δώδεκα *thotheka*
13 δεκατρία *theka-tria*
14 δεκατέσσερα *theka-tesera*
15 δεκαπέντε *theka-pende*
16 δεκαέξι *theka-exi*
17 δεκαεπτά *theka-epta*
18 δεκαοκτώ *theka-ohto*
19 δεκαεννιά *theka-enia*
20 είκοσι *ikosi*
21 εικοσιένα *ikosi-ena*
22 εικοσιδύο *ikosi-thio*
30 τριάντα *trianda*
31 τριανταένα *trianda-ena*
32 τριανταδύο *trianda-thio*
40 σαράντα *saranda*
50 πενήντα *peninda*
60 εξήντα *exinda*
70 εβδομήντα *evthomida*
80 ογδόντα *ogthonda*
90 ενενήντα *eneninda*
100 εκατό *ekato*
110 εκατόν δέκα *ekaton theka*
200 διακόσια *thiakosia*
1,000 χίλια *hilia*
1,000,000 ένα εκατομμύριο *ena ekatomirio*

# TIME

| | | |
|---|---|---|
| today | σήμερα | *simera* |
| yesterday | χτες | *htes* |
| tomorrow | αύριο | *avrio* |
| the day before yesterday | προχτές | *prohtes* |
| the day after tomorrow | μεθαύριο | *meTHavrio* |
| this week | αυτή την εβδομάδα | *afti tin evthomatha* |
| last week | την περασμένη εβδομάδα | *tin perasmeni evthomatha* |
| next week | την επόμενη εβδομάδα | *tin epomeni evthomatha* |
| this morning | το πρωί | *to proi* |
| this afternoon | το απόγευμα | *to apoyevma* |
| this evening | το βράδυ | *to vrathi* |
| tonight | απόψε | *apopse* |
| yesterday afternoon | χτες το απόγευμα | *htes t'apoyevma* |
| last night | χτες τη νύχτα | *htes ti nihta* |
| tomorrow morning | αύριο το πρωί | *avrio to proi* |
| tomorrow night | αύριο το βράδυ | *avrio to vrathi* |
| in three days | σε τρεις μέρες | *se tris meres* |
| three days ago | πριν τρεις μέρες | *prin tris meres* |
| late | αργά | *arga* |
| early | νωρίς | *noris* |
| soon | σύντομα | *sindoma* |
| later on | αργότερα | *argotera* |
| at the moment | προς το παρόν | *pros to paron* |
| second | το δευτερόλεπτο | *to thefterolepto* |
| minute | το λεπτό | *to lepto* |
| ten minutes | δέκα λεπτά | *theka lepta* |
| quarter of an hour | ένα τέταρτο | *ena tetarto* |
| half an hour | μισή ώρα | *misi ora* |

| three quarters of | τρία τέταρτα | tria tetarta |
| an hour | της ώρας | tis oras |
| hour | ώρα | ora |
| day | μέρα | mera |
| week | εβδομάδα | evthomatha |
| two weeks | σε δύο εβδομάδες | se thio evthomathes |
| month | μήνας | minas |
| year | χρόνος | hronos |

## TELLING TIME

In Greek you always put the hour first and then use the word
**ke** (και) to denote the minutes "past" the hour and **para** (παρά)
for the minutes "to" the hour (eg "five-twenty" = **5 ke** 20;
"five-forty" = **6 para** 20). The 24-hour clock is used officially
in timetables and enquiry offices.

Don't forget that Greek Standard Time is always seven hours
ahead of Eastern Standard Time.

| one o'clock | μία η ώρα | mia i ora |
| ten past one | μία και δέκα | mia ke theka |
| quarter past one | μία και τέταρτο | mia ke tetarto |
| twenty past one | μία και είκοσι | mia ke ikosi |
| half past one | μία και μισή | mia ke misi |
| twenty to two | δύο παρά είκοσι | thio para ikosi |
| quarter to two | δύο παρά τέταρτο | thio para tetarto |
| ten to two | δύο παρά δέκα | thio para theka |
| two o'clock | δύο η ώρα | thio i ora |
| 13:00 (1 pm) | δεκατρείς | theka-tris |
| 16:30/4:30 pm | δεκαέξι και | theka-exi ke |
| | τριάντα | trianda |
| 20:10/8:10 pm | είκοσι και δέκα | ikosi ke theka |
| at half past five | στις πέντε και μισή | stis pede ke misi |
| at seven o'clock | στις επτά | stis epta |
| noon | το μεσημέρι | to mesimeri |
| midnight | τα μεσάνυχτα | ta mesanihta |

# COMMUNICATIONS

## Useful Words and Phrases

| | | |
|---|---|---|
| code | ο κωδικός | o kothik_o_s |
| to dial | καλώ | kal_o_ |
| emergency | η επείγουσα ανάγκη | i epig_o_osa an_a_gi |
| directory assistance | οι πληροφορίες | i plirofor_i_es |
| extension | το εσωτερικό | to esoterik_o_ |
| mobile phone | το κινητό τηλέφωνο | tokinit_o_ til_e_fono |
| number | ο αριθμός | o ariTHm_o_s |
| phonecard | η τηλεφωνική κάρτα | i tilefonik_i_ karta, |
| collect call | το τηλεφώνημα | to tilef_o_nima |
| | κολέκτ | kol_e_kt |
| telephone | το τηλέφωνο | to til_e_fono |
| telephone booth | ο τηλεφωνικός | o tilefonik_o_s |
| | θάλαμος | TH_a_lamos |
| wrong number | λάθος νούμερο | l_a_THos n_oo_mero |

**Where is the nearest phone booth?**
Που είναι ο πλησιέστερος τηλεφωνικός θάλαμος;
*poo ine o plisi-esteros tilefonik_o_s TH_a_lamos*

**Hello, this is … speaking**
Χαίρετε, είμαι ο/η …
*h_e_rete, _i_me o/i*

**Is that …?**
Ο/η …;
*o/i*

**Speaking**
ο ίδιος
*o _i_thios*

**I would like to speak to …**
Θα ήθελα να μιλήσω στον …
*THa _i_THela na mil_i_so ston*

**Please tell him … called**
Παρακαλώ του λέτε ότι τηλεφώνησε ο/η …
*parakalo too lete oti tilefonise o/i*

**Ask him to call me back, please**
Πέστε του να με ξαναπάρει παρακαλώ
*peste too na me xanapari parakalo*

**My number is …**
το τηλέφωνό μου είναι …
*to tilefono moo ine*

**Do you know where he is?**
Ξέρετε που είναι;
*xerete poo ine*

**Could you leave him a message?**
Μπορείτε να του αφήσετε ένα μήνυμα;
*borite na too afisete ena minimas*

**I'll call back later**
Θα σε ξαναπάρω αργότερα
*THa se xanaparo argotera*

**Sorry, wrong number**
Πήρατε λάθος αριθμό
*pirate laTHos ariTHmo*

**How much is a call to …?**
Πόσο στοιχίζει ένα τηλεφώνημα στο …;
*poso sti-hizi ena tilefonima sto*

**I would like to make a collect call**
Θα ήθελα τα έξοδα να πληρωθούν εκεί
*THa iTHela ta exotha na pliroTHoon eki*

**I would like a number in …**
Θέλω ένα αριθμό στην …
THΕ̱lo ΕΝΑ ariTHMΟ̱ stin

**What's your fax number/What's your email address?**
Ποιός είναι ο αριθμός του φαξ/Ποιά είναι η διεύθυνση (email);
piΟ̱s iΝΕ o arithmΟ̱s tΟ̱Ο̱ fax/piΑ iΝΕ i thiΕfTHΙΝsi 'email'

**May I send a fax/email from here?**
Μπορώ να στείλω φαξ/email από εδώ;
borΟ̱ na stΙ̱lo fax/'email' apΟ̱ ethΟ̱

---

### THINGS YOU'LL SEE OR HEAR

| | | |
|---|---|---|
| ακουστικό | akoostikΟ̱ | receiver |
| άμεσος δράσις | Α̱mesos thrΑ̱sis | emergencies, police |
| αριθμός | ariTHMΟ̱s | number |
| δεν λειτουργεί | then litooryΙ̱ | out of order |
| καλεί | kalΙ̱ | ringing |
| καλέσατε | kalΕ̱sate | dial |
| κέρματα | kΕ̱rmata | coins |
| κωδικός | kothikΟ̱s | code |
| λάθος νούμερο | lΑ̱THos nΟ̱Ο̱mero | wrong number |
| μιλάει | milΑ̱i | busy |
| μονάδες | monΑ̱thes | units |
| νούμερο | nΟ̱Ο̱mero | number |
| πυροσβεστική | pirosvestikΙ̱ | fire department |
| σηκώσατε | sikΟ̱sate | pick up |
| τηλεφώνημα | tilefΟ̱nima | call |
| τηλεφωνώ | tilefonΟ̱ | to call |
| τοπικό | topikΟ̱ | local call |
| χαίρετε | hΕ̱rete | hello |
| χρυσός οδηγός | hrisΟ̱s othigΟ̱s | Yellow Pages |
| υπεραστικό | iperastikΟ̱ | long-distance call, international call |

# HOTELS

## Useful Words and Phrases

| | | |
|---|---|---|
| balcony | το μπαλκόνι | to balk<u>o</u>ni |
| bathroom | το λουτρό | to lootr<u>o</u> |
| bed | το κρεβάτι | to krev<u>a</u>ti |
| bedroom | το υπνοδωμάτιο | to ipnothom<u>a</u>tio |
| breakfast | το πρωινό | to proin<u>o</u> |
| check | ο λογαριασμός | o logariasm<u>o</u>s |
| dining room | η τραπεζαρία | i trapezar<u>i</u>a |
| dinner | το δείπνο | to th<u>i</u>pno |
| double room | το διπλό δωμάτιο | to thipl<u>o</u> thom<u>a</u>tio |
| elevator | το ασανσέρ | to asans<u>e</u>r |
| full board | η φουλ-πανσιόν | i fool-pansi<u>o</u>n |
| half board | η ντεμί-πανσιόν | i demi-pansi<u>o</u>n |
| hotel | το ξενοδοχείο | to xenothoh<u>i</u>o |
| key | το κλειδί | to klith<u>i</u> |
| lobby | το φουαγέ | to fooay<u>e</u> |
| lounge | το σαλόνι | to sal<u>o</u>ni |
| lunch | το γεύμα | to y<u>e</u>vma |
| manager | ο διευθυντής | o thi-efτHindi<u>s</u> |
| receipt | η απόδειξη | i ap<u>o</u>thixi |
| reception | η ρεσεψιόν | i resepsi<u>o</u>n |
| receptionist | ο ρεσεψιονίστας | o resepsion<u>i</u>stas |
| restaurant | το εστιατόριο | to estiat<u>o</u>rio |
| restroom | η τουαλέτα | i tooal<u>e</u>ta |
| room | το δωμάτιο | to thom<u>a</u>tio |
| room service | το σέρβις δωματίου | to s<u>e</u>rvis thomati<u>oo</u> |
| shower | το ντους | to doos |
| single room | το μονό δωμάτιο | to mon<u>o</u> thom<u>a</u>tio |
| twin room | το δωμάτιο με δύο κρεβάτια | to thom<u>a</u>tio me thio krev<u>a</u>tia |

**Do you have any vacancies?**
Εχετε κενά δωμάτια;
ehete kena thomatia

**I have a reservation**
Εχω κλείσει δωμάτιο
eho klisi thomatio

**I'd like a single room**
Θα ήθελα ένα μονό δωμάτιο
THa iTHela ena mono thomatio

**I'd like a double room**
Θα ήθελα ένα δωμάτιο με διπλό κρεβάτι
THa iTHela ena thomatio me thiplo krevati

**I'd like a twin room**
Θα ήθελα ένα δωμάτιο με δύο κρεβάτια
THa iTHela ena thomatio me thio krevatia

**I'd like a room with a bathroom/balcony**
Θα ήθελα ένα δωμάτιο με μπάνιο/μπαλκόνι
THa iTHela ena thomatio me banio/balkoni

**Is there satellite/cable TV in the rooms?**
Τα δωμάτια έχουν δορυφοκή/καλωδιακή τηλεόραση;
ta thomatia ehoon thoriforiki/kalothiaki tileorasi

**I'd like a room for one night/three nights**
Θα ήθελα ένα δωμάτιο για μία νύχτα/τρεις νύχτες
THa iTHela ena thomatio ya mia nihta/tris nihtes

**What is the charge per night?**
Πόσο στοιχίζει η διανυκτέρευση;
poso stihizi i thianihterefsi

**When is breakfast/dinner?**
Πότε έχει πρωινό/δείπνο;
*pote ehi proino/thipno*

**Would you have my luggage brought up?**
Θα μου φέρετε τις βαλίτσες μου;
*tha moo ferete tis valitses moo*

**Please call me at … o'clock**
Παρακαλώ ειδοποιήστε με στις …
*parakalo ithopi-isteme stis*

**May I have breakfast in my room?**
Μπορώ να πάρω το πρωινό στο δωματιό μου;
*boro na paro to proino sto thomatio moo*

**I'll be back at … o'clock**
Θα επιστρέψω στις …
*tha epistrepso stis*

**My room number is …**
Ο αριθμός του δωματιού μου είναι …
*o arithmos too thomatioo moo ine*

**I'm leaving tomorrow**
Φεύγω αύριο
*fevgo avrio*

**May I have the check, please?**
Τον λογαριασμό παρακαλώ
*ton logariasmo parakalo*

**Can you get me a taxi?**
Μου καλείτε ένα ταξί;
*moo kalite ena taxi*

## Things You'll See

| | | |
|---|---|---|
| **ασανσέρ** | *asanser* | elevator |
| **δείπνο** | *thipno* | dinner |
| **δωμάτια** | *thomatia* | rooms |
| **είσοδος** | *isothos* | entrance |
| **έξοδος κινδύνου** | *exothos kinthinoo* | emergency exit |
| **εστιατόριο** | *estiatorio* | restaurant |
| **λογαριασμός** | *logariasmos* | check |
| **λουτρό** | *lootro* | bathroom |
| **ντους** | *doos* | shower |
| **ξενοδοχείο** | *xenothohio* | hotel |
| **πρωινό** | *proino* | breakfast |
| **ρεσεψιόν** | *resepsion* | reception |
| **σκάλες** | *skales* | stairs |
| **σύρατε** | *sirate* | pull |
| **τουαλέτες** | *tooaletes* | restrooms |
| **υπόγειο** | *ipoyio* | basement |
| **φαγητό** | *fayito* | meal, lunch |
| **ωθήσατε** | *oTHisate* | push |

## Things You'll Hear

**Then iparhoon mona/thipla thomatia kena**
There are no single/double rooms left

**Imaste yemati**
No vacancies

**Parakalo, plironete prokatavolika**
Please pay in advance

**Parakalo, afinete to thiavatsrio sas etho**
Please leave your passport here

# SHOPPING

**Where is the … department?**
Που είναι το τμήμα των …;
*poo ine to tmima ton*

**Do you have …?**
Έχετε …;
*ehete*

**How much is this?**
Πόσο κάνει αυτό;
*poso kani afto*

**Where do I pay?**
Πού πληρώνω;
*poo plirono*

**Do you have something less expensive?**
Έχετε τίποτα φτηνότερο;
*ehete tipota ftinotero*

**Could you wrap it for me?**
Μου το τυλίγετε;
*moo to tiliyete*

**May I have a receipt?**
Μου δίνετε μία απόδειξη;
*moo thinete mia apothixi*

**I'd like to change this, please**
Θα ήθελα να το αλλάξω αυτό, παρακαλώ
*THa iTHela na to alaxo afto, parakalo*

**I'm just looking**
Απλώς κοιτάζω
*aplos kitazo*

**I'll come back later**
Θα επιστρέψω αργότερα
*THa epistrepso argotera*

# EATING OUT

Some examples of places to eat and drink are shown below
(notice that signs in Greek capital letters often look different
from the same words in lower-case.)

ΕΣΤΙΑΤΟΡΙΟΝ Εστιατόριον *estiatorion* (restaurant)
In all tourist places, you will find the menu printed in English
as well as in Greek, and the staff will almost certainly speak
English. If you feel more adventurous, you might prefer to try
some of the many Greek delicacies available, and in smaller
places you will be welcomed into the kitchen to see what's
cooking. The menu will usually give you two prices for each
item – the higher one includes a service charge.

ΤΑΒΕΡΝΑ Ταβέρνα *taverna*
A typical Greek restaurant, where draft wine is available.

ΨΑΡΟΤΑΒΕΡΝΑ Ψαροταβέρνα *psarotaverna*
A restaurant specializing in seafood.

ΨΗΣΤΑΡΙΑ Ψησταριά *psistaria*
A restaurant specializing in charcoal-grilled food.

ΟΥΖΕΡΙ Ουζερί *oozeri*
A bar that serves ouzo (a strong, aniseed-flavored spirit) and
beer with snacks (**mezethes**), which could be savouries or
sometimes, especially in the islands, octopus or local seafood.

ΖΑΧΑΡΟΠΛΑΣΤΕΙΟ Ζαχαροπλαστείο *zaharoplastio*
A pastry shop or café that serves cakes and soft drinks and is
also an ideal place to have breakfast.

ΚΑΦΕΝΕΙΟ Καφενείο *kafenio*
A coffee house, where Greek coffee is served with traditional
sweets. Here you can play a game of cards or backgammon.

## USEFUL WORDS AND PHRASES

| | | |
|---|---|---|
| beer | η μπύρα | i b<u>i</u>ra |
| bottle | το μπουκάλι | to book<u>a</u>li |
| cake | το γλυκό | to glik<u>o</u> |
| check | ο λογαριασμός | o logariasm<u>o</u>s |
| chef | ο μάγειρας | o m<u>a</u>yiras |
| coffee | ο καφές | o kaf<u>e</u>s |
| cup | το φλυτζάνι | to flitz<u>a</u>ni |
| fork | το πιρούνι | to pir<u>oo</u>ni |
| glass | το ποτήρι | to pot<u>i</u>ri |
| knife | το μαχαίρι | to mah<u>e</u>ri |
| menu | το μενού | to men<u>oo</u> |
| milk | το γάλα | to g<u>a</u>la |
| napkin | η χαρτοπετσέτα | i hartopets<u>e</u>ta |
| plate | το πιάτο | to pi<u>a</u>to |
| receipt | η απόδειξη | i ap<u>o</u>thixi |
| sandwich | το σάντουιτς | to s<u>a</u>ndooits |
| soup | η σούπα | i s<u>oo</u>pa |
| spoon | το κουτάλι | to koot<u>a</u>li |
| sugar | η ζάχαρη | i z<u>a</u>hari |
| table | το τραπέζι | to trap<u>e</u>zi |
| tea | το τσάι | to ts<u>a</u>i |
| teaspoon | το κουταλάκι | to kootal<u>a</u>ki |
| tip | το πουρμπουάρ | to poorboo<u>a</u>r |
| waiter | ο σερβιτόρος | o servit<u>o</u>ros |
| waitress | η σερβιτόρα | i servit<u>o</u>ra |
| water | το νερό | to ner<u>o</u> |
| wine | το κρασί | to kras<u>i</u> |
| wine list | ο κατάλογος | o kat<u>a</u>logos |
| | κρασιών | kras<u>io</u>n |

**A table for one/two/three, please**
Ένα τραπέζι για ένα/δύο/τρία άτομα, παρακαλώ
<u>e</u>na trap<u>e</u>zi ya <u>e</u>na/th<u>i</u>o/tr<u>i</u>a <u>a</u>toma, parakal<u>o</u>

**May we see the menu?**
Μπορούμε να δούμε το μενού;
*boroome na thoome to menoo*

**Is there a highchair?**
Υπάρχει παιδική καρέκλα;
*parhi pethiki karekla*

**What would you recommend?**
Τι θα προτείνατε;
*ti tha protinate*

**Is this suitable for vegetarians?**
Είναι για χορτοφάγους;
*ine ya hortofagoos*

**I'd like …**
Θα ήθελα …
*tha ithela*

**Waiter!**
Γκαρσόν!
*garson*

**May we have the check, please?**
Μας φέρνετε τον λογαριασμό, παρακαλώ;
*mas fernete ton logariasmo, parakalo*

**I didn't order this**
Δεν παράγγειλα αυτό
*then parangila afto*

**The meal was very good, thank you**
Το φαγητό ήταν πολύ καλό, ευχαριστούμε
*to fayito itan poli kalo, efharistoome*

# MENU GUIDE

**αλάτι** *alati* salt

**αλλαντικά** *alandika* sausages, salami, meats

**αμύγδαλα** *amigthala* almonds

**ανανάς** *ananas* pineapple

**ανθότυρο** *anthotiro* kind of cottage cheese

**αντζούγιες** *antsooyies* anchovies

**αρακάς λαδερός** *arakas* peas

**αρνί** lamb

**αρνί κοκκινιστό** *arni kokkinisto* lamb in tomato sauce

**αρνί μπριζόλες** *arni brizoles* lamb chops

**αρνί της σούβλας** *arni tis soovlas* spit-roast lamb

**αστακός** *astakos* lobster

**αυγά** *avga* eggs

**αυγά μάτια** *avga matia* fried eggs

**αυγά ομελέτα** *avga omeleta* omelette

**αυγοτάραχο** *avgotaraho* roe

**αχλάδι χυμός** *ahlathi himos* pear juice

**αχλαδιά** *ahlathia* pears

**βερύκοκκα** *verikoka* apricots

**βούτυρο** *vootiro* butter

**βρασμένος, βραστός** *vrasmenos, vrastos* boiled

**βύσσινο** *visino* cherries

**βοδινό** *vothino* beef

**γάβρος τηγανιτός** *gavros tiganitos* fried small fish

**γάλα** *gala* milk

**γαλακτομπούρεκο** *galaktobooreko* cream pie with honey

**γαλλικός καφές** *galikos kafes* French (filtered) coffee

**γαλοπούλα** *galopoola* turkey

**γαρίδες** *garithes* shrimps

**γαρνιτούρα με** *garnitoora* sautéed

**γιαλατζή ντολμάδες** *yalantzi dolmathes* vine leaves stuffed with rice

**γιαούρτι** *yaoorti* yogurt

**γιαούρτι πρόβειο** *yaoorti provio* sheep's yogurt

**γιουβαρλάκια** *yioovarlakia* meatballs

**γιουβέτσι** *yoovetsi* oven-cooked lamb with a kind of pasta

**γκοφρέττα** *gofreta* chocolate wafer

**γκρέϊπ φρουτ** *'grapefruit'* grapefruit

**γλυκό** *gliko* preserve in syrup

**γλυκό μαστίχα** *gliko mastiha* fudge

**γλώσσα** *glosa* sole

**γόπα τηγανητή** *gopa tiganiti* type of fried fish

**γραβιέρα τυρί** *graviera tiri* kind of savory cheese

**γρανίτα** *granita* sorbet

**δαμάσκηνα** *thamaskina* prunes

**δίπλες, τηγανητές** *thiples, tiganites* pancakes

**ελαιόλαδο** *eleolatho* olive oil

**ελιές** *elies* olives

**ελληνικός καφές** *elinikos kafes* Greek coffee

**εσκαλόπ** *eskalop* escalope

**ζαμπόν** *zabon* ham

**ζάχαρη** *zahari* sugar

**ζελέ** *zele* jelly

**ζυμαρικά** *zimarika* pasta

**ηλιέλαιο** *iligleo* sunflower oil

**θαλασσινά** *thalassina* seafood

**καβούρια ψητά** *kavooria psita* grilled crab

**κακαβιά** *kakavia* fish soup

**κακάο** *kakao* cocoa

**κακάο ρόφημα** *kakao rofima* hot chocolate

**καλαμαράκια** _kalamarakia_ squid

**καλαμποκέλαιο** _kalabokeleo_ corn oil

**καλαμπόκι** _kalaboki_ corn

**καναπέ** _kanape_ canapés

**καπαμάς αρνί** _kapamas arni_ lamb cooked in spices and tomato sauce

**καραβίδες** _karavithes_ shrimp

**καραμέλες** _karameles_ candy

**καρμπονάρα** _karbonara_ spaghetti carbonara

**καρότα** _karota_ carrots

**καρπούζι** _karpoozi_ watermelon

**καρύδα** _karitha_ coconut

**καρύδια** _karithia_ walnuts

**καρυδόπιττα** _karithopita_ cake with nuts and syrup

**κασέρι** _kaseri_ type of Greek cheese

**κάστανα** _kastana_ chestnuts

**καταΐφι** _kataifi_ sweet with honey and nuts

**καφές βαρύς γλυκός** _kafes varis glikos_ sweet Greek coffee

**καφές με γάλα** _kafes me gala_ coffee with milk

**κέϊκ** _keik_ cake

**κεράσια** _kerasia_ cherries

**κέτσαπ** _ketsap_ ketchup

**κέφαλος** _kefalos_ mullet

**κεφαλοτύρι** _kefalotiri_ type of Greek parmesan-style cheese

**κεφτέδες** _keftethes_ meatballs

**κόλα** _kola_ cola

**κολιοί** _koli-i_ mackerel

**κολοκυθάκια** _kolokiΤΗakia_ zucchini

**κολοκυθοτυρόπιττα** _kolokiΤΗotiropita_ zucchini and cheese pie

**κομπόστα** _komposta_ compôte

**κορν φλέϊκς** _korn fleiks_ corn flakes

**κότα** _kota_ chicken

**κότα κοκκινιστή** _kota kokkinisti_ chicken in tomato sauce

**κότα ψητή σούβλας** _kota psiti soovlas_ spit-roast chicken

**κότολέτες** _kotolete_ cutlets

**κοτόπιττα** _kotopita_ chicken pie

**κοτόπουλο** _kotopoolo_ chicken

**κοτόσουπα** _kotosoopa_ chicken soup

**κουκιά λαδερά** _kookia lathera_ broad beans in tomato sauce

**κουνέλι** _kooneli_ rabbit

**κρασί** _krasi_ wine

**κρασί άσπρο** _krasi aspro_ white wine

**κρασί κόκκινο** _krasi kokino_ red wine

**κρασί ρετσίνα** _krasi retsina_ dry white Greek wine

**κρασί ροζέ** _krasi roze_ rosé

**κρέας** _kreas_ beef

**κρεατόπιττες** _kreatopites_ ground meat pies

**κρέμα καραμελέ** _krema karamele_ crème caramel

**κρέμα** _krema_ cream

**κρεμμύδια** _kremithia_ onions

**κροκέτες** _kroketes_ croquettes

**κρουασάν** _krooasan_ croissants

**κυδωνόπαστο** _kithonopasto_ thick quince jelly

**κωκ** _kok_ cream cake with chocolate topping

**λαγός** _lagos_ hare

**λάδι** _lathi_ oil

**λαχανάκια μικτά** _lahanika mikta_ mixed vegetables

**λάχανο** _lahano_ cabbage

**λάχανο ντολμάδες με σάλτσα ντομάτας** _lahano dolmathes me saltsa domatas_ stuffed vine leaves in tomato sauce

**λαχανοσαλάτα** _lahanosalata_ cabbage salad

**λεμόνι** _lemoni_ lemon

**λιθρίνι ψητό** _liΤΗrini psito_ grilled mullet

λουκάνικα *lookanika* sausages
λουκουμάδες *lookoomathes* doughnuts
λουκούμια *lookoomia* Turkish delight
μαγιά *mayia* yeast
μαγιονέζα *mayoneza* mayonnaise
μαϊντανός *maidanos* parsley
μακαρόνια *makaronia*
  spaghetti/macaroni
μανιτάρια *manitaria* mushrooms
μανταρίνι *madarini* tangerine
μαργαρίνη *margarini* margarine
μαρίδες τηγανητές *marithes tiganites*
  small fried fish
μαρμελάδα *marmelatha* jam
μαρούλια σαλάτα *maroolia salata*
  lettuce salad
μέλι *meli* honey
μελιτζάνες *melitzanes* eggplant
μελιτζανοσαλάτα *melitzanosalata*
  eggplant salad
μελομακάρονα *melomakarona* sweet
  cakes with cinnamon, nuts and syrup
μήλα *mila* apples
μηλόπιττα *milopita* apple pie
μηλοχυμός *milohimos* apple juice
μοσχάρι κοκκινιστό *mos-hari* veal
μοσχαρίσιος κιμάς *mos-harisios kimas*
  ground beef
μουσακά *moosaka* moussaka
μουστοκούλουρα *moostokooloora* kind of
  Greek cookie
μουστάρδα *moostarta* mustard
μπακαλιάρος πλακί *bakaliaros* salt cod
μπακλαβάς *baclavas* layers of filo pastry
  with nuts and syrup
μπάμιες *bamies* okra
μπανάνα *banana* banana
μπαρμπούνια πανέ *barboonia pane*
  breaded red mullet
μπεσαμέλ σάλτσα *besamel saltsa*
  béchamel sauce

μπισκότα σοκολάτας *biskota sokolatas*
  chocolate cookies
μπισκοτάκια αλμυρά *biskotakia almira*
  savory cookies
μπιφτέκι *bifteki* grilled meatballs
μπον φιλέ *bon file* fillet steak
μπουγάτσα γλυκιά *boogatsa glikia* puff
  pastry with cream filling
μπουρεκάκια *boorekakia* cheese or
  mince pies
μπριάμι με κολοκυθάκια *briami me
  kolokiΤΗakia* zucchini cooked with
  potatoes in the oven
μπριζόλες στο τηγάνι *brizoles sto tigani*
  fried T-bone steak
μπριζόλες χοιρινές *brizoles hirines* pork
  chops
μπρόκολο *brokolo* broccoli
μπύρα *bira* beer
μυαλά πανέ *miala pane* breaded cow's
  brains
μύδια τηγανητά *mithia tiganita* fried
  mussels
νες καφέ *nes kafe* any instant coffee
ντολμάδες γιαλαντζή *dolmathes
  yialantzi* stuffed vine leaves with rice
ντοματόσουπα *domatosoopa* tomato
  soup
ντοματοσαλάτα *domatosalata* tomato
  salad
ντομάτα *domata* tomato
ντόνατς *donats* doughnuts
ξηροί καρποί *xiri karpi* all types of nuts
ξιφίας *xifias* sword fish
ξύδι *xithi* vinegar
ομελέτα *omeleta* omelette
ορεκτικά *orektika* hors d'oeuvres
ούζο *oozo* ouzo
παγωτό *pagoto* ice cream
παγωτό κρέμα *pagoto krema* vanilla ice
  cream

**παγωτό με σαντυγί** *pagoto me sandiyi* ice cream with whipped cream

**πάπρικα** *paprika* paprika

**πάστα** *pasta* gâteau

**παστίτσιο λαζάνια** *pastitsio lazania* lasagne

**πατάτες** *patates* potatoes

**πατάτες πουρέ** *patates poore* mashed potatoes

**πατάτες σουφλέ** *patates soofle* potato soufflé

**πατάτες τηγανητές** *patates tiganites* french fries

**πατάτες τσιπς** *patates tsips* potato chips

**πατατοσαλάτα** *patatosalata* potato salad

**πατζάρια** *patzaria* beets

**πατσάς σούπα** *patsas soopa* tripe soup

**πεπόνι** *peponi* melon

**πέστροφα** *pestrofa* trout

**πηχτή** *pihti* headcheese

**πιλάφι με σάλτσα ντομάτα** *pilafi me saltsa domata* rice with tomato sauce

**πιπέρι** *piperi* pepper

**πιπεριές πράσινες/κόκκινες** *piperies prasines/kokines* green/red peppers

**πιροσκί** *piroski* mince or sausage rolls

**πίτσα** *pitsa* pizza

**πίττα με κιμά** *pita me kima* ground meat pie

**πορτοκαλάδα** *portokalatha* orange juice

**πορτοκάλι** *portokali* orange

**πούτιγκα με ανανά** *pootiga me anana* pineapple pudding

**πούτιγκα με καρύδια** *pootiga me karithia* pudding with walnuts

**πούτιγκα με σταφίδες** *pootiga me stafithes* sultana pudding

**πρασσόπιττα** *prasopita* leek pie

**πράσσα** *prasa* leeks

**παρμεζάνα** *parmezana* parmesan cheese

**ραβανί** *ravani* very sweet sponge cake

**ρίγανη** *rigani* oregano

**ροδάκινα** *rothakina* peaches

**ροσμπίφ αρνί μοσχάρι** *rozbif arni mos-hari* roast beef, veal or lamb

**ρυζόγαλο** *rizogalo* rice pudding

**ρώσικη σαλάτα** *rosiki salata* vegetable salad

**σαλάμι** *salami* salami

**σαλάτα** *salata* salad

**σαλάτα με σπαράγγια** *salata me sparagia* asparagus salad

**σαλάτα χωριάτικη** *salata horiatiki* Greek salad—tomatoes, cucumber, feta cheese, peppers, and olives

**σαλιγκάρια** *saligaria* snails

**σάλτσα** *saltsa* sauce

**σάλτσα ντομάτα** *saltsa domata* tomato sauce

**σαμάλι** *samali* semolina cake with honey

**σαντιγή** *sandiyi* whipped cream

**σαρδέλλες** *sartheles* sardines

**σέλινο** *selino* celery

**σιμιγδάλη** *simigthali* semolina

**σιρόπι** *siropi* syrup

**σκορδαλιά με ψωμί** *skorthalia me psomi* thick garlic sauce with bread

**σκόρδο** *skortho* garlic

**σοκολάτα** *sokolata* chocolate

**σολομός καπνιστός** *solomos kapnistos* smoked salmon

**σουβλάκι καλαμάκι** *soovlaki kalamaki* shish kabob

**σουβλάκι ντονέρ με** *soovlaki doner* doner kabob

**σούπα ρεβύθια** *soopa reviThia* chickpea soup

**σούπα τραχανάς** *soopa trahanas* milk broth with flour

**σούπα φακές** *soopa fakes* lentil soup

**σουπιές τηγανητές** *soopies tiganites* fried cuttlefish

**σουσάμι** *soosami* sesame

**σουτζουκάκια** *sootzookakia* spicy meatballs in red sauce

**σπαγέτο** *spageto* spaghetti

**σπαράγγια σαλάτα** *sparangia salata* asparagus salad

**σταφίδες** *stafithes* raisins

**σταφιδόψωμο** *stafithopsomo* bread with raisins

**σταφύλι χυμός** *stafili himos* grape juice

**σταφύλια** *stafilia* grapes

**στιφάδο** *stifatho* chopped meat in onions

**στρείδια** *strithia* oysters

**σύκα** *sika* figs

**συκωτάκια** *sikotakia* liver

**συναγρίδα** *sinagritha* sea bream

**σφυρίδα** *sfiritha* pike

**ταραμοκεφτέδες** *taramokeftethes* roe pâté balls with spices

**ταραμοσαλάτα** *taramosalata* roe pâté

**τάρτα** *tarta* tart

**τας-κεμπάπ** *tas kebab* spicy lamb cutlets

**τζατζίκι** *tzatziki* yogurt, cucumber, garlic, dried mint, and olive oil

**τηγανητός** *tiganitos* fried

**τηγανήτες** *tiganites* pancakes

**τόνος** *tonos* tuna

**τοστ** *tost* toasted sandwich

**τούρτα** *toorta* gâteau

**τρουφάκια** *troofakia* small chocolate balls

**τσάι** *tsai* tea

**τσιπούρες** *tsipoores* flatfish

**τσίπουρο** *tsipooro* kind of ouzo

**τσουρέκια** *tsoorekia* sweet Easter bread with fresh butter

**τυρί** *tiri* cheese

**τυρόπιττα** *tiropita* cheese pie

**τυροπιττάκια** *tiropitakia* small cheese pies

**φάβα** *fava* continental lentils

**φασολάδα** *fasolatha* thick bean soup

**φασολάκια** *fasolakia* green beans

**φέτα** *feta* feta cheese

**φιλέτο** *fileto* fillet steak

**φοντάν** *fodan* candy

**φουντούκι** *foodooki* hazelnut

**φράουλες** *fraooles* strawberries

**φρουί-γκλασέ** *frooi-glase* dried assorted fruits with sugar

**φρουτοσαλάτα** *frootosalata* fruit salad

**φρυγανιές** *friganies* French toast

**φύλλο πίττας** *filo pitas* thin pastry

**φυστίκια** *fistikia* peanuts

**φυστίκια Αιγίνης** *fistikia eyinis* pistachios

**χαβιάρι** *haviari* caviar

**χαλβάς** *halvas* halva, candy made from sesame seeds and nuts

**χάμπουργκερ** *hamboorger* hamburger

**χοιρινό** *hirino* pork

**χοιρινό σούβλας** *hirino soovlas* pork on the spit

**χορτόσουπα** *hortosoopa* vegetable soup

**χταπόδι** *htapothi* octopus

**χυλοπίττες** *hilopites* tagliatelle

**χυμός** *himos* juice

**χωριάτικη σαλάτα** *horiatiki salata* Greek salad—tomatoes, cucumber, feta cheese, peppers, and olives

**ψάρι βραστό μαγιονέζα** *psari vrasto mayoneza* steamed fish with mayonnaise

**ψάρια μαρινάτα** *psaria marinata* marinated fish

**ψάρια τηγανητά** *psaria tiganita* fried fish

**ψαρόσουπα** *psarosoopa* fish soup

**ψητός** *psitos* grilled

**ψωμί άσπρο/μαύρο** *psomi aspro/mavro* white/brown bread

# HUNGARIAN

## CONTENTS

INTRODUCTION 202
USEFUL PHRASES 204
DAYS, MONTHS, SEASONS 209
NUMBERS 210
TIME 211
COMMUNICATIONS 213
HOTELS 216
SHOPPING 220
EATING OUT 221
MENU GUIDE 225

# INTRODUCTION

## PRONUNCIATION

When reading the imitated pronunciation, pronounce each syllable as if it formed part of an English word, and you will be understood sufficiently well. Remember the points below, and your pronunciation will be even closer to correct Hungarian. The first syllable of each word should be stressed, and double consonants should be pronounced (eg as in Ben Nevis).

| | |
|---|---|
| *a* | as the long "a" in father |
| *ay* | as in "pay" |
| *e* | as in "Ted" |
| *ew* | similar to the sound in "hew" |
| *g* | always as in "goat" |
| *i* | as in "bit" |
| *o* | as in the "ou" in "ought" |
| *u* | as in "tuck" |
| *y* | always as in "yes" (except as in *ay* above) |
| *yuh* | as the "yu" in "yucca" but only slightly sounded |
| *zh* | like the "s" in leisure |

## SUMMARY OF SPECIAL CHARACTERISTICS IN HUNGARIAN

In Hungarian, every vowel forms a syllable, so all vowels must be pronounced individually, even when several follow each other. The acute accent is often only an indication of length, as in the pairs **o/ó**, **u/ú**, **ö/ő** and **ü/ű** (yes, you have to look closely to see the difference in the last two pairs!). However, this is not the case with **a/á** and **e/é**; here, each letter has a completely different sound – as also happens with **o/ö** and **u/ü**. It is very important, therefore, to distinguish between these sounds, as failure to do so may result in lack of comprehension. The sounds of Hungarian vowels (**a, e, i, o, u**) as modified by various accents are approximated below, together with those consonants that are not pronounced as in English.

| | |
|---|---|
| a | is similar to the "u" in "tuck" |
| á | is a long "a" as in 'father' |
| c | "ts" as in "lots" |
| cs | "ch" as in "church" |
| é | "ay" as in "pay" |
| gy | is similar to the "de" in "dew" or the "du" in "duration" |
| í | as "ee" in "weed" |
| j | as the "y" in "yet" or "yawn" |
| ly | as the "y" in "yet" or "yawn" |
| ny | is similar to the "nu" in "tenure" or the "ni" in "onion" |
| o | is similar to the "ou" in "ought" |
| ó | as the word "awe" |
| ö | similar to the "ur" in "fur" |
| ő | similar to the "ur" in "fur" but longer |
| s | "sh" as in "shop" |
| sz | "s" as in "soap" |
| ty | as the "tu" in "tune" or "Tuesday" |
| u | as the "oo" in "look" |
| ú | as the "oo" in "moon" |
| ü | similar to the "ew" in "hew" |
| ű | similar to the "ew" in "hew" but longer |
| zs | similar to the "s" in "vision" or "measure" |

There are three words for "you" in Hungarian: **te** *teh* (informal), **maga** *muguh* (commonly used), and **ön** *urn* (formal). **Te** (or **ti**, in the plural) is only appropriate with children, close friends, and acquaintances of your own age. Although the more general **maga** is widely used in addressing all types of people, it may be considered impolite by some Hungarians. To be on the safe side, we recommend that you use the polite form **ön** (plural **önök** *urnurk*) in all cases.

## USEFUL PHRASES

**Yes/no**
Igen/nem
*igen/nem*

**Thank you/no, thank you**
Köszönöm/köszönöm nem
*kurssurnurm/kurssurnurm nem*

| **Please** *(offering)* | *(asking for something)* |
|---|---|
| Tessék | Kérem |
| *teshayk* | *kayrem* |

**I don't understand**
Nem értem
*nem ayrtem*

**Do you speak English/French/German?**
Beszél angolul/franciául/németül?
*bessayl ungolool/fruntsia-ool/naymet-ewl*

**I can't speak Hungarian**
Nem beszélek magyarul
*nem bessaylek mud-yarool*

**I don't know**
Nem tudom
*nem toodom*

**Please speak more slowly**
Tessék lassabban beszélni
*teshayk lushubbun bessaylni*

**Please write it down for me**
Legyen szíves leírni
*led-yen sseevesh leh-eerni*

**My name is …**
A nevem …
*uh nevem*

**How do you do, pleased to meet you**
Örülök hogy megismerhettem
*ur-rewlurk hod-yuh megishmerhettem*

**Good morning**
Jó reggelt kívánok
*yawreggelt keevanok*

**Good afternoon/good evening**
Jó napot/jó estét
*yawnupot/yaw-eshtayt*

**Good night**
Jó éjszakát/jó éjt
*yaw-ayssukat/yaw-ayt*

**Goodbye**
Viszontlátásra
*vissontlatashruh*

**How are you?** *(formal)*
Hogy van?
*hod-yuh vun*

*(informal)*
Hogy vagy?
*hod-yuh vud-yuh*

**Excuse me, please**
Bocsánatot kérek
*bochanutot kayrek*

**Sorry!**
Elnézést!
*elnayzaysht*

**I'm really sorry**
Igazán nagyon sajnálom
*iguzan nud-yon shuh-ynalom*

**Can you help me?**
Kérhetem a segítségét?
*kayrhetem uh shegeechaygayt*

**Can you tell me …?**
Meg tudná mondani, hogy …?
*meg toodnah monduni hod-yuh*

**May I have …?**
Kaphatnék egy …?
*kuphutnayk ed-yuh*

**I would like …**
Szeretnék egy …
*seretnayk ed-yuh*

**Is there … here?**
Van itt …?
*vun itt*

**Where can I get …?**
Hol kaphatok …-t?
*hol kuphutok …-t*

**How much is it?**
Mennyibe kerül?
*menn-yibeh kerewl*

**What time is it?**
Hány óra van?
*han-yuh awruh vun*

**I must go now**
Mennem kell
*vmennem kell*

**I'll be late**
Elkésck
*elkayshek*

**I've lost my way**
Eltévedtem
*eltayved-tem*

**Cheers!** *(formal)*             *(informal)*
Egészségére!                Egészségedre!
*egayss-shaygayreh*        *egayss-shaygedreh*

**Do you take credit cards?**
Elfogadják a hitelkártyákat?
*elfogud-yak uh hitelkart-yakut*

**Where is the restroom?**
Hol van a WC?
*hol vun uh vaytsay*

**Where is the US embassy?**
Merre van az amerikai nagykövetség?
*merre vun az amerikai nad-ykurvetshayg*

**I've lost my passport/money/key/credit cards**
Elvesztettem az útlevelem/pénzem/szobakulcsom/hitelkártyáim
*elvestettem az ootlevelem/paynzem/sobuh-kulchom/hitelkart-yaim*

**Go away!**
Hagyjon békén!
*hud-yon baykayn*

**Excellent!**
Nagyszerű!
*nud-yusserew*

---

### THINGS YOU'LL HEAR

| | |
|---|---|
| **bocsánat!** | sorry! |
| **bocsánatot kérek!** | excuse me! |
| **elnézést (kérek)!** | sorry! |
| **helló!** | hey! |
| **hogy van?** | how are you? |
| **igaza van** | you're right, he is right |
| **kezitcsókolom** | hello (literally "kiss-the-hand," a polite greeting used by children, and to women by men) |
| **kösz** | thanks |
| **köszönöm nagyon jól – és ön?** | very well, thank you – and you? |
| **nem értem** | I don't understand |
| **nem tudom** | I don't know |
| **pardon** | excuse me |
| **örvendek** | how do you do, nice to meet you |
| **szevasz!/szia!** | hi! |
| **szívesen** | you're welcome |
| **tényleg?** | is that so? |
| **tessék?** | excuse me? |
| **tessék (parancsolni)** | can I help you? |
| **tessék befáradni** | come straight in |
| **tessék vigyázni!** | look out! |
| **úgy van** | that's right |
| **vigyázz/vigyázzon** | look out! |

# DAYS, MONTHS, SEASONS

| Sunday | vasárnap | *vusharnup* |
|---|---|---|
| Monday | hétfő | *haytfur* |
| Tuesday | kedd | *kedd* |
| Wednesday | szerda | *serduh* |
| Thursday | csütörtök | *chewturturk* |
| Friday | péntek | *payntek* |
| Saturday | szombat | *sombut* |

| January | január | *yunoo-ar* |
|---|---|---|
| February | február | *febroo-ar* |
| March | március | *martsi-oosh* |
| April | április | *aprilish* |
| May | május | *mah-yoosh* |
| June | június | *yooni-oosh* |
| July | július | *yooli-oosh* |
| August | augusztus | *owgoosstoosh* |
| September | szeptember | *september* |
| October | október | *oktawber* |
| November | november | *november* |
| December | december | *detsember* |

| Spring | tavasz | *tuvuss* |
|---|---|---|
| Summer | nyár | *n-yar* |
| Fall | ősz | *urss* |
| Winter | tél | *tayl* |

| Christmas | karácsony | *kurachon-yuh* |
|---|---|---|
| Christmas Eve | szenteste | *senteshteh* |
| Good Friday | nagypéntek | *nud-yupayntek* |
| Easter | húsvét | *hooshvayt* |
| Pentecost | pünkösd | *pewnkurshd* |
| New Year | újév | *oo-yayv* |
| New Year's Eve | szilvester | *silvester* |

# NUMBERS

| | | | | |
|---|---|---|---|---|
| 0 | nulla *noolluh* | 10 | tíz *teez* |
| 1 | egy *ed-yuh* | 11 | tizenegy *tizened-yuh* |
| 2 | kettő, két *kettur, kayt* | 12 | tizenkettő *tizenkettur* |
| 3 | három *harom* | 13 | tizenhárom *tizenharom* |
| 4 | négy *nayd-yuh* | 14 | tizennégy *tizen-nayd-yuh* |
| 5 | öt *urt* | 15 | tizenöt *tizenurt* |
| 6 | hat *hut* | 16 | tizenhat *tizenhut* |
| 7 | hét *hayt* | 17 | tizenhét *tizenhayt* |
| 8 | nyolc *n-yolts* | 18 | tizennyolc *tizenn-yolts* |
| 9 | kilenc *kilents* | 19 | tizenkilenc *tizenkilents* |

| | |
|---|---|
| 20 | húsz *hooss* |
| 21 | huszonegy *hoossoned-yuh* |
| 22 | huszonkettő *hoossonkettur* |
| 30 | harminc *hurmints* |
| 40 | negyven *ned-yuven* |
| 50 | ötven *urtven* |
| 60 | hatvan *hutvun* |
| 70 | hetven *hetven* |
| 80 | nyolcvan *n-yoltsvun* |
| 90 | kilencven *kilentsven* |
| 100 | száz *saz* |
| 110 | száztíz *sazteez* |
| 200 | kétszáz *kayt-saz* |
| 300 | háromszáz *haromssaz* |
| 400 | négyszáz *nayd-yussaz* |
| 500 | ötszáz *urt-saz* |
| 600 | hatszáz *hut-saz* |
| 700 | hétszáz *hayt-saz* |
| 800 | nyolcszáz *n-yolts-saz* |
| 900 | kilencszáz *kilents-saz* |
| 1000 | ezer *ezer* |
| 100,000 | százezer *sazezer* |
| 1,000,000 | millió *milliaw* |

# TIME

| | | |
|---|---|---|
| today | ma | *muh* |
| yesterday | tegnap | *tegnup* |
| tomorrow | holnap | *holnup* |
| this week | a héten | *uh hayten* |
| last week | múlt héten | *moolt hayten* |
| next week | jövő héten | *yurvur hayten* |
| this morning | | |
| (4 to 9 am) | ma reggel | *muh reggel* |
| (9 am to noon) | délelőtt | *daylelurt* |
| (midnight to 4 am) | ma éjjel | *muh ay-yel* |
| this afternoon | ma délután | *muh daylootan* |
| this evening | ma este | *muh eshteh* |
| tonight | ma éjjel | *muh ay-yel* |
| in three days | három nap múlva | *harom nup moolvuh* |
| three days ago | három nappal ezelőtt | *harom nuppul ezelurt* |
| this year | idén | *idayn* |
| last year | tavaly | *tuvuh-yuh* |
| next year | jövőre | *yurvur-reh* |
| late | késő | *kayshur* |
| early | korán | *koran* |
| soon | nemsokára | *nemshokaruh* |
| later on | később | *kayshurb* |
| at the moment | pillanatnyilag | *pillunutn-yilug* |
| second | másodperc | *mashodperts* |
| minute | perc | *perts* |
| quarter of an hour | negyedóra | *ned-yedawruh* |
| half an hour | félóra | *faylawruh* |
| three quarters of an hour | háromnegyedóra | *haromned-yedawruh* |
| hour | óra | *awruh* |
| that day | aznap | *uznup* |
| every day | mindennap | *mindennup* |
| the next day | másnap | *mashnup* |

## TELLING TIME

Minutes past the hour are expressed by ... **perccel múlt** ...
(*pertsel moolt*), so "ten past three" is **tíz perccel múlt három**
(*teez pertsel moolt harom*). For minutes to the hour, the
expression ... **perc múlva** ... (*perts moolvuh*) is used, so "ten
to three" is **tíz perc múlva három** (*teez perts moolvuh harom*).

Half past and quarter hours are referred to the hour
approaching, so "half past three" becomes **fél négy** (*fayl nayd-yuh*),
literally "half four"; "quarter past three" is **negyed négy**
(*ned-yed nayd-yuh*), literally "quarter four"; and "quarter to
four" is **háromnegyed négy** (*haromned-yed nayd-yuh*), literally
"three quarters four."

In the simplest, though not as common, way of telling the time
the word for the hours comes first, followed by **óra** (*awruh*)
"hour" and the number of the minutes; thus "three ten" can also
be expressed as **három óra tíz** (*harom awruh teez*); "three fifty" as
**három óra ötven** (*harom awruh urtven*); "three fifteen" as **három
óra tizenöt** (*harom awruh tizenurt*); "three thirty" as **három óra
harminc** (*harom awruh harmints*); and "three forty five" as **három
óra negyvenöt** (*harom awruh nedyuvenurt*).

| | | |
|---|---|---|
| am | d.e./délelőtt | *daylelurt* |
| pm | d.u./délután | *daylootan* |
| one o'clock | egy óra | *ed-yuh awruh* |
| ten past one | tíz perccel múlt egy | *teez pertsel moolt ed-yuh* |
| | | |
| quarter past one | negyed kettő | *ned-yed kettur* |
| half past one | fél kettő | *fayl kettur* |
| twenty to two | húsz perc múlva kettő | *hooss perts moolvuh kettur* |
| quarter to two | háromnegyed kettő | *haromned-yed kettur* |
| two o'clock | két óra | *kayt awruh* |
| at half past five | fél hatkor | *fayl hutkor* |
| at seven o'clock | hét órakor | *hayt awrukor* |
| noon | dél | *dayl* |
| midnight | éjfél | *ayfayl* |

# COMMUNICATIONS

## Useful Words and Phrases

| | | |
|---|---|---|
| code | körzethívószám | kur-rzetheevawssam |
| collect call | R-beszélgetés | er bessaylgetaysh |
| dial tone | tárcsahang | tarchuh-hung |
| directory assistance | tudakozó | toodukozaw |
| email address | e-mail cím | eemayl tseem |
| extension | mellék | mellayk |
| fax machine | faxkészülék | foks-kaysewlaykut |
| internet | internet | 'internet' |
| mobile phone | mobiltelefon, bunkó | mobiltelefon, bunkaw |
| number | szám | sam |
| operator | telefonközpont | telefonkurzpont |
| phone card | telefonkártya | telefonkartya |
| telephone | telefon | telefon |
| telephone booth | telefonfülke | telefonfewlkeh |
| website | hálószem | halawsem |
| wrong number | téves kapcsolás | tayvesh kupcholash |

**Where is the nearest phone booth?**
Hol van a legközelebbi telefonfülke?
*hol van uh legkurzelebbi telefonfewlkeh*

**I would like a number in …**
Egy …-i telefonszámra lenne szükségem
*ed-yuh …-i telefonssamruh lenneh sewkshaygem*

**I would like to speak to …**
Szeretnék …-val beszélni
*seretnayk …-vul bessaylni*

**My number is …**
A telefonszámon …
*un telefonssamom*

**Could you leave him a message?**
Hagyhatnék egy üzenetet?
*hud-yuhutnayk ed-yuh ewzenetet*

**Sorry, wrong number**
Sajnálom, téves kapcsolás
*shuh-yunalom tayvesh kupcholash*

**What's your fax number/email address?**
Faxszáma/e-mail címe van?
*fokssama/ee-mayl tseemeh vun*

**Can I send a fax/email from here?**
Küldhetnék innen e-mailt/faxot?
*kewldhetnayk innen ee-maylt/foksot*

---

## THINGS YOU'LL HEAR

**Téves számot hívott**
You've got the wrong number

**Kivel beszélek?**
Who's speaking?

**Sajnos a vonal foglalt**
Unfortunately, the line is busy

**Sajnálom, nincs benn**
Sorry, he's not in

**Mi az ön telefonszáma?**
What is your number?

**Tessék holnap újra hívni**
Please call again tomorrow

**Megmondom, hogy ön kereste**
I'll tell him you called

**Tessék talán később újra megpróbálni**
Perhaps you can try a little later

---

## THINGS YOU'LL SEE

| | |
|---|---|
| a hívott fél fizet | collect call |
| ár | price |
| azonnali beszélgetés | immediate call |
| belföldi távhívás | domestic long-distance call |
| díj | charges |
| helyi beszélgetés | local call |
| hibaelhárító szolgálat | repairs service |
| hitelkártyával fizetett beszélgetés | call paid by credit card |
| igen sürgős beszélgetés | very urgent call |
| interurbán hívás | long-distance call |
| kézi kapcsolással | through the operator |
| körzethívószám | code |
| közvetlen tárcsázás | direct dialing |
| nem működik | out of order |
| nemzetközi hívás | international call |
| R-beszélgetés | collect call |
| sürgős beszélgetés | urgent call |
| távbeszélő | telephone (booth) |
| távhívás | long-distance call |
| távolsági beszélgetés | long-distance call |
| telefonfülke | telephone booth |
| telefonközpont | operator |
| tudakozó | directory assistance |
| balesetbejelentés | emergency call |

# HOTELS

## USEFUL WORDS AND PHRASES

| | | |
|---|---|---|
| balcony | erkély | *erkay* |
| bath | fürdő | *fewrdur* |
| bathroom | fürdőszoba | *fewrdurssobuh* |
| bed | ágy | *ad-yuh* |
| bedroom | hálószoba | *halawssobuh* |
| breakfast | reggeli | *reggeli* |
| check | számla | *samluh* |
| dining room | étterem | *aytterem* |
| dinner | vacsora | *vuchoruh* |
| double room | dupláágyas szoba | *doopluh-ad-yush sobuh* |
| elevator | lift | *lift* |
| lobby | hall | *hull* |
| full board | teljes ellátás | *tel-yesh ellatash* |
| half board | fél panzió | *fayl punzi-aw* |
| hotel | szálloda | *salloduh* |
| key | kulcs | *koolch* |
| lounge | szalon | *sulon* |
| lunch | ebéd | *ebayd* |
| manager | igazgató | *iguzgutaw* |
| reception | recepció | *retseptsi-aw* |
| receptionist | recepciós, portás | *retseptsi-awsh, portash* |
| restaurant | étterem | *aytterem* |
| restroom | WC | *vaytsay* |
| room | szoba | *sobuh* |
| room service | szobaszervíz | *sobusserveez* |
| shower | zuhany | *zoohun-yuh* |
| shower room | zuhanyozó | *zoohun-yozaw* |
| single room | egyágyas szoba | *ed-yad-yush sobuh* |
| suite | lakosztály | *lukossta-yuh* |
| TV | tévé | *tayvay* |
| twin room | kétágyas szoba | *kaytad-yush sobuh* |

**Do you have any vacancies?**
Van kiadó szobájuk?
*vun ki-udaw soba-yook*

**I have a reservation**
Foglaltam egy szobát
*foglultum ed-yuh sobat*

**I'd like a single/double room**
Szeretnék egy egyágyas/duplaágyas szobát kivenni
*seretnayk ed-yuh ed-yad-yush/doopluh-ad-yush sobat kivenni*

**I'd like a room with a bathroom/balcony**
Fürdőszobás/erkélyes szobát szeretnék
*fewrdurssobash/erkay-yesh sobat seretnayk*

**I'd like a room for one night/three nights**
Egy/három éjszakára szeretnék egy szobát kivenni
*ed-yuh/harom ayssukaruh seretnayk ed-yuh sobat kivenni*

**What is the charge per night?**
Mennyibe kerül a szoba egy éjszakára?
*menn-yibeh kerewl uh sobuh ed-yuh ayssukaruh*

**Is there satellite/cable TV in the rooms?**
A szobákban fogható-e kábel/műholdas tv?
*a sobakban foghato-eh kabel/mewholdash tayvay*

**Is there a reduction for children?**
Adnak engedményt gyerek számára?
*odnok engedmaynt d-yerek samaruh*

**Is there wheelchair access?**
Tolószékkel hozzáférhető?
*tolowsaykkul hozzafayrhetew*

**Can you warm this bottle/baby food for me?**
Felmelegítené ezt a cuclisüveget/babapempőt?
*felmelegeetenay est o tsutslish-ewveget/bobopempurt*

**Please call me at … o'clock**
Legyen szíves … órakor felhívni
*led-yen ssivesh … awrukor felheevni*

**May I have breakfast in my room?**
Kérem a reggelit a szobámban felszolgálni
*kayrem uh reggelit uh sobambun felssolgalni*

**My room number is …**
Szobaszámom …
*sobussamom*

**I'm leaving tomorrow**
Holnap elutazom
*holnup elootuzom*

**May I have the check, please?**
Legyen szíves elkészíteni a számlát?
*led-yen ssivesh elkaysseeteni uh samlat*

**I'll pay by credit card**
Hitelkártyával fizetek
*hitelkart-yavul fizetek*

**I'll pay cash**
Készpénzzel fizetek
*kaysspaynzel fizetek*

**Can you get me a taxi?**
Rendeljen kérem egy taxit
*rendel-yen kayrem ed-yuh tuxit*

## THINGS YOU'LL SEE

| | |
|---|---|
| ebéd | lunch |
| étterem | restaurant |
| felvonó | elevator |
| fürdőszoba | bathroom |
| hölgyek | women |
| húzni | pull |
| megtelt | no vacancies |
| mosdók | restrooms |
| porta | reception |
| reggeli | breakfast |
| számla | check |
| tolni | push |
| vacsora | dinner, supper |
| vészkijárat | emergency exit |

## THINGS YOU'LL HEAR

**Sajnálom, megtelt**
I'm sorry, we're full

**Nincs több egyágyas szobánk**
There are no single rooms left

**Nincs több duplaágyas szobánk**
There are no double rooms left

**Hány éjszakára?**
For how many nights?

**Hogyan szándékozik fizetni?**
How will you be paying?

**Előre kell fizetni**
Please pay in advance

## SHOPPING

**Where is the … department?**
Hol találom a … osztályt?
*hol tulalom uh … ossta-yut*

**Do you have …?**
Kapható önöknél …?
*kuphutaw urnurknayl*

**How much is this?**
Ez mennyibe kerül?
*ez menn-yibeh kerewl*

**Where do I pay?**
Hol lehet fizetni?
*hol lehet fizetni*

**Do you have anything less expensive?**
Ennél olcsóbb nincs?
*ennayl olchawb ninch*

**Could you wrap it for me?**
Legyen szíves becsomagolni
*led-yen ssivesh bechomugolni*

**May I have a receipt?**
Kaphatnék róla számlát?
*kuphutnayk rawluh samlat*

**May I have a refund?**
Visszakaphatnám a pénzemet?
*vissukuphutnam uh paynzemet*

**I'm just looking**
Csak körülnézek
*chuk kur-rewlnayzek*

**I'll come back later**
Később visszajövök
*kayshurb vissuh-yurvurk*

# EATING OUT

Most main dishes are cooked with pork-fat and seasoned with paprika, but the food in Hungary is not exclusively Hungarian: you may find dishes of Austrian, Slovakian, Serbian, Italian, and even French origin in local restaurants.

Although there are a few dishes without meat (primarily made with pasta **tészta** (*taysstuh*) or mushrooms **gomba** (*gombuh*), vegetarians will find most menus rather forbidding: Hungarians eat various forms of meat from early morning to late evening. The main type of meat is pork. Poultry and beef are also popular, but steak is something of a rarity. You will see many dishes prepared with a variety of freshwater fish: do not miss **halászlé** (*hulasslay*) – a thick fish soup flavored with paprika.

Hungarians are fond of soups and, traditionally, meals always start with a bowl of soup. The variety is astonishing – some are even made from fruits. Even the famous Hungarian goulash started life as (an admittedly very rich) soup, as **gulyásleves** (*goo-yashlevesh*), its local name, bears witness. Meat stews are the most popular main courses and there are three main variations: **pörkölt** (*purkurlt*) – stewed, diced meat with paprika; **paprikás** (*puprikash*), similar to **pörkölt** but with more paprika, and with sour cream added; and **tokány** (*tokan-yuh*) where the meat is sliced very thinly and stewed in its own juices.

Pastry (**sütemény** *shewtemayn-yuh*) is simply wonderful in Hungary. Visit a **cukrászda** – a type of teashop that sells its own cakes and pastries, freshly baked on the premises. Local sweets are enhanced by Viennese patisserie, many recipes for which originated in Hungary anyway. Particularly enticing are the various fillings used for Hungarian pancakes (**palacsinta** *puluchintuh*), which can be sweet or savoury: jam, cottage cheese, chocolate, cream, ham, cheese, or mushrooms.

There are various categories of restaurant: an **étterem** is generally a quite smart restaurant, while a **vendéglő** is more mundane, even sober. A **csárda** is a country inn with regional specialities, and a **sörkert** or **söröző** is a cross between a pub and a restaurant. Self-service (**önkiszolgáló**) and fast-food (**ételbár, snack-bár, bisztró, büfé**) establishments are also common in most towns and holiday resorts. The opening hours vary but, in general, restaurants are open from 11:30 am to 11 pm or later. Some restaurants have gypsy music from about 6 pm onward. A tip of about 15 percent is customary.

Between meals, look out for small kiosks on street corners, where you can buy hamburgers and hot dogs. Around Lake Balaton similar kiosks offer more local food, such as a variety of broiled meats (**lacikonyha** *lutsikon-yuhuh*), fried fish (**sült hal** *shewlt hul*), or fried crispy doughnuts called **lángos** (*langosh*).

Traditionally a wine-growing region, Hungary's wines are quite outstanding. Between the world-famous Tokay and the fiery red Bull's Blood, there's a whole range of excellent whites and reds ready to be explored – go to a **borkostoló** (wine cellar) or **borozó** (wine bar) to sample these. If beer is more to your taste, try the local **söröző** (*shururzur*).

## USEFUL WORDS AND PHRASES

| beer | sör | *shur* |
|------|-----|--------|
| bottle | üveg | *ewveg* |
| bread | kenyér | *ken-yayr* |
| cake | sütemény | *shewtemayn-yuh* |
| check | számla | *samluh* |
| chef | szakács | *sukach* |
| coffee | kávé | *kavay* |
| cup | csésze | *chaysseh* |
| fork | villa | *villuh* |
| glass | pohár | *pohar* |
| knife | kés | *kaysh* |
| menu | étlap | *aytlup* |
| milk | tej | *tay* |
| napkin | kéztörlő, szalvéta | *kayzturlur, sulvaytuh* |
| pepper | bors | *borsh* |
| plate | tányér | *tan-yayr* |
| receipt | nyugta | *n-yoogtuh* |

| | | |
|---|---|---|
| **red wine** | vörösbor | *vurrurshbor* |
| **salt** | só | *shaw* |
| **sandwich** | szendvics | *sendvich* |
| **soup** | leves | *levesh* |
| **spoon** | kanál | *kunal* |
| **sugar** | cukor | *tsookor* |
| **table** | asztal | *usstul* |
| **tea** | tea | *teh-uh* |
| **teaspoon** | kávéskanál | *kavayshkunal* |
| **tip** | borravaló | *borruvulaw* |
| **waiter** | pincér | *pintsayr* |
| **waitress** | pincérnő | *pintsayrnur* |
| **water** | víz | *veez* |
| **white wine** | fehérbor | *fehayrbor* |
| **wine** | bor | *bor* |
| **wine list** | itallap | *itullup* |

### A table for one/two/four, please
Egy asztalt szeretnék egy/két/négy személyre
*ed-yuh usstult seretnayk ed-yuh/kayt/nayd-yuh semayreh*

### May I see the menu/wine list?
Az étlapot/itallapot, legyen szíves?
*uz aytlupot/itullupot led-yen ssivesh*

### What would you recommend?
Mit tud ajánlani?
*mit tood uh-yanluni*

### I'd like …
Szeretnék egy …-t
*seretnayk ed-yuh …-t*

### Just a cup of coffee, please
Csak egy csésze kávét kérek
*chuk ed-yuh chaysseh kavayt kayrek*

**Waiter!/Waitress!**
Főúr!/Kisasszony! Legyen szíves!
*fur-oor/kishusson-yuh led-yen ssivesh*

**Is this suitable for vegetarians?**
Ezt vegetáriánus eheti?
*est vegetarianush eheti*

**Do you do children's portions?**
Gyerekadag is kapható?
*d-yerekodog ish kophotaw*

**I didn't order this**
Én nem ezt rendeltem
*ayn nem ezt rendeltem*

**May we have some more …?**
Kaphatnánk még …-t?
*kuphutnank mayg …-t*

**The meal was very good, thank you**
Nagyon finom volt az étel, köszönöm szépen
*nud-yon finom volt uz aytel kurssurnurm saypen*

**May we have the check, please?**
Legyen szíves elkészíteni a számlát?
*led-yen ssivesh elkaysseeteni uh samlat*

---

### THINGS YOU'LL HEAR

**Jó étvágyat (kívánok)!**
Enjoy your meal!

**Mit parancsolnak az urak/hölgyek?**
What would the gentlemen/ladies like to order?

---

# MENU GUIDE

**alma** apple
**almás rétes** apple strudel
**ásványvíz** mineral water
**bab** beans
**banán** banana
**barack** apricot
**barackosfánk** apricot doughnut
**bárány** lamb
**bécsi szelet** veal cutlet in breadcrumbs
**bélszínfilé** boneless tenderloin steak
**besamelmártás** white cream sauce
**betyárleves** "outlaw" ragoût – a thick
  spicy broth with vegetables
**birka** mutton
**bográcsgulyás** goulash soup – thick
  spicy meat and vegetable soup
**bor** wine
**borjú(lús)** veal
**bors** pepper
**borsostokány** beef casserole
**buggyantott tojás** poached eggs
**bukta** jam-filled sweet roll
**bundás alma** apple fritter
**burgonya** potatoes
**burgonyapüré** mashed potatoes
**cékla** beets
**citrom** lemon
**cukkini** zucchini
**cseresznye** cherry
**csikóstokány** beef casserole with diced
  bacon, onions, tomatoes, and peppers
**csirke** chicken
**csirke becsinált** chicken ragoût
**csontleves** clear meat soup
**csuka** pike
**daragaluska** small cornmeal dumplings
**daragombóc** cornmeal dumpling
**datolya** dates

**derelye** ravioli filled with jam, cheese,
  or meat
**dió** walnuts
**disznóhús** pork
**disznócsülök káposztával** smoked
  knuckle of pork with sauerkraut
**édességek** sweets, desserts
**egres** gooseberry
**előételek** appetizers
**eper** strawberries
**erdélyi tokány** Transylvanian beef
  casserole with bacon
**erőleves** broth
**fácán** pheasant
**fánk** jam doughnut
**fehérbab** dried white beans
**fejes saláta** lettuce
**felfújt** soufflé
**felvágott** salami, cold meats
**finommetélt** thin egg noodles
**fokhagyma** garlic
**főételek** main courses
**főtt** boiled
**füge** figs
**fürjtojás** quail's egg
**galuska** small soft dumplings
**gesztenye** chestnuts
**gomba** mushrooms
**gombóc** ball, dumpling
**gőngyölt felsál** beef olive
**görögdinnye** watermelon
**gulyásleves** goulash soup
**gyömbér** ginger
**gyümölcs** fruit
**gyümölcslé** fruit juice
**hab** mousse
**habosszilva** plum and chocolate mousse
**hagyma** onions

hal fish
halászlé fish soup
harcsa catfish
hideg előételek cold appetizers
hús meat
húsleves broth
húspástétom meat pie
ízestekercs jam roll
joghurt yogurt
kacsa duck
kapor dill
káposzta cabbage
karfiol cauliflower
kávé coffee
kelbimbó Brussels sprouts
keménytojás hard-boiled egg
kenyér bread
képviselőfánk custard-filled doughnut
  sometimes with chocolate icing
keszeg bream
kifli crescent-shaped roll
kókusz coconut
kókusztekercs coconut roll
kolbász spicy paprika sausage
kolozsvári gulyás Transylvanian goulash
  stew with cabbage
kovászos uborka pickles
körömpörkölt pork knuckle casserole
kőrözött ewe's cheese spread
körte pears
krumpli potatoes
kukorica sweetcorn
lágy sajt soft cheese
lágytojás soft-boiled egg
lángos savory doughnuts
lé juice
lecsó green pepper and tomato stew
lekvár jam
lencse lentils
lepény pie
leves soup

liba goose
libapecsenye roasted goose
limonádé lemonade
magyaros hidegtál assorted cold meats
máj liver
májgaluska small liver dumplings
majonézmártás mayonnaise
mák poppy seed
malac suckling pig
málna raspberry
mandula almonds
marha beef
marhapörkölt beef casserole
mártás sauce
meggy morello cherry
meggyes rétes morello cherry strudel
melegszendvics toasted sandwiches
metélt sweet pasta
menü menu
méz honey
mogyorótorta hazelnut gâteau
mustár mustard
napi ajánlatunk today's special
narancs orange
nyúl rabbit, hare
olaj oil
omlett omelette
orjaleves pork broth
őszibarack peaches
őzhúsleves venison soup
padlizsán eggplant
padlizsánpástétom eggplant purée
palacsinta pancakes
palócgulyás lamb goulash stew
paprikás diced meat stewed in paprika
  and sour cream
paradicsom tomatoes
paradicsomos tökfőzelék squash in
  thick tomato sauce
paradicsomsaláta tomato salad
paraj spinach

árolt braised
ászkagombóc dumpling made of bread
irítós toast
irított burgonya roasted potatoes
irított máj sautéed liver
irospaprika paprika
iskóta sponge cake
iskótatekercs jam roll
onty carp
ogácsa savory scone
örkölt casserole made with diced meat
uliszka cornmeal porridge
ulyka turkey
uncstorta rich rum-flavored gâteau
ablóhús mixed kabob
akott layered
ántott breaded
etek radish
étes strudel
ibizli redcurrant
ingló greengages
izibizi rice mixed with peas
izsfelfújt rice soufflé
izskóret rice garnish
ostélyos braised steak
oston/rostonsült broiled
ozmaring rosemary
ajt cheese
aláta salad
árgabarack apricot
árgaborsó dried peas
árgadinnye honeydew melon
árgarépa carrots
avanyú káposzta sauerkraut
avanyúság pickles
ertés pork
ertéshúspogácsa ground pork balls
ó salt
onka ham
ós sütemény savory cakes made from
    thin flaky pastry

sör beer
spárga asparagus
specialitások specialities
spenót spinach
spenótbomba spinach fritters
süllő pike/perch
sült fried, roasted
sült burgonya french fries
sütemények pastry
svájci sajtfondue cheese fondue
szalmakrumpli potato chips
szalonna fat bacon
szamóca wild strawberries
szárazbableves haricot bean soup
szárnyas poultry, fowl
szárnyaskrémleves cream of fowl soup
szarvasgomba truffles
szarvas magyarosan haunch of venison
    in paprika and sour cream sauce
szegedi gulyás beef goulash with bacon
    and sauerkraut
szegfűszeg cloves
székelygulyás Transylvanian sauerkraut
    and pork stew with sour cream
szendvicsek sandwiches
szerb gulyás Serbian goulash stew with
    cabbage
szerecsendió nutmeg
szódavíz soda water
szőlő grapes
szörp fruit juice
szűzpecsenye roasted pork tenderloin
tarhonya fine grains of pasta made from
    eggs and barley
tárkony tarragon
tartármártás tartar sauce
tavaszi saláta spring salad – cucumbers,
    tomatoes, turnips, radish, and lettuce
tea tea
tej milk
tejberizs rice pudding

**tejeskávé** coffee with milk
**tejföl** sour cream
**tejfölös bableves** bean soup with sour
cream
**tejszín** cream
**tejszínhab** whipped cream
**téliszalámi** Hungarian salami
**tengeri hal** saltwater fish
**tészták** pastry, sweet pasta dish
**tojás** egg
**tokány** casserole made with onions and
diced meat
**tonhal Orly módra** tuna fried in batter
and served with tomato sauce
**torta** gâteau
**tök** squash
**tökfőzelék** squash in thick sour cream
sauce
**töltött** stuffed
**töltött fasírozott** meat loaf stuffed with
hard-boiled eggs
**töltött paprika** stuffed green peppers in
tomato sauce
**töpörtyű** pork or goose crackling
**tüdő** cow's lungs
**túró** cottage cheese
**túrós metélt** pasta with soft white
cheese, bacon, and sour cream
**túrós palacsinta** pancakes with sweet
cottage cheese and raisin filling
**túrós pite** sweet cottage cheese pie
**túróspogácsa** scone containing soft
white cheese
**túrós puliszka** cornmeal porridge with
cottage cheese
**túrós rétes** cheese strudel
**tűzdelt fehérpecsenye** greased
tenderloin steak
**tűzdelt nyúlgerinc** greased hare saddle
**tyúkhúsleves** chicken broth
**uborka** cucumber

**uborkasaláta** cucumber salad
**ürü** mutton
**ürüborda** mutton chop
**ürücomb** leg of mutton
**vadas** sauce served with game or beef,
made from lemon juice, mustard, sour
cream, and diced vegetables
**vadasan** meat braised with red onions,
vegetables, and spices, and served with
game sauce
**vaddisznó erdész módra** haunch of
wild boar with mushrooms, bacon,
and potatoes
**vadszárnyas** fowl
**vagdalt libamelle** goose meat loaf
**vaj** butter
**vanília** vanilla
**vargabéles** cake made with curd,
vanilla, and raisins
**vegyes saláta** mixed salad
**velő** brains
**véres hurka** fried black pudding
**virsli** hot dogs
**vitaminsaláta** grated cabbage, carrot,
radish, and onion salad
**vörösbor** red wine
**vöröshagyma** purple onions
**zabpehely** oat flakes
**zeller** celery
**zellerkrémleves** cream of celery soup
**zöldbab** green beans
**zöldborsó** peas
**zöldpaprika** green pepper
**zöldségleves** mixed vegetable broth
**zsemle** bread roll
**zsemlegombóc** potato and bread
dumplings
**zserbószelet** cake with chocolate icing,
made up of alternate layers of apricot
jam, nuts, and chocolate cream
**zsiványpecsenye** mixed roasted meat

# ITALIAN

## CONTENTS

| | |
|---|---|
| INTRODUCTION | 230 |
| USEFUL PHRASES | 231 |
| DAYS, MONTHS, SEASONS | 237 |
| NUMBERS | 238 |
| TIME | 239 |
| COMMUNICATIONS | 241 |
| EMERGENCIES | 243 |
| HOTELS | 244 |
| SHOPPING | 248 |
| EATING OUT | 249 |
| MENU GUIDE | 253 |

# INTRODUCTION

## Pronunciation

The pronunciation of an Italian word is very similar to the way
it is written. When reading the imitated pronunciation, stress
the part that is underlined. Pronounce each syllable as if it
formed part of an English word and you will be understood.
Remember the points below, and your pronunciation will be
even closer to the correct Italian.

| | |
|---|---|
| *ai* | as in "fair" |
| *ay* | as in "pay" |
| *e* | as in "bed" |
| | (pronounced as a separate syllable at the end of a word) |
| *g* | always hard as in "get" |
| *I* | as in "I" |
| *ow* | as in "cow" |
| *r* | always strongly pronounced |
| *y* | always pronounced as in "yet" except in *ay* as above |

Note that when there are two identical consonants separated
by a hyphen, eg **vorrei** – *vor-ray*, both consonants must be
pronounced as if you were pronouncing two separate English
words: eg "just two," "full length."

## Genders and Articles

Italian has two genders for nouns – masculine and feminine.
In the vocabulary sections, we generally give the definite
article ("the"). For masculine nouns, the definite article is **il**
(plural **i**) before nouns beginning with a consonant, **lo** (plural
**gli**) before nouns beginning with **s** + consonant or with **z**, and
**l'** (plural **gli**) before nouns beginning with a vowel.
For feminine nouns, use **la** before a noun beginning with
a consonant and **l'** before a vowel (plural **le**).

The masculine indefinite article ("a/an") is **uno** before a noun
beginning with a consonant and **un** before a vowel. The
feminine is **una** before a consonant and **un'** before a vowel.

# USEFUL PHRASES

## Yes, No, OK, etc.

**Yes/No**
Sì/No
*see/no*

**OK**
OK
*"ok"*

**That's fine**
Va bene
*va bene*

**That's right**
È vero
*eh vayro*

## Greetings, Introductions

**How do you do, pleased to meet you**
Piacere di conoscerla
*pee-achaire dee konoshairla*

**Good morning/good evening/good night**
Buon giorno/Buona sera/Buona notte
*bwon jorno/bwona saira/bwona not-te*

**Goodbye**
Arrivederci
*ar-reevedairchee*

**How are you?**                    *(familiar)*
Come sta?                           Come stai?
*kome sta*                          *kome stɪ*

**My name is …**
Mi chiamo …
*mee k-yamo*

**What's your name?**      *(familiar)*
Come si chiama?      Come ti chiami?
*k<u>o</u>me see k-y<u>a</u>ma*      *k<u>o</u>me tee k-y<u>a</u>mee*

**This is …** *(introducing male/female)*
Questo è …/Questa è …
*kw<u>e</u>sto eh/kw<u>e</u>sta eh*

**Hello/Hi!**
Ciao/Salve!
*chow/s<u>a</u>lve*

## PLEASE, THANK YOU, APOLOGIES

**Thank you/No, thank you**
Grazie/No grazie
*gr<u>a</u>tzee-e/no gr<u>a</u>tzee-e*

**Please** *(offering)*      *(asking for something)*
Prego      Per favore/per piacere
*pr<u>e</u>go*      *pair fav<u>o</u>re/pair pee-ach<u>ai</u>re*

**Sorry!/Excuse me!**      *(familiar)*
Scusi!      Scusa!
*sk<u>oo</u>zee*      *sk<u>oo</u>za*

## WHERE, HOW, ASKING

**Excuse me, please** *(to get past etc)*
Permesso
*pairm<u>e</u>sso*

**Can you tell me …?**
Potrebbe dirmi …?
*potr<u>e</u>b-be d<u>ee</u>rmee*

**May I have …?**
Potrei avere …?
*potr<u>ay</u> av<u>ai</u>re*

**Would you like a ...?**
Vorrebbe un/una ...?
*vor-reb-be oon/oona*

**Would you like to ...?**
Le piacerebbe ...?
*le pee-achaireb-be*

**Is there ... here?**
C'è ...?
*cheh*

**What's that?**
Che cos'è?
*ke kozeh*

**How much is it?**
Quanto costa?
*kwanto kosta*

**Where is the ...?**
Dov'è il/la ...?
*doveh eel/la*

**Is there wheelchair access?**
È possibile l'accesso con la sedia a rotelle?
*eh pos-see-bee-leh l'aches-so kon la saidee-a rotail-le*

**Are guide dogs allowed?**
È permesso portare i cani guida?
*eh pairmes-so portarai ee kanee gweeda*

**ABOUT ONESELF**

**I'm from ...**
Sono di ...
*sono dee*

**I'm ... years old**
Ho ... anni
*o ... an-nee*

**I'm a …** *(occupation)*
Faccio il/la …
*facho eel/la*

**I'm married/single/divorced** *(said by a man)*
Sono sposato/celibe/divorziato
*sono spozato/cheleebe/deevortz-yato*

*(said by a woman)*
Sono sposata/nubile/divorziata
*sono spozata/noobeele/deevortz-yata*

**I have … sisters/brothers/children**
Ho … sorelle/fratelli/bambini
*o … sorel-le/fratel-lee/bambeenee*

## HELP, PROBLEMS

**Can you help me?**
Può aiutarmi?
*pwo i-ootarmee*

**I don't understand**
Non capisco
*non kapeesko*

**Does anyone here speak English?**
C'è qualcuno che parla inglese?
*cheh kwalkoono ke parla eengleze*

**I can't speak Italian**
Non parlo italiano
*non parlo eetal-yano*

**I don't know**
Non so
*non so*

**Please speak more slowly**
Per favore, parli più lentamente
*pair favore parlee p-yoo lentamente*

**Please write it down for me**
Me lo scriva, per favore
*me lo skreeva pair favore*

**I'm lost** *(said by a man/woman)*
Mi sono perso/persa
*mee sono pairso/pairsa*

**Go away!** *(familiar)*
Se ne vada!      Vattene!
*se ne vada*      *vat-tene*

## LIKES, DISLIKES, SOCIALIZING

**I like/love …**
Mi piace …
*mee pee-ache*

**I don't like …**
Non mi piace …
*non mee pee-ache*

**Do you like …?**
Le piace …?
*le pee-ache*

**It's delicious/awful!**
È buonissimo/terribile!
*eh bwonees-seemo/ter-reebeele*

**I don't drink/smoke**
Non bevo/fumo
*non bevo/foomo*

**Do you mind if I smoke?**
Le dispiace se fumo?
*le deespee-ache se foomo*

**What would you like (to drink)?**
Cosa desidera (da bere)?
*koza dezeedaira da baire*

**I would like a …**
Vorrei un/una …
*vor-re oon/oona*

**Nothing for me, thanks**
Per me niente, grazie
*pair me nee-ente gratzee-e*

**Cheers!** *(toast)*
Alla salute!/Cin cin!
*al-la saloote/cheen cheen*

---

### THINGS YOU'LL HEAR

| | |
|---|---|
| **a più tardi** | see you later |
| **arrivederci** | goodbye |
| **attenzione!** | look out! pay attention! |
| **avanti!** | come in! |
| **bene** | good, fine |
| **buon viaggio!** | have a good trip! |
| **cosa hai/ha detto?** | what did you say? |
| **ecco-ti qua!** | here you are! |
| **mi dispiace tanto!** | I'm so sorry! |
| **mi scusi** | excuse me |
| **molte grazie** | thank you very much |
| **non capisco** | I don't understand |
| **prego** | you're welcome, don't mention it |
| **prego?** | excuse me? |
| **serviti/si serva/servitevi** | help yourself |
| **scusi?, come?** | excuse me? |
| **va bene** | that's right |

---

# DAYS, MONTHS, SEASONS

| | | |
|---|---|---|
| Sunday | domenica | *domeneeka* |
| Monday | lunedì | *loonedee* |
| Tuesday | martedì | *martedee* |
| Wednesday | mercoledì | *mairkoledee* |
| Thursday | giovedì | *jovedee* |
| Friday | venerdì | *venairdee* |
| Saturday | sabato | *sabato* |
| | | |
| January | gennaio | *jen-na-yo* |
| February | febbraio | *feb-bra-yo* |
| March | marzo | *martzo* |
| April | aprile | *apreele* |
| May | maggio | *maj-jo* |
| June | giugno | *joon-yo* |
| July | luglio | *lool-yo* |
| August | agosto | *agosto* |
| September | settembre | *set-tembre* |
| October | ottobre | *ot-tobre* |
| November | novembre | *novembre* |
| December | dicembre | *deechembre* |
| | | |
| Spring | primavera | *preemavaira* |
| Summer | estate | *estate* |
| Fall | autunno | *owtoon-no* |
| Winter | inverno | *eenvairno* |
| | | |
| Christmas | Natale | *natale* |
| Christmas Eve | la Vigilia di Natale | *veejeel-ya dee natale* |
| Good Friday | Venerdì Santo | *venairdee santo* |
| Easter | Pasqua | *paskwa* |
| New Year | Capodanno | *kapodan-no* |
| New Year's Eve | San Silvestro | *san seelvestro* |
| Pentecost | Pentecoste | *pentekoste* |

# NUMBERS

| | | | |
|---|---|---|---|
| 0 | zero *tzairo* | 10 | dieci *dee-echee* |
| 1 | uno *oono* | 11 | undici *oon-deechee* |
| 2 | due *doo-e* | 12 | dodici *doh-deechee* |
| 3 | tre *tre* | 13 | tredici *tre-deechee* |
| 4 | quattro *kwat-tro* | 14 | quattordici *kwat-tor-deechee* |
| 5 | cinque *cheenkwe* | 15 | quindici *kween-deechee* |
| 6 | sei *say* | 16 | sedici *say-deechee* |
| 7 | sette *set-te* | 17 | diciassette *deechas-set-te* |
| 8 | otto *ot-to* | 18 | diciotto *deechot-to* |
| 9 | nove *no-ve* | 19 | diciannove *deechan-no-ve* |

20 venti *ventee*
21 ventuno *vent-oono*
22 ventidue *ventee-doo-e*
30 trenta *trenta*
31 trentuno *trentoono*
32 trentadue *trentadoo-e*
40 quaranta *kwaranta*
50 cinquanta *cheenkwanta*
60 sessanta *ses-santa*
70 settanta *set-tanta*
80 ottanta *ot-tanta*
90 novanta *novanta*
100 cento *chento*
110 centodieci *chento-dee-echee*
200 duecento *doo-e-chento*
1,000 mille *meele*
10,000 diecimila *dee-echeemeela*
20,000 ventimila *venteemeela*
50,000 cinquantamila *cheenkwantameela*
100,000 centomila *chentomeela*
1,000,000 un milione *oon meel-yone*

Note that thousands are written 1.000, 10.000, etc, in Italian.

# TIME

| today | oggi | *oj-jee* |
|---|---|---|
| yesterday | ieri | *yaire* |
| tomorrow | domani | *domanee* |
| this week | questa settimana | *kwesta set-teemana* |
| last week | la settimana scorsa | *set-teemana skorsa* |
| next week | la settimana prossima | *set-teemana pros-seema* |
| this morning | stamattina | *stamat-teena* |
| this afternoon | questo pomeriggio | *kwesto pomereej-jo* |
| this evening | stasera | *stasaira* |
| tonight | stanotte | *stanot-te* |
| in three days | tra tre giorni | *tra tre jornee* |
| three days ago | tre giorni fa | *tre jornee fa* |
| late | tardi | *tardee* |
| early | presto | *presto* |
| soon | presto | *presto* |
| later on | più tardi | *p-yoo tardee* |
| at the moment | in questo momento | *een kwesto momento* |
| second | un secondo | *sekondo* |
| minute | un minuto | *meenooto* |
| two minutes | due minuti | *doo-e meenootee* |
| quarter of an hour | un quarto d'ora | *kwarto dora* |
| half an hour | mezz'ora | *medzora* |
| three quarters of an hour | tre quarti d'ora | *tre kwartee dora* |
| hour | un'ora | *ora* |
| day | un giorno | *jorno* |
| week | una settimana | *set-teemana* |
| two weeks | quindici giorni | *kween-deechee jornee* |
| month | un mese | *meze* |
| year | un anno | *an-no* |
| that day | quel giorno | *kwel jorno* |
| every day | ogni giorno | *on-yee jorno* |
| the next day | il giorno dopo | *jorno dopo* |

## TELLING TIME

The hour is expressed in Italian by the ordinal number only:
**sono le due** "it's two o'clock," **alle due** "at two o'clock." There
is no equivalent of "o'clock." To denote the half hour, add **e
mezza** after the hour: **sono le due e mezza** "it's 2:30." To say
"quarter past," add **e un quarto** "and a quarter" to the hour:
**sono le tre e un quarto** is "it's a quarter past three."

Quarter to the hour is expressed either by adding **e tre quarti**
"and three quarters" to the hour, or adding **meno un quarto**
"less a quarter" to the next hour. "It's a quarter to eight" is
**sono le sette e tre quarti** or **sono le otto meno un quarto**.

To express minutes after the hour, add the minutes to the
hour: **sono le sette e quaranta** "it's seven forty." For minutes to
the hour use **meno** followed by the number of minutes to the
next hour: **sono le otto meno venti** "it's twenty to eight."

There are no equivalents of am/pm, although you can use **di
mattina/del mattino** "in the morning," **di/del pomeriggio** "in
the afternoon," **di sera** "in the evening," or **di notte** "at night."

| | | |
|---|---|---|
| **what time is it?** | che ore sono? | *ke ore sono?* |
| **it's one o'clock** | è l'una | *eh loona* |
| **it's two/three/four o'clock** | sono le due/tre/quattro | *sono le doo-e/tre/kwat-tro* |
| **ten past one** | l'una e dieci | *loona ay dee-echee* |
| **quarter past one** | l'una e un quarto | *loona ay oon kwarto* |
| **1:30** | l'una e mezza | *loona ay medza* |
| **twenty to two** | le due meno venti | *lay doo-e meno ventee* |
| **quarter to two** | le due meno un quarto | *le doo-e meno oon kwarto* |
| **two o'clock** | le due | *le doo-e* |
| **at 5:30** | alle cinque e mezza | *al-le cheenkwe ay medza* |
| **at seven o'clock** | alle sette | *al-le set-te* |
| **noon** | mezzogiorno | *medzojorno* |
| **midnight** | mezzanotte | *medzanot-te* |

# COMMUNICATIONS

## Useful Words and Phrases

| | | |
|---|---|---|
| **code** | il prefisso | *prefees-so* |
| **collect call** | la chiamata a carico | *k-yamata a kareeko* |
| | del destinatario | *del desteenataree-o* |
| **dial tone** | il segnale di libero | *sen-yale dee leebairo* |
| **email** | la posta elettronica | *posta ai-lait-tronee-ka* |
| **emergency** | l'emergenza | *emairjentza* |
| **extension** | l'interno | *eentairno* |
| **fax machine** | il fax | *'fax'* |
| **internet** | l'internet | *'internet'* |
| **mobile phone** | il telefonino | *telefonino* |
| **number** | il numero | *noomairo* |
| **operator** | l'operatore | *opairatore* |
| **payphone** | il telefono a gettoni | *telefono a jet-tonee* |
| **phonecard** | la scheda telefonica | *skeda telefoneeka* |
| **telephone** | il telefono | *telefono* |
| **telephone booth** | la cabina telefonica | *kabeena telefoneeka* |
| **website** | il sito internet | *seeto 'internet'* |
| **wrong number** | il numero sbagliato | *noomairo zbal-yato* |

### Where is the nearest telephone booth?
Dov'è la cabina telefonica più vicina?
*doveh la kabeena telefoneeka p-yoo veecheena*

### I would like a number in …
Ho bisogno del numero di un abbonato di …
*o beezon-yo del noomairo dee oon ab-bonato dee*

### I would like to speak to …
Vorrei parlare con …
*vor-ray parlare kon*

### My number is …
Il mio numero è …
*eel mee-o noomairo eh*

**Could you leave him/her a message?**
Potrebbe lasciargli/lasciarle un messaggio?
*potreb-be lasharl-yee/lasharle oon mes-saj-jo*

**I'll call back later**
Richiamero più tardi
*reekeeah-mayro p-yoo tardee*

**What's your fax number/email address?**
Qual'è il suo numero di fax/posta elettronica?
*kwal-ai eel soo-o noo-mairo dee fax/posta ai-lait-tronee-ka*

**May I send an email/fax from here?**
Posso inviare della posta elettronica/un fax da qui?
*pos-so eenvee-arai del-la posta ai-lait-tronee-ka/oon fax da kwee*

---

### THINGS YOU'LL HEAR

**Pronto**
Hello

**Sono io/pronto**
Speaking

**Con chi vuole parlare?**
Whom would you like to speak to?

**Ha sbagliato numero**
You've got the wrong number

**Chi parla?**
Who's calling?

**Attenda in linea, prego**
Hold, please

**Mi dispiace, non c'è**
I'm sorry, he/she's not in

**Gli dirò che ha chiamato**
I'll tell him you called

# EMERGENCIES

### USEFUL WORDS AND PHRASES

| | | |
|---|---|---|
| accident | l'incidente | *eencheedente* |
| ambulance | l'ambulanza | *amboolantza* |
| breakdown | il guasto | *gwasto* |
| burglary | il furto | *foorto* |
| crash | l'incidente | *eencheedente* |
| emergency | l'emergenza | *emairjentza* |
| fire | il fuoco | *fwoko* |
| fire department | i vigili del fuoco | *veejeelee del fwoko* |
| police | la polizia | *poleetzee-a* |
| police station | il commissariato | *kom-mees-sar-yato* |
| | di polizia | *dee poleetzee-a* |

**Help!**
Aiuto!
*I-ooto*

**Stop!**
Si fermi!
*see fairmee*

**Get an ambulance!**
Chiami un'ambulanza!
*k-yamee oon amboolantza*

**Hurry up!**
Presto!
*presto*

**My address is …**
Il mio indirizzo è …
*eel mee-o eendeereetzo eh*

**My passport/car has been stolen**
Mi hanno rubato il passaporto/la macchina
*mee an-no roobato eel pas-saporto/la mak-keena*

# HOTELS

## Useful Words and Phrases

| | | |
|---|---|---|
| balcony | il balcone | *bal-kone* |
| bathroom | il bagno | *ban-yo* |
| bed | il letto | *let-to* |
| bed and breakfast | camera con colazione | *kamaira kon kolatz-yone* |
| bedroom | la camera da letto | *kamaira da let-to* |
| breakfast | la prima colazione | *preema kolatz-yone* |
| check | il conto | *konto* |
| car park | il parcheggio | *parkej-jo* |
| dining room | la sala da pranzo | *sala da prantzo* |
| dinner | la cena | *chena* |
| double bed | il letto matrimoniale | *let-to matreemonyale* |
| double room | la stanza doppia | *stantza doppee-a* |
| elevator | l'ascensore | *ashen-sore* |
| full board | la pensione completa | *pens-yone kompleta* |
| guesthouse | la pensione, la locanda | *pens-yone, lokanda* |
| half board | la mezza pensione | *medza pens-yone,* |
| hotel | l'albergo, l'hotel | *albairgo, oh-tel* |
| key | la chiave | *k-yave* |
| maid | la cameriera | *kamair-yaira* |
| manager | il direttore | *deeret-tore* |
| receipt | la ricevuta | *reechevoota* |
| reception | la reception | *'reception'* |
| receptionist | il/la receptionist | *'receptionist'* |
| restroom | la toilette | *twalet* |
| room | la camera, la stanza | *kamaira, stantza* |
| room service | il servizio in camera | *serveetz-yo een kamaira* |
| shower | la doccia | *docha* |
| single bed | il letto singolo | *let-to seengolo* |
| single room | la stanza singola | *stantza seengola* |

**Do you have any vacancies?**
Avete una stanza libera?
*avete oona stantza leebaira*

**I have a reservation**
Ho prenotato una stanza
*o prenotato oona stantza*

**I'd like a single room**
Vorrei una stanza singola
*vor-ray oona stantza seengola*

**I'd like a room with a bathroom/balcony**
Vorrei una stanza con bagno/con il balcone
*vor-ray oona stantza kon ban-yo/kon eel bal-kone*

**Is there satellite/cable TV in the rooms?**
C'è la TV satellite/cavo in queste stanze?
*Cheh la tee-vee satail-lee-te/kavo een kwaiste stantze*

**I'd like a room for one night/three nights**
Vorrei una stanza per una notte/tre notti
*vor-ray oona stantza pair oona not-te/tre not-tee*

**What is the charge per night?**
Quanto si paga per notte?
*kwanto see paga pair not-te*

**When is breakfast/dinner?**
A che ora viene servita la colazione/la cena?
*a ke ora v-yene serveeta la kolatz-yone/la chena*

**Please wake me at … o'clock**
Mi svegli, per favore, alle …
*mee zvel-yee pair favore al-le*

**May I have breakfast in my room?**
Potrei avere la colazione in camera?
*potray avaire la kolatz-yone een kamaira*

**My room number is …**
Il mio numero di stanza è …
*eel mee-o noomero dee stantza eh*

**There is no toilet paper in the bathroom**
Non c'è carta igienica in bagno
*non cheh karta eej-yeneeka een ban-yo*

**The window won't open**
La finestra non si apre
*la feenestra non see apre*

**There isn't any hot water**
Non c'è acqua calda
*non cheh akwa kalda*

**I'm leaving tomorrow**
Parto domani
*parto domanee*

**When do I have to vacate the room?**
Entro che ora devo liberare la camera?
*entro ke ora devo leebairare la kamaira*

**May I have the check, please?**
Mi da il conto, per favore?
*mee da eel konto pair favore*

**I'll pay by credit card**
Pago con la carta di credito
*pago kon la karta dee kredeeto*

**I'll pay cash**
Pago in contanti
*pago een kontantee*

**Can you get me a taxi, please?**
Potrebbe chiamarmi un taxi, per favore?
*potreb-be k-yamarmee oon 'taxi' pair favore*

## THINGS YOU'LL SEE

| | |
|---|---|
| ascensore | elevator |
| bagno | bathroom |
| cena | dinner |
| colazione | breakfast |
| completo | no vacancies |
| conto | check |
| entrata | entrance |
| parcheggio | car park |
| pranzo | lunch |
| prenotazione | reservation |
| scale | stairs |
| spingere | push |
| tirare | pull |
| uscita d'emergenza | emergency exit |

## THINGS YOU'LL HEAR

**Mi spiace, siamo al completo**
I'm sorry, we're full

**Non ci sono più camere singole/doppie**
There are no single/double rooms left

**Per quante notti?**
For how many nights?

**Come vuole pagare?**
How will you be paying?

**Pagamento anticipato, per favore**
Please pay in advance

**Dovete liberare la stanza entro mezzogiorno**
You must vacate the room by midday

# SHOPPING

**Excuse me, where is/where are …?**
Mi scusi, dov'è/dove sono …?
*mee skoozee doveh/dove sono*

**Do you have …?**
Avete …?
*avete*

**How much is this?**
Quanto costa questo?
*kwanto kosta kwesto*

**Where do I pay?**
Dove si paga?
*dove see paga*

**Do you take credit cards?**
Accettate carte di credito?
*ach-chet-tate karte dee kredeeto*

**May I have a receipt/a bag, please?**
Potrebbe darmi lo scontrino/un sacchetto?
*potreb-be darmee lo skontreeno/oon sak-ket-to*

**Do you have anything less expensive?**
Non ha niente di più economico?
*non a n-yente dee p-yoo ekonomeeko*

**May I have a refund?**
Posso riavere indietro i soldi?
*pos-so ree-avaire endee-etro ee soldee*

**That's fine. I'll take it!**
Va bene. Lo prendo!
*va bene. lo prendo*

**It isn't what I wanted**
Non è quello che volevo
*non eh kwel-lo ke volevo*

# EATING OUT

There are various types of places to eat in Italy. For snacks, the most common is the bar. These are open all day from early morning until about 10 pm. They are all licensed to sell alcohol and usually offer a variety of sandwiches, rolls, cakes, and hot and cold drinks. In most bars you are required to first go to the cashier, place your order, pay, and get a receipt (**scontrino**.) Then hand the receipt to the bartender and repeat your order. You will notice that most Italians stand up in bars – sitting down costs extra. The sign **tavola calda** means that hot dishes are also served.

For full meals there are **osteria**, **pizzeria**, **trattoria**, **taverna**, and **ristorante**. Wherever possible, it's a good idea to choose the **menu turistico** (tourist menu) or the **menu fisso** (fixed-price menu.) Although the variety is more restricted, the food is of the same standard and you get a good deal more for your money, without having to face any service charge shocks at the end of the meal. Always ask for the local culinary specialities and local wine. These are generally excellent, and wine is less expensive and of superior quality in its place of origin.

In Italy, you can order the following types of coffee: **espresso** (small, strong, black coffee), **caffè macchiato** (espresso with a dash of milk), **cappuccino** (frothy, milky coffee sprinkled with cocoa), **caffelatte** (coffee with milk.) These are the most common, but there is also **caffè corretto** (espresso with a liqueur,) **caffè decaffeinato** (decaffeinated coffee), **caffè lungo** (weak espresso), and **caffè ristretto** (strong espresso.) Remember that if you ask for "Un caffè, per favore," you will be served an **espresso**.

## Useful Words and Phrases

| | | |
|---|---|---|
| **beer** | la birra | b*ee*r-ra |
| **bottle** | la bottiglia | bot-t*ee*l-ya |
| **bread** | il pane | p*a*ne |
| **butter** | il burro | b*oo*r-ro |
| **café** | il bar | bar |

249

| cake | la torta | *torta* |
| carafe | la caraffa | *karaf-fa* |
| check | il conto | *konto* |
| child's portion | una porzione per bambini | *portz-yone pair bambeenee* |
| coffee | il caffè | *kaf-feh* |
| cup | la tazza | *tatza* |
| dessert | il dessert | *desser* |
| fork | la forchetta | *forket-ta* |
| glass | il bicchiere | *beek-yaire* |
| half liter | da mezzo litro | *da metzo leetro* |
| knife | il coltello | *koltel-lo* |
| liter | un litro | *leetro* |
| main course | il piatto principale | *p-yat-to preencheepale* |
| menu | il menù | *menoo* |
| milk | il latte | *lat-te* |
| napkin | il tovagliolo | *toval-yolo* |
| pepper | il pepe | *pepey* |
| plate | il piatto | *p-yat-to* |
| restaurant | il ristorante | *reestorante* |
| salt | il sale | *sale* |
| sandwich | il panino | *paneeno* |
| snack | lo spuntino | *spoonteeno* |
| soup | la minestra | *meenestra* |
| spoon | il cucchiaio | *kook-ya-yo* |
| appetizer | l'antipasto | *anteepasto* |
| sugar | lo zucchero | *dzookairo* |
| table | il tavolo | *tavolo* |
| tea | il tè | *teh* |
| teaspoon | il cucchiaino | *kook-ya-eeno* |
| tip | la mancia | *mancha* |
| waiter | il cameriere | *kamair-yaire* |
| waitress | la cameriera | *kamair-yaira* |
| water | l'acqua | *akwa* |
| wine | il vino | *veeno* |
| wine list | la lista dei vini | *leesta day veenee* |

**A table for one/two/three, please**
Un tavolo per una persona/per due/per tre, per favore
*oon tavolo pair oona pairsona/pair doo-e/pair tray pair favore*

**Is there a highchair?**
Si può avere un seggiolone?
*see pwo avaire oon seg-gee-olone*

**May I see the menu/wine list?**
Potrei vedere il menu/la lista dei vini?
*potray vedaire eel menoo/la leesta day veenee*

**What would you recommend?**
Cosa ci consiglia?
*koza chee konseel-ya*

**I'd like …**
Vorrei …
*vor-ray*

**Just an espresso/cappuccino/coffee with milk, please**
Solo un caffè/un cappuccino/un caffelatte, per favore
*solo oon kaf-feh/oon kap-poocheeno/oon kaf-felat-te pair favore*

**I only want a snack**
Vorrei solo uno spuntino
*vor-ray solo oono spoonteeno*

**Is there a fixed-price menu?**
C'è un menù fisso?
*cheh oon menoo fees-so*

**A liter of house red, please**
Un litro di vino rosso della casa, per favore
*oon leetro dee veeno ros-so del-la kaza pair favore*

**Do you have any vegetarian dishes?**
Avete piatti vegetariani?
*avete p-yat-tee vejetar-yanee*

**I'm allergic to nuts/shellfish**
Sono allergico/a alle noci/ai frutti di mare
*sono al-lairjeeko/a al-lai nochee/aee froot-tee dee marai*

**Could we have some water?**
Potremmo avere un po' d'acqua?
*potrem-mo avaire oon po dakwa*

**Do you do children's portions?**
Fate porzioni per bambini?
*fatai porzeeonee pair bambeenee*

**Can you warm this bottle/baby food for me?**
Mi può riscaldare il biberon/il pasto del bambino?
*mee pwo reeskaldarai eel bee-bairon/eel pazto del bambeeno*

**Waiter/waitress!**
Cameriere/cameriera!
*kamair-yaire/kamair-yaira*

**We didn't order this!**
Non lo abbiamo ordinato!
*non lo abb-yamo ordeenato*

**May we have some more …?**
Potremmo avere ancora un po' di …?
*potrem-mo avaire ankora oon po dee*

**May I have another knife/spoon?**
Potrei avere un altro coltello/cucchiaio?
*potray avaire oon altro koltel-lo/kook-ya-yo*

**May we have the check, please?**
Può portarci il conto, per favore?
*pwo portarchee eel konto pair favore*

**May I have a receipt, please?**
Potrei avere la ricevuta/lo scontrino, per favore?
*potray avaire la reechevoota/lo skontreeno pair favore*

# MENU GUIDE

**acqua** water
**acqua minerale gassata** carbonated mineral water
**acqua minerale non gassata** still mineral water
**aglio** garlic
**agnello** lamb
**albicocche** apricots
**anatra** duck
**anguria** watermelon
**antipasti** appetizers
**antipasti misti** variety of appetizers
**aragosta** lobster
**arancia** orange
**aranciata** orangeade
**aringa** herring
**arrosto di ...** roasted ...
**baccalà** dried cod
**bavarese** ice-cream cake with cream
**besciamella** white sauce
**bistecca (di manzo)** steak
**braciola di maiale** pork steak
**branzino al forno** baked sea bass
**brasato** braised beef with herbs
**bresaola** dried, salted beef sliced thinly, and eaten cold with oil and lemon
**brodo** clear broth
**brodo di pollo** chicken broth
**brodo vegetale** clear vegetable broth
**budino** pudding
**burro** butter
**caffè** coffee
**caffè corretto** espresso with a dash of liqueur
**caffè lungo** weak espresso
**caffè macchiato** espresso with a dash of milk
**caffè ristretto** strong espresso

**caffelatte** half coffee, half hot milk
**calamaro** squid
**calzone** folded pizza with tomato and mozzarella or ricotta inside
**cannella** cinnamon
**capretto al forno** roasted kid
**carciofi** artichokes
**carne** meat
**carote** carrots
**cassata siciliana** Sicilian ice-cream cake with glacé fruit, chocolate, and ricotta
**castagne** chestnuts
**cavoletti di Bruxelles** Brussels sprouts
**cavolfiore** cauliflower
**cavolo** cabbage
**cefalo** mullet
**cicoria** chicory
**ciliege** cherries
**cioccolata** chocolate
**cipolle** onions
**coniglio** rabbit
**contorni** vegetables
**cotechino** spiced pork sausage
**cotoletta** veal, pork, or lamb chop
**cozze** mussels
**crema** custard dessert
**crema di funghi** cream of mushroom soup
**crema di piselli** cream of pea soup
**crema pasticciera** confectioner's custard
**crespelle** type of savory pancake filled with white sauce and other fillings
**dolci** sweets, desserts, cakes
**fagiano** pheasant
**fagioli** beans
**fagiolini** long, green beans
**fegato** liver
**fettuccine** ribbon-shaped pasta

**fichi** figs
**filetti di pesce persico** fillets of perch
**filetti di sogliola** fillets of sole
**filetto (di manzo)** fillet of beef
**finocchio** fennel
**formaggi misti** variety of cheeses
**fragole** strawberries
**frappé** whisked fruit or milk iced drink
**frittata** type of omelette
**fritto misto** mixed seafood in batter
**frittura di pesce** variety of fried fish
**frutta** fruit
**frutti di mare** seafood
**funghi** mushrooms
**gamberetti** shrimp
**gamberi** large shrimp
**gamberoni** jumbo shrimp
**gazzosa** clear lemonade
**gelatina** gelatin
**gelato** ice cream
**gnocchi** flour and potato dumplings
**granchio** crab
**granita** drink with crushed ice
**grigliata di pesce** broiled fish
**grigliata mista** mixed grill (meat or fish)
**grissini** thin, crisp breadsticks
**indivia** endive
**insalata** salad
**insalata di mare** seafood salad
**insalata di pomodori** tomato salad
**insalata mista** mixed salad
**insalata verde** green salad
**lamponi** raspberries
**latte** milk
**lattuga** lettuce
**legumi** legumes
**lenticchie** lentils
**limone** lemon
**lingua** tongue
**macedonia di frutta** fruit salad
**maiale** pork

**maionese** mayonnaise
**mandorla** almond
**manzo** beef
**marroni** chestnuts
**medaglioni di vitello** veal medallions
**mela** apple
**melanzane** eggplant
**melone** melon
**menta** mint
**menu turistico** tourist menu
**meringata** meringue pie
**merluzzo** cod
**millefoglie** layered pastry slice with
    confectioner's custard
**minestra in brodo** noodle soup
**mirtilli** bilberries
**more** mulberries or blackberries
**nasello** hake
**nocciole** hazelnuts
**noci** walnuts
**nodino** veal chop
**olio** oil
**origano** oregano
**ossobuco** stewed shin of veal
**ostriche** oysters
**pane** bread
**panino** filled roll
**panna** cream
**parmigiano** parmesan cheese
**pasta e piselli** pasta with peas
**pasticcio di maccheroni** baked macaroni
**pastina in brodo** noodle soup
**patate** potatoes
**patate fritte** french fries
**pecorino** strong, hard sheep's milk cheese
**pepe** pepper (spice)
**peperoni** peppers
**pera** pear
**pesca** peach
**pesce** fish
**pesce in carpione** marinaded fish

**piselli** peas
**pollo** chicken
**pollo al forno/arrosto** roasted chicken
**polpette** meatballs
**polpettone** meatloaf
**pomodori** tomatoes
**pomodori ripieni** stuffed tomatoes
**pompelmo** grapefruit
**porri** leeks
**primi piatti** first courses
**prosciutto cotto** cooked ham
**prosciutto e fichi** cured ham with figs
**prugne** plums
**purè di patate** mashed potatoes
**quaglie** quails
**radicchio** chicory
**rapanelli** radishes
**razza** skate
**risi e bisi** risotto with peas and ham
**riso** rice
**risotto ai funghi** mushroom risotto
**risotto alla castellana** risotto with
  mushroom, ham, cream, and cheese
**risotto alla milanese** risotto flavored
  with saffron
**salame** salami
**sale** salt
**salmone affumicato** smoked salmon
**salsa di pomodoro** tomato sauce
**salsa tartara** tartar sauce
**salsiccia** sausage
**saltimbocca alla romana** slices of veal
  stuffed with ham and sage and fried
**salvia** sage
**sarde ai ferri** broiled sardines
**scaloppine** veal escalopes
**scamorza alla griglia** broiled soft cheese
**scampi alla griglia** broiled scampi
**secondi piatti** second courses, main
  courses
**sedano** celery

**senape** mustard
**sogliola** sole
**sorbetto** sorbet, soft ice cream
**spaghetti aglio, olio e peperoncino**
  spaghetti with garlic, oil, and
  crushed chili pepper
**spaghetti al pesto** spaghetti in crushed
  basil, garlic, oil, and parmesan dressing
**spaghetti al pomodoro** spaghetti in
  tomato sauce
**spaghetti al ragù** spaghetti with meat
  sauce
**spaghetti alla carbonara** spaghetti with
  egg, chopped bacon, and cheese sauce
**spaghetti alla puttanesca** spaghetti with
  anchovies, capers, and black olives in
  tomato sauce
**spaghetti alle vongole** spaghetti
  with clams
**spaghetti all'amatriciana** spaghetti with
  chopped bacon and tomato sauce,
  typical of Rome
**spezzatino di vitello** veal stew
**spinaci** spinach
**stracciatella** soup of beaten eggs cooked
  in boiling, clear broth
**strudel di mele** apple strudel
**succo** juice
**tacchino ripieno** stuffed turkey
**tagliata** finely cut beef fillet cooked
  in the oven
**tagliolini** thin soup noodles
**tartine** small sandwiches
**tartufo** round ice cream covered in
  cocoa or chocolate
**tè** tea
**tè con latte** tea with milk
**tè con limone** lemon tea
**tiramisù** dessert made with coffee-
  soaked sponge fingers, eggs, Marsala,
  mascarpone, and cocoa powder

255

tonno tuna
torta tart, flan
torta salata savory flan
torta ai carciofi artichoke flan
torta al cioccolato chocolate tart
torta al formaggio cheese flan
torta di mele apple tart
torta di noci walnut tart
torta di ricotta type of cheesecake
torta di zucchine zucchini flan
torta gelato ice-cream tart
tortellini pasta shapes with ground pork, ham, parmesan, and spiced with nutmeg
tortellini alla panna tortellini with cream
tortellini al pomodoro tortellini with tomato sauce
tortellini al ragù tortellini with ground meat and tomato sauce
tortellini in brodo tortellini in clear broth
tortelloni di magro/di ricotta pasta shapes filled with cheese, parsley, and chopped vegetables
trancio di pesce spada swordfish steak
trenette col pesto type of flat spaghetti with crushed basil, garlic, oil, and cheese sauce
triglie mullet (fish)
trippa tripe
trota trout
trota affumicata smoked trout
trota al burro trout cooked in butter
trota alle mandorle trout with almonds
trota bollita boiled trout
uova eggs
uova al tegamino con pancetta fried eggs and bacon
uova alla coque boiled eggs
uova farcite eggs with tuna and capers

uova sode hard-boiled eggs
uva grapes
uva bianca white grapes
uva nera black grapes
vellutata di asparagi creamed asparagus with egg yolks
vellutata di piselli creamed peas with egg yolks
verdura vegetables
vermicelli very fine, thin pasta, often used in soups
vino wine
vino bianco white wine
vino da dessert dessert wine
vino da pasto table wine
vino da tavola table wine
vino rosso red wine
vitello veal
vitello tonnato cold sliced veal in tuna, anchovy, oil, and lemon sauce
vongole clams
würstel hot dog
zabaione creamy, whipped dessert made from beaten eggs, sugar, and Marsala wine
zafferano saffron
zucca pumpkin
zucchine zucchini
zucchine al pomodoro chopped zucchini in tomato, garlic, and parsley sauce
zucchine ripiene stuffed zucchini
zuccotto ice-cream cake with sponge fingers, cream, and chocolate
zuppa soup
zuppa di cipolle onion soup
zuppa di cozze mussel soup
zuppa di lenticchie lentil soup
zuppa di pesce fish soup
zuppa di verdura vegetable soup
zuppa inglese trifle

# NORWEGIAN

## CONTENTS

INTRODUCTION 258
USEFUL PHRASES 260
DAYS, MONTHS, SEASONS 265
NUMBERS 266
TIME 267
COMMUNICATIONS 269
HOTELS 272
SHOPPING 276
EATING OUT 277
MENU GUIDE 281

# INTRODUCTION

## PRONUNCIATION

When reading the imitated pronunciation, stress that part that is underlined. Pronounce each syllable as if it formed part of an English word, and you will be understood sufficiently well. Remember the points below, and your pronunciation will be closer to the correct Norwegian.

| | |
|---|---|
| EW | say "ee" with your lips rounded (or the French "u") |
| Hy | the "hu" sound as in "huge" |
| I | the "i" sound as in "high" |
| ow | as in "cow" |
| ur | the "uv sound as in "fur" |

## NORWEGIAN ALPHABETICAL ORDER

In the lists called *Things You'll See* and in the Menu Guide we have followed Norwegian alphabetical order. The following letters are listed after z: æ, ø, å.

## "YOU"

There are two words for "you": **du** (addressing one person) and **dere** (addressing two or more people). The polite form **De** is seldom used.

## GENDERS AND THE DEFINITE/INDEFINITE ARTICLE

Norwegian has three genders for nouns – masculine, feminine, and neuter. Since most feminine words can also have a masculine form, in this phrase book we have mainly used masculine and neuter forms, giving only essential feminine ones.

The definite article (English "the") is used as an ending in Norwegian and shows the gender of the noun: **-en** (masculine), **-et** (neuter).Where used, **-a** is the feminine word ending.

When you see translations given in the form **gutt(en)** or **hus(et)**, the form **gutten** will mean "the boy" and **huset** "the house." Note that the final **-t** of the definite article ending is always silent: **huset** *hoosseh*. The indefinite article ending (English "a," "an") is the same as the definite article but is placed before the noun as a separate word: **en** or **et**. For example, "a boy" is **en gutt** and "a house" is **et hus**.

### VERBS

Verbs are given in the infinitive form: "(to) speak" (**å**) **snakke**. To form the present tense for all persons, add "r" to the infinitive: **jeg snakker** "I speak," **du snakker** "you speak," and so on.

## USEFUL PHRASES

**Yes/no**
Ja/nei
*yah/nɪ*

**Thank you**
Takk
*takk*

**No, thank you**
Nei takk
*nɪ takk*

**Please** *(offering)*
Vær så god
*varshawgo*

**I don't understand**
Jeg forstår ikke
*yɪ forshtawr ikkeh*

**Do you speak English/French/German?**
Snakker du engelsk/fransk/tysk?
*snakker doo eng-elsk/fransk/tɛwsk*

**I can't speak Norwegian**
Jeg snakker ikke norsk
*yɪ snakker ikkeh norshk*

**I don't know**
Jeg vet ikke
*yɪ vayt ikkeh*

**Please speak more slowly**
Kan du snakke langsommere
*kan doo sn̪akkeh l̪ang-sawmereh*

**Please write it down for me**
Kan du skrive det opp for meg?
*kan doo skr̪eeveh deh op for mɪ*

**My name is …**
Jeg heter …
*yɪ h̪ayter*

**How do you do, pleased to meet you**
God dag, hyggelig å hilse på deg
*go dahg h̪ɛwgeli aw h̪ilseh paw dɪ*

**Good morning/good afternoon/good evening**
God mor'n/god dag/god kveld
*go-mawrn/go-d̪ahg/go-kvell*

**Good night** *(when leaving late at night/at bedtime)*
God natt
*go-n̪att*

**Goodbye**
Morn'a; *(informal)* ha det
*morna; h̪ah-deh*

**Excuse me, please**
Unnskyld
*oonsh̪ɛwl*

**Sorry!**
Om forlatelse!
*om forl̪ahdelseh*

**I'm really sorry!**
Jeg er virkelig lei meg!
*yɪ ar vɪrkeli lɪ mɪ*

**Can you help me?**
Kan du hjelpe meg?
*kan doo yelpeh mɪ*

**Can you tell me …?**
Kan du si meg …?
*kan doo see mɪ*

**May I have …?**
Kan jeg få …?
*kan yɪ faw*

**I would like a …**
Jeg vil gjerne ha en/et …
*yɪ vil yarneh hah ayn/et*

**I would like to …**
Jeg vil gjerne …
*yɪ vil yarneh*

**Would you like a …?**
Vil du ha en/et …?
*vil doo hah ayn/et*

**Is there … here?**
Er det … her?
*ar deh … har*

**Where can I get …?**
Hvor kan jeg få …?
*vohr kan yɪ faw*

**How much is it?**
Hvor mye koster det?
*vohr mEW-eh koster deh*

**What time is it?**
Hvor mange er klokken?
*vohr mang-eh ar klokken*

**I must go now**
Jeg må gå nå
*yı maw gaw naw*

**I've lost my way** (*on foot*)
Jeg har gått meg bort
*yı hahr gawt mı bohrt*

**Cheers!**
Skål!
*skawl*

**Do you take credit cards?**
Tar du kredittkort?
*tahr doo kredittkort*

**Where is the US embassy?**
Hvor er den amerikanske ambassade?
*vohr ar den amayreekahnskeh ambassadeh*

**Where is the restroom?**
Hvor er toalettet?
*vohr ar toh-a-letteh*

**Excellent!**
Fint!
*feent*

**I've lost my passport/money/room key/traveler's checks/
  credit cards**
Jeg har mistet /mitt pass/mine penger/nøkkelen til rommet
  mitt/mine reisesjekker/mine kredittkort
yı hahr _mee_stet /m_i_tt pass/m_ee_neh p_e_ng-er/n_u_rkel-en til r_oh_m-eh
  m_i_tt/m_ee_neh ray-seh-sh_e_kker/m_ee_neh kred_i_ttk_o_rt

---

## THINGS YOU'LL HEAR

| | |
|---|---|
| bare hyggelig! | you're welcome! |
| bra | good |
| det er riktig | that's right |
| fint | fine |
| god tur | have a good trip |
| hils …! | regards to …! |
| hva? | excuse me? |
| hva sa du? | excuse me, what did you say? |
| hvordan går det? | how are things? |
| hvordan har du det? | how are you? |
| ja | yes |
| jaså? | is that so? |
| jeg forstår ikke | I don't understand |
| jeg vet ikke | I don't know |
| kom inn | come in |
| morn'a | cheerio |
| nei | no |
| om forlatelse! | I'm so sorry! |
| pass deg! | look out! |
| takk | thanks |
| tusen takk | thank you very much |
| unnskyld | excuse me |
| velkommen | welcome |
| vi ses | see you later |
| vær så god | here you are; please help yourself |

# DAYS, MONTHS, SEASONS

| | | |
|---|---|---|
| Sunday | søndag | *surndag* |
| Monday | mandag | *mandag* |
| Tuesday | tirsdag | *teerssdag* |
| Wednesday | onsdag | *ohnssdag* |
| Thursday | torsdag | *tawrssdag* |
| Friday | fredag | *fraydag* |
| Saturday | lørdag | *lurrdag* |
| | | |
| January | januar | *yanoo-ahr* |
| February | februar | *febroo-ahr* |
| March | mars | *marsh* |
| April | april | *apreel* |
| May | mai | *mɪ* |
| June | juni | *yooni* |
| July | juli | *yooli* |
| August | august | *owgoost* |
| September | september | *september* |
| October | oktober | *oktawber* |
| November | november | *november* |
| December | desember | *desember* |
| | | |
| Spring | vår | *vawr* |
| Summer | sommer | *sommer* |
| Fall | høst | *hurst* |
| Winter | vinter | *vinter* |
| | | |
| Christmas | Jul | *yool* |
| Christmas Eve | Julaften | *yoolaften* |
| New Year | Nyttår | *newtawr* |
| New Year's Eve | Nyttårsaften | *newtawrsaften* |
| Easter | Påske | *pawskeh* |
| Good Friday | Langfredag | *langfraydag* |
| Pentecost | Pinse | *pinseh* |
| Midsummer Day | Sankthans | *sangt-hanss* |

# NUMBERS

Compound numbers are found in two forms in Norwegian. The newer form puts the tens before the units, eg: **tjueen** is "twenty one." The older form puts the units first, eg: **enogtyve** literally means 'one and twenty'. The old system is still used by many Norwegians and some use a mixture of both systems.

| | | | |
|---|---|---|---|
| 0 | null *nooll* | 10 | ti *tee* |
| 1 | en (ett*) *ayn (ett)* | 11 | elleve *elveh* |
| 2 | to *toh* | 12 | tolv *tawll* |
| 3 | tre *tray* | 13 | tretten *tretten* |
| 4 | fire *feereh* | 14 | fjorten *fyohrten* |
| 5 | fem *fem* | 15 | femten *femten* |
| 6 | seks *seks* | 16 | seksten *sisten* |
| 7 | sju/syv *shoo/sEWv* | 17 | sytten *surtten* |
| 8 | åtte *awtteh* | 18 | atten *atten* |
| 9 | ni *nee* | 19 | nitten *neetten* |

20 tjue/tyve Hyoo-eh/tEWveh
21 tjueen/enogtyve Hyoo-eh-ayn/ayn-aw-tEWveh
22 tjueto/toogtyve Hyoo-eh-toh/toh-aw-tEWveh
30 tretti/tredve tretti/tredveh
40 førti/førr furtti/furr
50 femti femti
60 seksti seksti
70 sytti surtti
80 åtti awtti
90 nitti neetti
100 (ett) hundre hoondreh
110 hundre og ti hoondreh aw tee
200 to hundre toh hoondreh
300 tre hundre tray hoondreh
400 fire hundre feereh hoondreh
1,000 (ett) tusen toossen
10,000 ti tusen tee toossen
100,000 hundre tusen hoondreh toossen          *ett is the neuter
1,000,000 (en) million milliyohn               form of en

# TIME

| today | i dag | *ee-dahg* |
|---|---|---|
| yesterday | i går | *ee-gawr* |
| tomorrow | i morgen | *ee-mawern* |
| this week | denne uken | *den-eh ooken* |
| last week | i forrige uke | *ee forri-eh ookeh* |
| next week | neste uke | *nest-eh ookeh* |
| this morning | i morges | *ee-morges* |
| this afternoon | i ettermiddag | *ee-ettermiddag* |
| this evening/ tonight | i kveld | *ee-kvell* |
| in three days | om tre dager | *om tray dahger* |
| three days ago | for tre dager siden | *for tray dahger seeden* |
| late | sent | *saynt* |
| early | tidlig | *teeli* |
| soon | snart | *snahrt* |
| later on | senere | *saynereh* |
| at the moment | for øyeblikket | *for oyeblikkeh* |
| second | sekund(et) | *sekoon* |
| minute | minutt(et) | *minoott* |
| one minute | et minutt | *et minoott* |
| two minutes | to minutter | *toh minootter* |
| quarter of an hour | et kvarter | *et kvartayr* |
| half an hour | en halv time | *ayn hal teemeh* |
| three quarters of an hour | tre kvarter | *tray kvartayr* |
| hour | time(n) | *teemeh* |
| that day | den dagen | *den dahgen* |
| every day | hver dag | *var dahg* |
| all day | hele dagen | *hayleh dahgen* |
| the next day | neste dag | *nesteh dahg* |
| week | uke(n) | *ookeh* |
| month | måned(en) | *mawned* |
| year | år(et) | *awr* |

## TELLING TIME

Norway conforms to Central European Time, which is one hour in advance of GMT. The Norwegians put their clocks forward by an hour from the end of March until the end of September. When telling time, it is important to note that, instead of saying "half past" an hour, the Norwegians refer to the next hour coming, for example: "half past one" in Norwegian is "half two."

Also, the minutes after "quarter past" and before "quarter to" the hour are linked to the half hour, for example: for "twenty past three" the Norwegians would say "ten to half four" and for "twenty-five to one" they would say "five past half one." The 24-hour clock is used quite commonly in timetables, on radio and television, and often when making appointments.

| | | |
|---|---|---|
| am | om formiddagen | *om formiddagen* |
| pm | om ettermiddagen | *om ettermiddagen* |
| one o'clock | klokken ett | *klokken ett* |
| ten past one | ti over ett | *tee awver ett* |
| quarter past one | kvart over ett | *kvart awver ett* |
| twenty past one | ti på halv to | *tee paw hal toh* |
| twenty-five past one | fem på halv to | *fem paw hal toh* |
| half past one | halv to | *hal toh* |
| twenty-five to two | fem over halv to | *fem awver hal toh* |
| twenty to two | ti over halv to | *tee awver hal toh* |
| quarter to two | kvart på to | *kvart paw toh* |
| ten to two | ti på to | *tee paw toh* |
| two o'clock | klokken to | *klokken toh* |
| 13:00 (1 pm) | klokken tretten | *klokken tretten* |
| 16:30/4:30 pm | seksten tretti | *sisten tretti* |
| at half past five | klokken halv seks | *klokken hal seks* |
| at seven o'clock | klokken sju | *klokken shoo* |
| noon | klokken tolv | *klokken tawll* |
| midnight | midnatt | *midnatt* |

# COMMUNICATIONS

## Useful Words and Phrases

| busy | opptatt | *opptat* |
|---|---|---|
| call | telefonsamtale(n) | *telefohnsamtahleh* |
| collect call | noteringsover-føring(en) | *nohtayringssawver-furring* |
| dial tone | summetone(n) | *soommetohneh* |
| directory assistance | opplysningen | *opplEWssning-en* |
| inquiries | opplysninger | *opplEWssning-er* |
| extension | linje(n) | *leen-yeh* |
| internet | internett(et) | *internett(eh)* |
| mobile phone | mobiltelefon(en) | *mohbeel-telefohn(ayn)* |
| number | nummer(et) | *noommer* |
| payphone | telefon-automat(en) | *telefohn-owtohmaht* |
| phone book | telefonkatalog(en) | *telefohnkatalawg* |
| phonecard | telefonkort(et) | *telefohn-kort(eh)* |
| telephone | telefon(en) | *telefohn* |
| website | web side(n) | *vebb seedeh(n)* |
| wrong number | feil nummer | *fil noommer* |

### Where is the nearest phone booth?
Hvor er nærmeste telefonkiosk?
*vohr ar narmesteh telefohnHyawsk*

### I would like a number in …
Jeg skal ha et nummer i …
*yı skal hah et noommer ee*

### I would like to speak to …
Kan jeg få snakke med …?
*kan yı faw snakkeh may*

### My number is …
Mitt nummer er …
*mit noommer ar*

**I would like a number in …**
Må jeg bede om et nummer i …
*maw yi bay om it nawmor ee*

**Hello, this is … speaking**
Hallo, det er …
*hahloh, day air*

**Speaking**
Det er (+ *name*)
*day air*

**I would like to speak to …**
Jeg vil gerne tale med …
*yi vil gairner tahler meth*

**My number is …**
Mit nummer er …
*mit nawmor air*

**Could you leave him/her a message?**
Kan du gi ham/henne en beskjed?
*kan doo yee ham/henneh ayn beshay*

**I'll call back later**
Jeg ringer igjen senere
*yi ring-er ee-yen saynereh*

**What's your fax number/email address?**
Hva er ditt fax nummer/epost adresse?
*vah ar ditt faks noommer/ay-pawst adresseh*

**May I send an email/fax from here?**
Kan jeg sende epost/en fax herfra?
*kan yi senneh ay-pawst/ayn faks hayr-frah*

## Things You'll Hear

**Hvem skal du snakke med?**
Whom would you like to speak to?

**Hvem er det som snakker?**
Who's speaking?

**Hva er ditt nummer?**
What is your number?

**Han/hun er dessverre ikke inne**
Sorry, he/she is not in

**Han/hun kommer tilbake klokken ett**
He/she will be back at one o'clock

**Kan du ringe igjen i morgen?**
Can you call back tomorrow?

**Jeg skal si fra at du har ringt**
I'll tell him/her you called

## Things You'll See

| | |
|---|---|
| **feilmelding** | repair service |
| **fjerntakst** | operator; long-distance calls |
| **fjernvalg** | direct dialing |
| **gebyr** | charge |
| **innenlands** | national |
| **i ustand** | out of order |
| **lokalsamtale** | local call |
| **retningsnummer** | dialing code |
| **takst** | charges |
| **utlandet** | international |

# HOTELS

## USEFUL WORDS AND PHRASES

| | | |
|---|---|---|
| **balcony** | balkong(en) | *balkong* |
| **bathroom** | bad(et) | *bahd* |
| **bed** | seng(en) | *seng* |
| **bedroom** | soverom(met) | *saw-verohm* |
| **breakfast** | frokost(en) | *frohkost* |
| **check** | regning(en) | *rining* |
| **dining room** | spisesal(en) | *spee-seh-sahl* |
| **dinner** | middag(en) | *middag* |
| **double bed** | dobbeltseng(en) | *dobbeltseng* |
| **double room** | dobbeltrom(met) | *dobbeltrohm* |
| **elevator** | heis(en) | *hiss* |
| **full board** | full pensjon | *full pangshohn* |
| **half board** | halv pensjon | *hal pangshohn* |
| **head waiter** | hovmester(en) | *hawvmester* |
| **hotel** | hotell(et) | *hotel* |
| **hotel manager** | hotellsjef(en) | *hotelshayf* |
| **key** | nøkkel(en) | *nurkel* |
| **lobby** | foyer(en) | *foh-a-yay* |
| **lounge** | salong(en) | *salong* |
| **lunch** | lunsj(en) | *'lunch'* |
| **reception** | resepsjon(en) | *resepshohn* |
| **receptionist** | resepsjonist(en) | *resepshohnist* |
| **restaurant** | restaurant(en) | *restoorang* |
| **restroom** | toalett(et) | *toh-a-lett* |
| **room** | rom(met) | *rohm* |
| **room service** | romservice(n) | *rohm-'service'* |
| **shower** | dusj(en) | *doosh* |
| **single room** | enkeltrom(met) | *engkeltrohm* |
| **twin room** | tomannsrom | *tohmanssrohm* |

**Do you have any vacancies?**
Har dere ledige rom?
*hahr dereh laydi-eh rohm*

**I have a reservation**
Jeg har reservert rom
*yɪ hahr ressarvayrt rohm*

**I'd like a single/twin room**
Kan jeg få et enkeltrom/tomannsrom?
*kan yɪ faw et engkeltrohm/tohmansrohm*

**I'd like a room with a bathroom/balcony**
Kan jeg få et rom med bad/balkong?
*kan yɪ faw et rohm may bahd/balkong*

**Is there satellite/cable TV in the rooms?**
Finnes det satelitt/kabel-TV på rommene?
*finnes deh sahtaylitt/kahbel tayh-vayh paw rohmmehneh*

**I'd like a room for one night/three nights/one week**
Kan jeg få et rom for en natt/tre netter/en uke?
*kan yɪ faw et rohm for ayn natt/tray netter/ayn ookeh*

**What is the charge per night?**
Hva koster det pr. natt?
*vah koster deh par natt*

**Are there facilities for the disabled?**
Er det tilrettelagt for funksjonshemmede?
*ayr deh tilretteh-lahgt for foonkshohns-hemmedeh*

**When is breakfast/lunch/dinner?**
Når er frokost/lunsj/middag?
*nawr ar frohkost/lunch/middag*

**Please wake me at 7 o'clock**
Kan du vekke meg klokken sju
*kan doo vekkeh mı klokken shoo*

**May I have breakfast in my room?**
Kan jeg få frokost på rommet?
*kan yı faw frohkost paw rohmeh*

**I'll be back at 10 o'clock**
Jeg vil være tilbake klokken ti
*yı vil var-eh tilbahkeh klokken tee*

**My room number is 205**
Jeg har rom nummer to hundre og fem
*yı hahr rohm noommer toh hoondreh aw fem*

**I'm leaving tomorrow**
Jeg reiser i morgen
*yı risser ee-mawern*

**May I have the check, please?**
Kan jeg få regningen, takk?
*kan yı faw rining-en takk*

**I'll pay by credit card**
Jeg betaler med kredittkort
*yı betahler may kredittkor*

**I'll pay cash**
Jeg betaler kontant
*yı betahler kontant*

**Can you get me a taxi?**
Kan du få tak i en taxi?
*kan doo faw tahk ee ayn taxi*

## Things You'll See

| | |
|---|---|
| **bad** | bath |
| **dusj** | shower |
| **frokost** | breakfast |
| **fullt** | no vacancies |
| **heis** | elevator |
| **inngang** | entrance |
| **ledig** | vacancies |
| **nødutgang** | emergency exit |
| **regning** | check |
| **rom** | room |
| **røyking forbudt** | no smoking |
| **skyv** | push |
| **trekk** | pull |
| **utgang** | exit |

## Things You'll Hear

**Det er dessverre fullt**
I'm sorry, we're full

**Vi har ingen enkeltrom igjen**
We have no single rooms left

**Hvor mange netter er det for?**
For how many nights?

**Kan du skrive navnet ditt her?**
Please sign your name here

**Hvordan vil du betale?**
How will you be paying?

**Kan du være så snill å betale på forhånd?**
Please pay in advance

# SHOPPING

**I'd like …**
Jeg skal ha …
*yi skal hah*

**Do you have …?**
Har du …?
*hahr doo*

**How much is this?**
Hvor mye koster denne (dette)?
*vohr mEW-eh koster denneh (dehtteh)*

**Do you have any more of these?**
Har du flere av disse?
*hahr doo flayreh av deesseh*

**Where do I pay?**
Hvor skal jeg betale?
*vohr skal yı betahleh*

**Do you have anything less expensive?**
Har du noe som er billigere?
*hahr doo no-eh som ar billi-ereh*

**May I have a receipt?**
Kan jeg få en kvittering?
*kan yı faw ayn kvittayring*

**May I have a refund?**
Kan jeg få pengene igjen?
*kan yı faw peng-eneh ee-yen*

**I'm just looking**
Jeg bare ser
*yı bahreh sayr*

# EATING OUT

The working day is from about 7 am to 3 or 4 pm and mealtimes are therefore quite early, with lunch mid-morning and dinner at about 4 pm. In hotels and restaurants, lunch is normally available between 12 and 2:30 and dinner is available all evening. Eating in hotels and restaurants can be quite expensive. However, you can get good-quality inexpensive meals at cafés that have a fixed-pricec menu **dagens rett** (*dahgenss ret*). Meatballs **kjøttkaker** (*Hyurt-kahker*), thick meat stew **brun lapskaus** (*broon lapskowss*), and pork chops with sweet and sour cabbage **svinekoteletter med surkål** (*sveeneh-koteletter may soorkawl*) are popular dishes. A service charge is usually included in the check and tipping is up to you.

Norwegians eat a substantial breakfast **frokost** (*frohkost*) usually consisting of bread, cold meats, cured fish, a variety of jams, and brown Norwegian goats' cheese.

Traditional dishes in Norway are plain and prepared from food that can be easily stored, ie salted, cured, smoked, and dried. In the past, the staple diet consisted of various kinds of porridge, and soured cream porridge **rømmegrøt** (*rurmegrurt*), served sprinkled with cinnamon and sugar, was eaten on special occasions like Midsummer's Day. Today, you are likely to come across **spekemat** (*spaykehmaht*), which is a selection of cold cured meats. These, together with sweet and sour salted herring **sursild** (*soorsill*), cured herring **spekesild** (*spaykehsill*), fermented trout **rakørret** (*rahkurret*), and cured salmon **gravlaks** (*grahvlaks*), are traditionally found in the Norwegian buffet **koldtbord** (*kawltbohr*).

Open sandwiches are available in most eating places. Waffles **vafler** (*vafler*), with soured cream and jam, are another favorite.

Licensing laws are strict, alcohol prices are high, and the state has a monopoly on the sale of alcohol. Bring your duty-free allowance with you; otherwise you may have to buy spirits at the state-owned **Vinmonopolet** at triple the price. Beer is sold at supermarkets but not wine and spirits.

## Useful Words and Phrases

| | | |
|---|---|---|
| beer | øl(et) | *url* |
| bottle | flaske(n) | *flaskeh* |
| buffet | koldtbord(et) | *kawltbohr* |
| cake | kake(n) | *kahkeh* |
| check | regning(en) | *rining* |
| chef | kokk(en) | *kokk* |
| children's portion | barneporsjon(en) | *barneporshohn* |
| coffee | kaffe(n) | *kaffeh* |
| cup | kopp(en) | *kopp* |
| fork | gaffel(en) | *gaffel* |
| glass | glass(et) | *glass* |
| knife | kniv(en) | *k-neev* |
| menu | meny(en) | *menEW* |
| milk | melk(en) | *melk* |
| napkin | serviett(en) | *sarvi-ett* |
| open sandwich | smørbrød(et) | *smurrbrur* |
| plate | tallerken(en) | *tal-arken* |
| receipt | kvittering(en) | *kvittayring* |
| schnapps | akevitt(en) | *akevitt* |
| snack | smårett(en) | *smawrett* |
| soup | suppe(n) | *sooppeh* |
| spoon | skje(en) | *shay* |
| sugar | sukker(et) | *sookker* |
| table | bord(et) | *bohr* |
| tea | te(en) | *tay* |
| teaspoon | teskje(en) | *tayshay* |
| tip | tips(et) | *tips* |
| waiter | kelner(en) | *kelner* |
| waitress | serveringsdame(n) | *sarvayringssdahmeh* |
| water | vann(et) | *vann* |
| wine | vin(en) | *veen* |
| wine list | vinkart(et) | *veenkart* |

**A table for one/two, please**
Kan jeg få et bord til en/to, takk?
*kan yı faw et bohr til ayn/too takk*

**May I see the menu?**
Kan jeg få se menyen?
*kan yı faw say men_Ewen*

**May I see the wine list?**
Kan jeg få se vinkartet?
*kan yı faw say v_eenkarteh*

**What would you recommend?**
Hva vil du anbefale?
*vah vil doo _ahnbefahleh*

**I'm allergic to nuts/shellfish**
Jeg er allergisk mot nøtter/skalldyr
*yı ar all_argisk moht n_urttehr/sk_all-dEwr*

**I'm vegetarian**
Jeg er vegetarianer
*yı ar vegget_ahreeahnehr*

**Do you have any vegetarian dishes?**
Har dere vegetarretter?
*hahr d_ayreh vegget_ahr-retter*

**I'd like …**
Kan jeg få …
*kan yı faw*

**Just a cup of coffee, please**
Bare en kopp kaffe, takk
*b_ahreh ayn kopp k_affeh takk*

**Waiter/waitress!**
Hallo!
*hallo*

**May we have the check, please?**
Kan vi få regningen, takk?
*kan vee faw rining-en takk*

**I only want a snack**
Jeg vil bare ha en smårett
*yı vil bahreh hah ayn smawrett*

**Is there a fixed-price menu?**
Er det en dagens rett?
*ar deh ayn dahgenss rett*

**I didn't order this**
Jeg har ikke bestilt dette
*yı hahr ikkeh behstilt detteh*

**May I have another knife/fork?**
Kan jeg få en kniv/gaffel til?
*kan yı faw ayn k-neev/gaffel til*

**May we have some more …?**
Kan vi få litt mer …?
*kan vee faw litt mayr*

**The meal was very good, thank you**
Maten smakte deilig, takk!
*mahten smahkteh dili takk*

**May we pay separately?**
Kan vi betale hver for oss?
*kan vee betahleh var for oss*

# MENU GUIDE

**agurk(er)** cucumber; pickles

**and** duck

**ansjos** anchovies

**appelsin** orange

**aprikos** apricot

**bakt** baked

**betasuppe** yellow pea, ham, and vegetable soup

**biff med løk** fried steak with onions

**bjørnebær** blackberries, brambles

**blandet kjøttrett** a variety of meats diced and fried

**blomkål** cauliflower

**bløtkokt egg** soft-boiled egg

**blåbær** blueberries

**blåskjell** mussels

**boller** buns; dumplings; fish/meatballs

**bringebær** raspberries

**brokkoli** broccoli

**brus** carbonated drinks

**bryst** breast

**brød** bread

**buljong** clear soup, consommé

**butterdeig** flaky pastry

**bønner** beans

**chips** potato chips

**dampet** steamed

**drikkevarer** drinks

**druer** grapes

**dyrestek** roasted reindeer

**eggekrem** thick custard

**eggeplomme** egg yolk

**eggerøre** cold scrambled eggs

**eple** apple

**erter** peas

**erter, kjøtt og flesk** yellow pea soup and ham (with the ham served as the second course with boiled potatoes)

**fasan** pheasant

**fenalår** cured leg of mutton

**fersken** peach

**filet** fillet

**fisk(e)** fish

**flaske** bottle

**flatbrød** thin crispbread

**flesk** pork belly

**flyndre** sole

**fløte** cream

**forloren** meat loaf served as a roast

**franskbrød** white bread with poppy seeds

**frisk(e)** fresh

**frityrstekt** deep-fried

**frokost** breakfast

**frokostblanding** breakfast cereal

**fromasj** cold soufflé, mousse

**frukt** fruit

**fylt** stuffed

**får** mutton

**gaffelbiter** small fillets of herring soaked in strong marinade

**grapefrukt** grapefruit

**grateng** savory hot soufflé

**gravlaks** cured salmon (gravad lax)

**gressløk** chives

**griljert** fried in breadcrumbs

**grillben** barbecued spareribs

**grovbrød** wholemeal bread

**gryte** casserole

**grønnsaker** vegetables

**grøt** porridge made from flour, oats, or rice; "gelatin" made from boiled fruits and fruit juice, and thickened with cornflour

**gulrot** carrot

**gås** goose

havre oatmeal
hellefisk halibut
helstekt fried or roasted whole
hjemmelaget homemade
honning honey
hovedrett main course
hummer lobster
hvalbiff whale steak
hveteboller buns
hvitløk garlic
hvit saus white sauce
hvitting whiting
hvitvin white wine
høns(e) chicken, poultry
hårdkokt egg hard-boiled egg
is ice cream, ice
jordbær strawberries
juice fruit juice
kaffe coffee
kake(r) cake(s); fish or meat cakes
kald cold
kaldrøkt cold smoked salmon
kalkun turkey
kalv(e) veal
kanel cinnamon
kapers capers
karbonade ground beef steak
karve caraway seeds
kavring rusk
kinakål Chinese leaves
kirsebær cherries
kjeks cookies
kjøtt meat
kjøttkaker ground beef balls
knakkpølse small, thick smoked
   sausage
kneipbrød crusty wheaten bread
knekkebrød crispbread
kokt boiled, poached
koldtbord cold buffet
kotelett chop, cutlet

krabbe crab
kreps crayfish
kringle pretzel-shaped cake filled with
   almond paste, apples, or raisins
kryddersild cured, spiced raw herring
kulturmelk, kulturmjølk soured milk
kveite halibut
kylling chicken
kål cabbage
kålrabi, kålrot rutabaga
laks salmon
lam(me) lamb
lammerygg saddle of lamb
leskedrikk squash
lever liver
loff white bread
lumpe thin potato scone
lunsj lunch
løk onion
lår leg
mais sweetcorn
majones mayonnaise
makaroni macaroni
makron macaroon
mandel almond
marengs meringues
marinert marinated
medisterkaker fried meatballs made
   from ground pork
medisterpølse fried or poached pork
   sausage
mel flour
melk milk
meny menu
middag dinner
mjølk milk
moreller cherries
multer cloudberries (wild orange berries)
mørbrad sirloin
nygrodde poteter new potatoes boiled
   in their skins

**nype** rosehip

**nypesuppe** rosehip soup (usually served with whipped cream as a dessert)

**nyrer** kidneys

**nøtter** nuts

**okse** beef

**oksehale** oxtail

**oksestek** roasted beef

**ost** cheese

**ovnsbakt** oven-baked

**panert** coated with breadcrumbs

**pannekaker** large thin pancakes

**pepperrot** horseradish

**persille** parsley

**persillerot** parsnip

**pinnekjøtt** salted, dried side of lamb, boiled and served with mashed turnip

**pisket krem** whipped cream

**platte** platter of cold meat or fish

**plukkfisk** poached cod in white sauce

**pochert** poached

**postei** pâté, vol-au-vent

**poteter** potatoes

**potet gull** french fries

**purre** leeks

**pytt i panne** fried, diced meat and potatoes, served with a fried egg

**pære** pear

**pølser** hot dogs

**pålegg** sandwich spread or cold meat for sandwiches

**rabarbra** rhubarb

**ragu** stew

**rakørret** fermented trout

**raspeball** dumpling made from grated potato

**reddiker** radishes

**reinsdyr** reindeer

**reke(r)** shrimp

**remulade** mayonnaise with chopped pickles and spices

**rett(er)** dish(es), course(es)

**reven, revet, revne** grated

**ribbe** side of either pork or lamb

**rips** redcurrants

**ris** rice

**rislapper** small rice porridge pancakes eaten hot with jam

**ristet** toasted, fried, roasted

**rogn** roe

**rosenkål** Brussels sprouts

**rosiner** raisins

**rugbrød** rye bread

**rullekake** swiss roll

**rundstykke** crusty roll

**rødbeter** beets

**rødgrøt med fløte** soft red berry "gelatin" with cream

**rødkål** sweet and sour boiled red cabbage with caraway seeds

**rødspette** plaice

**røkelaks** smoked salmon

**røket, røkt** smoked

**røkt svinekam** smoked loin of pork

**rømme** soured cream

**rørt(e)** uncooked fruits with sugar

**rå** raw

**råkostsalat** raw vegetable salad

**råkrem** whipped cream with yolks of egg

**saft** juice

**saftsuppe** red fruit juice soup

**salat** lettuce; salad

**saltpølse** salami

**sardiner** sardines

**saus** sauce

**sei** coley

**seibiff** coley steaks with fried onions

**selleri(rot)** celeriac

**semulegrøt** semolina pudding served with red fruit sauce

**sennep** mustard

**sild** herring
**sitron** lemon
**sitronbrus** lemonade
**sjokolade** chocolate
**skalldyr** shellfish
**skinke** ham
**skjell** shells; puff pastry "shells"
**slangeagurk** cucumber
**smultringer** doughnuts
**smør** butter
**smørbrød** open sandwich
**smørgrøt** sweet porridge made from white flour, served with cinnamon
**snitter** small open sandwiches
**solbær** blackcurrants
**sopp** mushroom
**speilegg** fried egg ("sunny side up")
**spekemat** tray of various kinds of cured and smoked cold meats and fish
**spekepølse** salami
**spekesild** cured, raw herring
**spekeskinke** cured leg of ham
**spinat** spinach
**spisekart** menu
**stangselleri** celery
**stappe** mashed
**stek** roasted
**stekt** fried, roasted
**stikkelsbær** gooseberries
**stuing** in white or cream sauce
**sukker** sugar
**sukkererter** snow pea
**sukrede rips** redcurrants with sugar
**suppe** soup
**surkål** sweet and sour boiled cabbage with caraway seeds (sauerkraut)
**sur og søt** sweet and sour
**sursild** cured pickled herring
**svin(e)** pork
**svinekam** loin of pork
**svor** pork crackling

**syltet** preserved, pickled
**syltetøy** jam
**søt** sweet
**tartarsaus** mayonnaise with chopped egg, onion, capers, and pickles
**te** tea
**terninger** diced
**terte** tart, pastry
**tilslørte bondepiker** stewed apples with toasted breadcrumbs and cream
**tiur** grouse
**tomat** tomato
**torsk** cod
**trollkrem** whipped cream with egg whites and a sweet sauce
**trøfler** truffles
**tunge** tongue
**tyttebær** cowberries (like cranberries)
**tørr** dry
**urter** herbs
**urtete** herb tea
**vafler** waffles
**valnøtter** walnuts
**vanilje** vanilla
**vaniljesaus** custard sauce
**vann** water
**vannbakkels** choux pastry cakes filled with whipped cream
**varm** warm, hot
**varm(e) retter** hot dishes
**varme pølser** hot dogs
**vegetarretter** vegetarian dishes
**vestkystsalat** shellfish salad
**vilt** game
**vindruer** grapes
**waleskringle** choux pastry ring
**wienerpølser** hot dogs
**øl** beer
**ørret** trout
**østers** oysters
**ål** eel

# POLISH

## CONTENTS

INTRODUCTION 286
USEFUL PHRASES 288
DAYS, MONTHS, SEASONS 293
NUMBERS 294
TIME 295
COMMUNICATIONS 297
HOTELS 300
SHOPPING 304
EATING OUT 305
MENU GUIDE 309

# INTRODUCTION

## Pronunciation

When reading the imitated pronunciation, stress the part that is underlined (usually the last but one syllable). Pronounce each syllable as if it formed part of an English word, and you will be understood sufficiently well. Note especially these points:

| | |
|---|---|
| *a* | as in "assist" |
| AWN | a nasal sound as in "sawn" but with the "n" barely sounded |
| *ay* | as in "pay" |
| *e, eh* | "e" as in "bed" |
| EN | as the "en" in "end" but a nasal sound and barely sounded |
| *g* | always hard as in "get" |
| H | as the "ch" in the Scottish word "loch" |
| I | as the "i" sound in "wine" |
| J | as the "s" sound in "leisure" |
| *o* | as in "lot" |
| *u* | as in "luck" |
| *wuh* | as the "w" in "well" but barely sounded |
| *y* | as in "yes" (apart from *ay* above) |
| *yuh* | as the "y" in "yes" but barely sounded |

## Summary of Special Characteristics in Polish

| | |
|---|---|
| ą | a nasal "awn" sound as in "sawn" or the French "an" |
| c | "ts" as in "cats" |
| ć, cz | "ch" as in "challenge" |
| ch | "ch" as in Scottish "loch" |
| dz | "j" as in "jeans" when followed by **i** or **e** but otherwise "dz" as in "adze" |
| dź | "j" as in "jeans" |
| dż | "d" as in "dog" followed by "s" as in "leisure" |
| ę | similar to "en" in "end" only nasal and barely sounded but, if at the end of the word, pronounced "e" as in "bed" |

| | |
|---|---|
| **h** | "ch" as in Scottish "loch" |
| **i** | "ee" as in "teeth" |
| **j** | "y" as in "yes" |
| **ł** | "w" as in "window" |
| **ń** | similar to the "ni" in "companion" |
| **ó** | "oo" as in "soot" |
| **rz** | similar to the "s" in "leisure" or, when it follows **p**, **t** or **k**, then it is pronounced "sh" as in "shut" |
| **ś, sz** | "sh" as in "shut" |
| **y** | similar to the "i" in "bit" |
| **ź, ż** | similar to the "s" in "leisure" |

Note also the following:

**i** in the middle of a word following **c**, **dz**, **n**, **s** or **z** softens these sounds and remains silent:

| | |
|---|---|
| **ci** | "ch" as in "cheap" |
| **dzi** | "j" as in "jeans" |
| **ni** | "n-yuh" sound as the "ni" in "companion" |
| **si** | "sh" as in "show" |
| **zi** | "s" as in "leisure" |

**i** at the end of a word following **c**, **dz**, **n**, **s**, or **z** softens the preceding sound but is also pronounced:

| | |
|---|---|
| **ci** | "chee" as in "cheese" |
| **dzi** | "jee" as in "jeep" |
| **ni** | "n-yee" as the "ni" in "companion" plus "ee," the "y" sound being barely perceptible |
| **si** | "shee" as in "sheet" |
| **zi** | "s" as in "leisure" plus "ee" |

## POLITE FORMS OF ADDRESS

Polite forms of address are commonly used in Polish. In the phrases, the alternatives shown by (*to a man*) and (*to a woman*) indicate the forms to be used. A man is addressed as **pan**, "Mr" or "sir," a woman as **pani**, "madam" or "Ms." The familiar forms for "you," **ty** (*singular*) and **wy** (*plural*), can be used among friends and when speaking to young people.

## USEFUL PHRASES

**Yes/No**
Tak/nie
*tak/n-yeh*

**Thank you**
Dziękuję
*jENkoo-yeh*

**No, thank you**
Nie, dziękuję
*n-yeh jENkoo-yeh*

**Please**
Proszę
*prosheh*

**I don't understand**
Nie rozumiem
*n-yeh rozoom-yem*

**Do you speak English/French/German?**
Czy mówi pan (*to a man*)/pani (*to a woman*) po angielsku/
  francusku/niemiecku?
*chi moovee pan/panee po ang-yelskoo/frantsooskoo/n-yem-yetskoo*

**I can't speak Polish**
Nie mówię po polsku
*n-yeh moov-yeh po polskoo*

**I don't know**
Nie wiem
*n-yeh v-yem*

**Please speak more slowly**
Proszę mówić wolniej
*prosheh mooveech voln-yay*

**Please write it down for me**
Proszę mi to napisać
*prosheh mee to napeesach*

**My name is …**
Nazywam się …
*nazivam sheh*

**Pleased to meet you**
Bardzo mi miło pana (*to a man*)/panią (*to a woman*) poznać
*pardzo mee meewo pana/pan-yAWN poznach*

**Good morning/afternoon**
Dzień dobry
*jen-yuh dobri*

**Good evening**
Dobry wieczór
*dobri v-yechoor*

**Good night**
Dobranoc
*dobranots*

**Goodbye**
Do widzenia
*do veedzen-ya*

**How are you?**
Jak się pan (*to a man*)/pani (*to a woman*) miewa?
*yak sheh pan/panee m-yeva*

**Very well, thank you**
Dziękuję, dobrze
*jENkoo-yeh dobjeh*

**Excuse me, please**
Przepraszam
*psheprasham*

**Sorry!**
Przepraszam!
*psheprasham*

**I'm really sorry**
Bardzo mi przykro
*bardzo mee pshikro*

**Can you help me?**
Czy mógłby pan (*to a man*)/mogłaby pani (*to a woman*) mi pomóc?
*chi moogwuhbi pan/mogwabi panee mee pomoots*

**Can you tell me …?**
Czy mógłby pan (*to a man*)/mogłaby pani (*to a woman*) mi
powiedzieć …?
*chi moogwuhbi pan/mogwabi panee mee pov-yejech*

**May I have …?**
Poproszę …?
*poprosheh*

**I would like …**
Chciałbym (*man*)/Chciałabym (*woman*) …
*Hchawuhbim/Hchawabim*

**Is there … here?**
Czy jest tu …?
*chi yest too*

**Where can I get …?**
Gdzie mogę dostać …?
*jeh mogeh dostach*

**How much is it?**
Ile kosztuje?
*eleh koshtoo-yeh*

**What time is it?**
Która jest godzina?
*ktoora yest gojeena*

**I must go now**
Muszę już iść
*moosheh yooj eesh-ch*

**I've lost my way**
Zgubiłem (*man*)/zgubiłam (*woman*) się
*zgoobeewem/zgoobeewam sheh*

**Cheers!**
Na zdrowie!
*na zdrov-yeh*

**Do you take credit cards?**
Czy przyjmuje pan (*to a man*)/pani (*to a woman*) karty kredytowe?
*chi pshi-yuhmoo-yeh pan/panee karti kreditoveh*

**Where is the restroom?**
Gdzie jest toaleta?
*jeh yest to-aleta*

**Go away!**
Proszę odejść!
*prosheh odaysh-ch*

### I've lost my passport/money/traveler's checks/credit cards
Zgubiłem (*man*)/zgubiłam (*woman*) paszport/pieniądze/czeki
   podróżne/karty kredytowe
*zgoobeewuhem/zgoobeewuham pashport/p-yenyAWNje/tshekee
   podroojne/karti kreditowe*

### Where is the US embassy?
Gdzie jest amerykańska ambasada?
*gjeh yest amerikan-yska ambasada*

### Is there wheelchair access?
Czy jest tam dostęp dla wózków inwalidzkich?
*chi yest tam dostehp dla voozkoov eenva-leejkeeH*

### Are guide dogs allowed?
Czy psy przewodnicy są dozwolone?
*chi psi pshewodneeci sAWN dozwolone*

---

#### THINGS YOU'LL HEAR

| | |
|---|---|
| Chwileczkę | One moment |
| Co słychać? | How are you? |
| Wszystko w porządku, dziękuję | Very well, thank you |
| – a co u pana/pani? | – and you? |
| Do zobaczenia | See you later |
| Naprawdę? | Is that so? |
| Nie ma | We haven't got any |
| Nie rozumiem | I don't understand |
| Proszę | Here you are, Please |
| Proszę bardzo | You're welcome |
| Słucham? | Excuse me? |
| Tak jest | That's right |
| Uwaga! | Look out! |
| Wspaniale! | Excellent! |

# DAYS, MONTHS, SEASONS

| | | |
|---|---|---|
| Sunday | niedziela | *n-yejela* |
| Monday | poniedziałek | *pon-yejawek* |
| Tuesday | wtorek | *vtorek* |
| Wednesday | środa | *shroda* |
| Thursday | czwartek | *chvartek* |
| Friday | piątek | *p-yAWNtek* |
| Saturday | sobota | *sobota* |
| | | |
| January | styczeń | *stichen-yuh* |
| February | luty | *looti* |
| March | marzec | *majets* |
| April | kwiecień | *kv-yechen-yuh* |
| May | maj | *mI* |
| June | czerwiec | *cherv-yets* |
| July | lipiec | *leep-yets* |
| August | sierpień | *sherp-yen-yuh* |
| September | wrzesień | *vjeshen-yuh* |
| October | październik | *paj-jerneek* |
| November | listopad | *leestopad* |
| December | grudzień | *groojen-yuh* |
| | | |
| Spring | wiosna | *v-yosna* |
| Summer | lato | *lato* |
| Fall | jesień | *yeshen-yuh* |
| Winter | zima | *jeema* |
| | | |
| Christmas | Boże Narodzenie | *boje narodzen-yeh* |
| Christmas Eve | Wigilia | *veegeel-ya* |
| New Year | Nowy Rok | *novi rok* |
| New Year's Eve | Sylwester | *silvester* |
| Easter | Wielkanoc | *v-yelkanots* |

# NUMBERS

| | | | |
|---|---|---|---|
| 0 | zero *zero* | 10 | dziesięć *jeshENCH* |
| 1 | jeden *yeden* | 11 | jedenaście *yedenash-cheh* |
| 2 | dwa *dva* | 12 | dwanaście *dvanash-cheh* |
| 3 | trzy *tshi* | 13 | trzynaście *tshinash-cheh* |
| 4 | cztery *chteri* | 14 | czternaście *chternash-cheh* |
| 5 | pięć *p-yENCH* | 15 | piętnaście *p-yENtnash-cheh* |
| 6 | sześć *shesh-ch* | 16 | szesnaście *shesnash-cheh* |
| 7 | siedem *sh-yedem* | 17 | siedemnaście *shedemnash-cheh* |
| 8 | osiem *oshem* | 18 | osiemnaście *oshemnash-cheh* |
| 9 | dziewięć *jev-yENCH* | 19 | dziewiętnaście *jev-yENtnash-cheh* |

| | |
|---|---|
| 20 | dwadzieścia *dvajesh-cha* |
| 21 | dwadzieścia jeden *dvajesh-cha yeden* |
| 22 | dwadzieścia dwa *dvajesh-cha dva* |
| 30 | trzydzieści *tshijesh-chee* |
| 40 | czterdzieści *chterjesh-chee* |
| 50 | pięćdziesiąt *p-yENchjeshAWNt* |
| 60 | sześćdziesiąt *shesh-chjeshAWNt* |
| 70 | siedemdziesiąt *shedemjeshAWNt* |
| 80 | osiemdziesiąt *oshemjeshAWNt* |
| 90 | dziewięćdziesiąt *jev-yENchjeshAWNt* |
| 100 | sto *sto* |
| 110 | sto dziesięć *sto jeshENCH* |
| 200 | dwieście *dv-yesh-cheh* |
| 300 | trzysta *tshista* |
| 400 | czterysta *chterista* |
| 500 | pięćset *p-yENchset* |
| 600 | sześćset *shesh-chset* |
| 700 | siedemset *shedemset* |
| 800 | osiemset *oshemset* |
| 900 | dziewięćset *jev-yENchset* |
| 1000 | tysiąc *tishAWNts* |
| 100,000 | sto tysięcy *sto tishENtsi* |
| 1,000,000 | milion *meel-yon* |

# TIME

| today | dzisiaj | *jeeshı* |
|---|---|---|
| yesterday | wczoraj | *vchorı* |
| tomorrow | jutro | *yootro* |
| this week | w tym tygodniu | *vtim tigodn-yoo* |
| last week | w zeszłym tygodniu | *vzeshwim tigodn-yoo* |
| next week | w przyszłym tygodniu | *vpshishwim tigodn-yoo* |
| this morning | dzisiaj rano | *jeeshı rano* |
| this afternoon | dzisiaj popołudniu | *jeeshı popowoodn-yoo* |
| this evening | dzisiaj wieczorem | *jeeshı v-yechorem* |
| tonight | dzisiejszej nocy | *jeeshayshay notsi* |
| late | późno | *poojno* |
| early | wcześnie | *vcheshn-yeh* |
| soon | nie długo | *n-yeh dwoogo* |
| minute | minuta | *meenoota* |
| quarter of an hour | kwadrans | *kvadrans* |
| half an hour | pół godziny | *poowuh gojeeni* |
| three quarters of an hour | trzy kwadranse | *tji kvadranseh* |
| hour | godzina | *gojeena* |
| every day | codziennie | *tsojen-yeh* |

## TELLING TIME

There are several ways of telling time in Polish. For time on the hour, use first, second, third for one, two, three, etc. So "one o'clock" is **pierwsza** (*p-yervsha*), "two o'clock" is **druga** (*drooga*) and so on. Poles leave out the words "hour" and "minutes."

For time past and to the hour, say the hour followed by the minutes: "ten past ten" is therefore **dziesiąta dziesięć** (*jeshawnta jeshench*). "Ten forty" is **dziesiąta czterdzieści** (*jeshawnta chterjesh-chee*). Time past the hour can also be expressed using **po** meaning "after," for example "ten past ten" is **dziesięć po dziesiątej** (*jeshench po jeshawntay*).

Another way of expressing time to the hour is to use **za** "before," followed by the minutes and the hour that is approaching: so "twenty to eleven" is **za dwadzieścia jedenasta** (*za dvajesh-cha yedenasta*).

For half past, use either the past hour followed by thirty, so "half past ten" is **dziesiąta trzydzieści** (*jeshAWNta tshijesh-chee*); or you can say "half to" the hour approaching – **w pół do jedenastej** (*v poowuh do yedenastay*).

**Kwadrans** ("quarter") is sometimes used, so "quarter past ten" is **kwadrans po dziesiątej** (*kvadrans po jeshAWNtay*).

| | | |
|---|---|---|
| 1 o'clock | pierwsza | *p-yervsha* |
| 2 o'clock | druga | *drooga* |
| 3 o'clock | trzecia | *tshecha* |
| 4 o'clock | czwarta | *chvarta* |
| 5 o'clock | piąta | *p-yAWNta* |
| 6 o'clock | szósta | *shoosta* |
| 7 o'clock | siódma | *shoodma* |
| 8 o'clock | ósma | *oosma* |
| 9 o'clock | dziewiąta | *jev-yAWNta* |
| 10 o'clock | dziesiąta | *jeshAWNta* |
| 11 o'clock | jedenasta | *yedenasta* |
| 12 o'clock | dwunasta | *dvoonasta* |
| **ten past one** | dziesięć po pierwszej | *jeshENCH po p-yervshay* |
| **quarter past one** | kwadrans po pierwszej | *kvadrans po p-yervshay* |
| **half past one** | w pół do drugiej | *vpoowuh do droog-yay* |
| **twenty to two** | za dwadzieścia druga | *za dvajesh-cha drooga* |
| **quarter to two** | za kwadrans druga, za piętnaście druga | *za kvadrans drooga, za p-yENTnash-cheh drooga* |
| **at seven o'clock** | o siódmej | *o shoodmay* |
| **noon** | południe | *powoodn-yeh* |
| **midnight** | północ | *poowuhnots* |

# COMMUNICATIONS

## Useful Words and Phrases

| | | |
|---|---|---|
| **code** | kod | *kod* |
| **collect call** | rozmowa R | *rozmova err* |
| **dial tone** | sygnał | *signawuh* |
| **directory assistance** | informacja | *eenformats-ya* |
| **email address** | adres email | *adres eemeyl* |
| **extension** | wewnętrzny | *vevnEntshni* |
| **mobile phone** | telefon komórkowy | *telefon komoorkovi* |
| **number** | numer | *noomer* |
| **operator** | centrala | *tsentrala* |
| **payphone** | automat telefoniczny | *awtomat telefoneechni* |
| **telephone** | telefon | *telefon* |
| **telephone booth** | budka telefoniczna | *boodka telefoneechna* |
| **telephone card** | karta telefoniczna | *karta telefoneechna* |
| **telephone token** | żeton | *jeton* |
| **website** | strona internetowa | *strona eenternetova* |
| **wrong number** | pomyłka | *pomiwuhka* |

### Where is the nearest phone booth?
Gdzie jest najbliższa budka telefoniczna?
*gjeh yest nıbleejsha boodka telefoneechna*

### I would like a number in …
Poproszę number w …
*poprosheh noomer v*

### I would like to speak to …
Chciałbym (*man*)/chciałabym (*woman*) rozmawiać z …
*Hchawuhbim/Hchawabim rozmav-yach z*

### My number is …
Mój numer jest …
*moo-yuh noomer yest*

**I would like to make a collect call**
Poproszę rozmowę R
*vpoprosheh rozmoveh err*

**Could you leave him a message?**
Czy można zostawić wiadomość?
*chi mojna zostaveech v-yadomosh-ch*

**I'll call back later**
Zadzwonię poźniej
*zadzvon-yeh poojn-yay*

**Sorry, wrong number**
Przepraszam, pomyłka
*psheprasham pomiwuhka*

**Please tell him … called** (*man/woman*)
Proszę powiedzieć mu, że … dzwonił/dzwoniła
*prosheh pov-yejech moo je … dzvon-yeewuh/dzvon-yeewa*

**Ask him to call me back, please**
Proszę, poprosić go żeby oddzwonił
*prosheh poprosheech go jebi odzvon-yeewuh*

---

### THINGS YOU'LL HEAR

**Z kim chce pan/pani mówić?**
Whom would you like to speak to?

**Pomyłka**
You've got the wrong number

**Kto mówi?**
Who's speaking?

---

**Jaki jest pana/pani numer?**
What is your number?

**Przepraszam, ale nie ma go**
Sorry, he's not in

**Wróci o …**
He'll be back at … o'clock

**Proszę zadwonić jutro**
Please call again tomorrow

**Przekażę mu, że pan dzwonił/pani dzwoniła**
I'll tell him you called

---

## THINGS YOU'LL SEE

| | |
|---|---|
| **adres email** | email address |
| **automatyczne połączenie** | direct dialing |
| **budka telefoniczna** | telephone booth |
| **centrala** | operator |
| **fotokopiarka** | photocopier |
| **informacja** | directory assistance |
| **karta telefoniczna** | phonecard |
| **kod** | code |
| **międzynarodowa** | international |
| **nieczynny** | out of order |
| **opłata** | charges |
| **pogotowie** | ambulance |
| **rozmowa miejscowa** | local call |
| **rozmowa międzymiastowa** | long-distance call |
| **rozmowa zagraniczna** | international call |
| **strona internetowa** | website |
| **żeton** | telephone token |

# HOTELS

## USEFUL WORDS AND PHRASES

| | | |
|---|---|---|
| balcony | balkon | *balkon* |
| bathroom | łazienka | *wajenka* |
| bed | łóżko | *woojko* |
| bedroom | sypialnia | *sip-yaln-ya* |
| breakfast | śniadanie | *shn-yadan-yeh* |
| check | rachunek | *raHoonek* |
| dining room | jadalnia | *yadaln-ya* |
| dinner | kolacja | *kolats-ya* |
| double room | pokój dwuosobowy | *pokoo-yuh dvoo-osobovi* |
| elevator | winda | *veenda* |
| full board | pełne utrzymanie | *pewuhneh ootjiman-yeh* |
| guest house | zajazd | *za-yazd* |
| hotel | hotel | *Hotel* |
| inn | gospoda | *gospoda* |
| key | klucz | *klooch* |
| lobby | foyer | *fo-yeh* |
| lounge | hall | *Hal* |
| lunch | obiad | *ob-yad* |
| manager | kierownik | *k-yerovneek* |
| reception | recepcja | *retsepts-ya* |
| receptionist (*male*) | recepcjonista | *retsepts-yoneesta* |
| (*female*) | recepcjonistka | *retsepts-yoneestka* |
| restaurant | restauracja | *restawrats-ya* |
| room | pokój | *pokoo-yuh* |
| shower | prysznic | *prishneets* |
| single room | pokój | *pokoo-yuh* |
| | jednoosobowy | *yedno-osobovi* |
| toilet | toaleta | *to-aleta* |
| twin room | pokój z dwoma | *pokoo-yuh z dvoma* |
| | łóżkami | *woojkamee* |
| youth hostel | schronisko | *sHroneesko* |
| | młodzieżowe | *muhwojejoveh* |

**Do you have any vacancies?**
Czy ma pan (*to a man*)/pani (*to a woman*) wolne pokoje?
*chi ma pan/p<u>a</u>nee v<u>o</u>lneh pok<u>o</u>-yeh*

**I have a reservation**
Mam rezerwację
*mam rezerv<u>a</u>ts-yeh*

**I'd like a single/double room**
Poproszę pokój jednoosobowy/dwuosobowy
*popr<u>o</u>sheh p<u>o</u>koo-yuh yedno-osob<u>o</u>vi/dvoo-osob<u>o</u>vi*

**I'd like a twin room**
Poproszę pokój z dwoma łóżkami
*popr<u>o</u>sheh pokoo-yuh z dvoma woojkamee*

**Is there satellite/cable TV in the rooms?**
Czy jest w pokojach telewizja satelitarna/kablowa?
*chi yest w pokoyaн tele-<u>viz</u>ya satelee-<u>tar</u>na/kabl<u>o</u>va*

**I'd like a room with a bathroom/balcony**
Poproszę pokój z łazienką/balkonem
*popr<u>o</u>sheh p<u>o</u>koo-yuh z waj<u>e</u>nkAWN/balk<u>o</u>nem*

**I'd like a room for one night/two/three nights**
Poproszę pokój na jedną dobę/dwie/trzy doby
*popr<u>o</u>sheh p<u>o</u>koo-yuh na <u>ye</u>dnAWN d<u>o</u>beh/dv-yeh/tshi d<u>o</u>bi*

**What is the charge per night?**
Ile kosztuje za dobę?
*<u>ee</u>leh kosht<u>oo</u>-yeh za d<u>o</u>beh*

**There's no hot water/toilet paper/soap**
Nie ma ciepłej wody/papieru toaletowego/mydła
*n-yeh ma ch<u>e</u>pway v<u>o</u>di/pap-<u>ye</u>roo to-aletov<u>e</u>go/m<u>i</u>dwa*

**What time is breakfast/dinner?**
O której jest śniadanie/kolacja?
*o ktooray yest shn-yadan-yeh/kolats-ya*

**Please call me at … o'clock**
Proszę mnie obudzić o … godzinie
*prosheh mn-yeh oboojeech o … gojeen-yeh*

**May I have breakfast in my room?**
Czy można zjeść śniadanie w pokoju?
*chi mojna z-yesh-ch shn-yadan-yeh vpoko-yoo*

**I'm leaving tomorrow**
Wyjeżdżam jutro
*vi-yejd-jam yootro*

**At what time do I have to be out of my room?**
O której trzeba opuścić pokój?
*o ktooray tsheba opoosh-cheech pokoo-yuh*

**May I have the check, please?**
Proszę o rachunek
*prosheh o raноonek*

**I'll pay by credit card**
Zapłacę kartą kredytową
*zapwatseh kartAWN kreditovAWN*

**I'll pay cash**
Zapłacę gotówką
*zapwatseh gotoovkAWN*

**Can you get me a taxi?**
Czy może pan (*to a man*)/pani (*to a woman*) sprowadzić mi
   taksówkę?
*chi mojeh pan/panee sprovajeech mee taksoovkeh*

## THINGS YOU'LL SEE

| | |
|---|---|
| ciągnąć | pull |
| łazienka | bathroom |
| obiad | lunch |
| pchnąć | push |
| prysznic | shower |
| rachunek | check |
| recepcja | reception |
| restauracja | restaurant |
| rezerwacja | reservation |
| śniadanie | breakfast |
| toaleta, W.C. | restroom |
| winda | elevator |
| wyjście | exit |

## THINGS YOU'LL HEAR

**Przepraszam, nie mamy wolnych pokoi**
I'm sorry, we're full

**Nie ma żadnych jednoosobowych pokoi**
There are no single rooms left

**Nie ma żadnych dwuosobowych pokoi**
There are no double rooms left

**Ile dób?**
How many nights?

**Proszę zapłacić z góry**
Please pay in advance

**Proszę wypełnić formularz**
Please fill in this form

# SHOPPING

**Where is the … department?**
Gdzie jest dział z …?
*gjeh yest jawuh z*

**Do you have …?**
Czy ma pan (*to a man*)/pani (*to a woman*) …?
*chi ma pan/panee*

**How much is this?**
Ile to kosztuje?
*eeleh to koshtoo-yeh*

**Where do I pay?**
Gdzie się płaci?
*gjeh sheh pwachee*

**Do you have anything less expensive?**
Czy jest coś tańszego?
*chi yest tsosh tan-yushego*

**May I have a receipt?**
Czy mogę otrzymać paragon?
*chi mogeh otshimach paragon*

**May I have a refund?**
Proszę o zwrot
*prosheh o zvrot*

**I'm just looking**
Chcę tylko popatrzyć
*Htseh tilko popatshich*

# EATING OUT

Poles usually have their main meal of the day relatively early, between 3 and 5 pm. Restaurants, **restauracja** (*restawrats-ya*), fall into four categories: **kat.S** (very high standard), **kat.I**, **kat.II**, and **kat.III**. In the better restaurants, you will now pay more but get a wider range of food. Most larger hotels have **kat.S** or **kat.I** restaurants. While small restaurants in the lower categories frequently offer high-quality food, **kat.S** restaurants are known for their slow service. There are various other places where you can get food and drink:

**Bar** – offers both soft and alcoholic drinks, and snacks.

**Mleczny bar** (*mlechni bar*) – literally a "milk bar" that is open during the day and where you can eat dishes based on dairy products, cereals, vegetables but no meat or fish. No alcoholic drinks are served. In the **mleczny bar** you go straight to the cashier, tell them what you want to eat, pay and take your receipt to the kitchen window. Then you are called to collect it. The **mleczny bar** is excellent value for money. The **Naleśniki z serem** (*naleshneekee zeh serem*) – pancakes with soft white cheese and sour cream – are well worth trying as are the different types of dumplings.

**Cocktail bar** – surprisingly these sell no alcoholic drinks, only milk shakes, cream cakes, and ice cream.

**Kawiarnia** (*kav-yarn-ya*) – basically a café offering coffee, tea, soft and alcoholic drinks as well as pastries, cakes, and often breakfasts and light snacks.

**Winiarnia** (*veen-yarn-ya*) – a wine bar. Food is not sold here.

**Piwiarnia** (*peev-yarn-ya*) – a bar that mainly sells beer. Again food is not usually served. Be careful of the company!

In addition to the traditional places, foreign fast-food chains can now be found in the larger towns.

Restaurants and most cafés have cloakroom facilities, and you are expected to tip the cloakroom attendant as well as the toilet attendant. (Don't be surprised if you are asked to pay extra for toilet paper and the use of soap.)

## Useful Words and Phrases

| beer | piwo | _peevo_ |
|------|------|---------|
| bottle | butelka | _bootelka_ |
| bowl | miska | _meeska_ |
| cake | ciasto | _chasto_ |
| check | rachunek | _raHoonek_ |
| chef | szef kuchni | _shef kooHnee_ |
| coffee | kawa | _kava_ |
| cup | filiżanka | _feeleejanka_ |
| fixed-price menu | obiad firmowy | _ob-yad feermovi_ |
| fork | widelec | _veedelets_ |
| glass | szklanka | _shklanka_ |
| knife | nóż | _nooj_ |
| menu | menu, | _men-yoo,_ |
| | jadłospis | _yadwospees_ |
| milk | mleko | _mleko_ |
| napkin | serwetka | _servetka_ |
| plate | talerz | _talej_ |
| receipt | przepis | _pshepees_ |
| sandwich | kanapka | _kanapka_ |
| snack | przekąska | _pshekAWNska_ |
| soup | zupa | _zoopa_ |
| spoon | łyżka | _wijka_ |
| sugar | cukier | _tsook-yer_ |
| table | stolik | _stoleek_ |
| tea | herbata | _Herbata_ |
| teaspoon | łyżeczka | _wijechka_ |
| tip | napiwek | _napeevek_ |
| vodka | wódka | _voodka_ |
| waiter | kelner | _kelner_ |
| waitress | kelnerka | _kelnerka_ |
| water | woda | _voda_ |
| wine | wino | _veeno_ |
| wine list | karta win | _karta veen_ |

**A table for one/two, please**
stolik dla jednej osoby/dwóch osób, proszę
*stoleek dla yednay osobi/dvooH osoob prosheh*

**May I see the menu?**
Czy mogé poprosić o jadłospis?
*chi mogeh poprosheech o yadwospees*

**May I see the wine list?**
Czy mogę poprosić o kartę win?
*chi mogeh poprosheech o karteh veen*

**What would you recommend?**
Co pan (*to a man*)/pani (*to a woman*) poleca?
*so pan/panee poletsa*

**Is this suitable for vegetarians?**
Czy to się nadaje dla wegetarianinów?
*chi to sheh nadaye dla vegetaryaneenoov*

**I'm allergic to nuts/shellfish**
jestem uczulony (*man*)/uczulona (*woman*) na orzechy/małże
*yestem oochooloni/oochoolona na ojeHi/mawuhje*

**Do you do children's portions?**
Czy ma Pan (*to a man*)/Pani (*to a woman*) porcje dla dzieci?
*chi ma pan/panee portsye dla jyechee*

**Just a cup of coffee, please**
Tylko kawę proszę
*tilko kaveh prosheh*

**Waiter/waitress!**
Proszę pana/panią!
*prosheh pana/pan-yAWN*

307

**I only want a snack**
Tylko przekąskę proszę
*tilko pshek<u>AWN</u>skeh pr<u>o</u>sheh*

**Is there a fixed-price menu?**
Czy jest obiad firmowy?
*chi yest <u>ob</u>-yad feerm<u>o</u>vi*

**I didn't order this**
Tego nie zamawiałem (*man*)/zamawiałam (*woman*)
*t<u>e</u>go n-yeh zamav-<u>ya</u>wem/zamav-<u>ya</u>wam*

**May we/I have some more …?**
Możemy/mogę poprosić o wjęcej …?
*moj<u>e</u>mi/mog<u>eh</u> popr<u>o</u>shech o v-y<u>EN</u>tsay*

**May we have the check, please?**
Poproszę o rachunek
*popr<u>o</u>sheh o ra<u>Hoo</u>nek*

**The meal was very good, thank you**
Bardzo było smaczne, dziękuję
*b<u>a</u>rdzo b<u>i</u>wo sm<u>a</u>chneh j<u>EN</u>k<u>oo</u>-yeh*

---

### THINGS YOU'LL SEE

| | |
|---|---|
| **restauracja** | restaurant |
| **samoobsługa** | self-service |
| **smacznego** | enjoy your meal |
| **szatnia** | cloakroom |
| **szatnia obowiązkowa** | cloakroom obligatory |
| **toaleta płatna 200 zt.** | charge for restroom 200 złotys |
| **toalety** | restrooms |

# MENU GUIDE

agrest gooseberries
babka cake made with eggs and butter
bakalie fruits and nuts
baranina mutton, lamb
barszcz czerwony beet soup
bawarka milky tea
bażant pheasant
befsztyk beef steak
bezy meringues
biała kiełbasa white sausage – pork
    sausage with garlic
biały ser white cheese
bita śmietana whipped cream
bitki wołowe beef cutlets
bliny blinis – small thick, rich pancakes
boczek bacon
bób broad beans
brukiew turnips
brukselki Brussels sprouts
brzoskwinia peach
budyń custard-like pudding
bułka white bread
bułeczka roll
buraki beets
bryzol broiled beef steak
cebula onion
chleb bread
chleb żytni rye bread
chrzan horseradish
ciasto cake, pastry
cielęcina veal
comber saddle
cukier sugar
cynaderki kidneys
cytryna lemon
czarna porzeczka blackcurrants
czekolada chocolate
czereśnia cherry

czosnek garlic
daktyle dates
dania mięsne meat dishes
dania rybne fish dishes
dania z drobiu poultry dishes
dania z jaj egg dishes
deser dessert
dorsz cod
drób poultry
dynia pumpkin
dziczyzna game
drożdżówka brioche, Danish pastry
dżem jam
faszerowany stuffed
fasola beans, kidney beans
fasola szparagowa French beans
filet cielęcy veal escalope
flądra flounder
frytki french fries
galaretka gelatin
gęś goose
gofry waffles
gołąbki stuffed cabbage leaves
golonka boiled leg of pork
gotowany boiled
grochówka pea soup
groch włoski chickpeas
groszek peas
gruszka pear
grzanki toast, croûtons, garlic bread
gulasz goulash
herbata tea
herbatniki cookies
homar lobster
indyk turkey
jabłko apple
jagody bilberries
jagnię lamb

jajecznica scrambled eggs
jajka przepiórcze quails' eggs
jajka sadzone fried eggs
jajko egg
jajko na miekko soft-boiled egg
jajko na twardo hard-boiled egg
jarski vegetarian
jarzyny vegetables
jeżyny blackberries
jogurt yogurt
kabanos dried, smoked pork sausage
kaczka duck
kakao cocoa
kalafior cauliflower
kalarepa kohlrabi
kanapka sandwich
kapuśniak cabbage soup
kapusta cabbage
kapusta czerwona red cabbage
kapusta kiszona sauerkraut
karczochy artichokes
karmazyn haddock
karp carp
kartofelki sauté sautéed potatoes
kartoflanka potato soup
kartofle potatoes
kartofle w mundurkach baked potatoes
kasza any type of boiled grain or cereal
kasza gryczana buckwheat
kasza jeczmienna barley porridge
kasza manna semolina
kasza perłowa pearl barley
kaszanka black pudding
kasztany chestnuts
kawa coffee
kawa po staropolsku traditional Polish-style coffee containing spices
kawior caviar
kefir drinking yogurt
kiełbasa sausage
kisiel a thickened kind of gelatin

klopsiki ground meatballs
klopsy ground meatballs
kluski dumplings, noodles
kminek caraway seed
knedle plum dumplings
kołacz rich cake made with eggs and butter
kołduny meatballs made of ground lamb or mutton and boiled
konfitury jam, preserves
koper dill
kopytka potato dumplings
kotlet chop, cutlet
kotlet mielony ground meat burger
kotlet siekany hamburger steak
kotlet wieprzowy pork chop
kotlet wołowy beef cutlet
krem z czekoladą cream sprinkled with chocolate
kremówka a type of millefeuille cake, custard slice
krewetki shrimp
krokiety croquettes
kromka chleba slice of bread
królik rabbit
krupnik barley soup, spiced hot mead
kukurydza corn on the cob
kulebiak pie with meat, fish, or cabbage
kura chicken
kurczę po polsku roasted chicken stuffed with liver and bread
kurczak pieczony roasted chicken
kuropatwa partridge
kwaśne mleko sour milk
leniwe pierogi dumplings with white cheese
leszcz bream
lody ice cream
łazanki dish similar to lasagne
łosoś salmon
łosoś wędzony smoked salmon

majeranek marjoram
majonez mayonnaise
makaron macaroni, pasta
makowiec poppy seed cake
makrela mackerel
maliny raspberries
mandarynki tangerines
marchew carrot
margaryna margarine
marynowany marinated
masło butter
masło roślinne hard margarine made
    from vegetable oil
maślaki large-cap wild mushrooms
maślanka buttermilk
mazurek a kind of thin cake
mielonka a type of luncheon meat
mielony ground
mięso meat
migdały almonds
miód honey
mizeria cucumber in sour cream
mleko milk
mocno wysmażony well-done
morele apricots
mostek cielęcy veal brisket
murzynek chocolate cake
mus jabłeczny apple mousse
mus owocowy fruit mousse
musztarda mustard
nadzienie stuffing
naleśniki pancakes
napoleonka a type of millefeuille cake,
    custard slice
nerki kidneys
ocet vinegar
ogórek cucumber
ogórek kiszony cucumber pickled in
    brine
ogórek konserwowy pickles in vinegars
olej oil

oliwa olive oil
oliwki olives
omlet omelette
oszczypek smoked ewes' milk
    cheese
orzechy włoskie walnuts
orzeszki peanuts
orzeszki laskowe hazelnuts
owoce fruit
ozorki cielęce veal tongue
ozór tongue
panierowany in breadcrumbs
papryka paprika
papryka zielona green peppers
parówki hot dogs
paszteciki savory pastries
pasztet terrine, pâté
pasztetówka liver sausage
pączki doughnuts
pieczarki button mushrooms
pieczeń roasted
pieprz pepper
piernik spiced honeycake
pierogi ravioli-like dumplings
pietruszka parsley
pikantny spicy
piwo beer
placek tart
płatki owsiane porridge oats
po angielsku rare
polędwica sirloin
polędwica sopocka smoked fish fillet
pomarańcza orange
pomidor tomato
pory leeks
porter stout
porzeczka czarna blackcurrants
porzeczka czerwona redcurrants
przecier purée
przekładaniec layer cake
przepiórki quail

przystawki entrées
pstrąg trout
ptyś cream puff
pyzy large dumplings
rabarbar rhubarb
racuszki kind of pancake with apple
rak crayfish
ratafia fruit liqueur
renklody greengages
rodzynki raisins
rolmopsy rollmop herrings
rosół broth
rozbef roasted beef
rozmaryn rosemary
rumsztyk rumpsteak
ryba fish
ryż rice
rzodkiewki radishes
salceson brawn
sałatka salad
sałatka owocowa fruit salad
sandacz perch
sardynki sardines
sarnina deer
schab joint of pork
ser cheese
sernik cheesecake
sezamki sesame seeds
sękacz fancy layer cake
seler celery
serdelki kind of sausage eaten hot
słodki sweet
smażony fried
sok juice
sola sole
solony salted
sos sauce, gravy
sól salt
stek steak
surówka crudités, raw vegetables
surowy raw

suszone śliwki prunes
szaszłyk mutton kabob
szczupak pike
sznycel escalope
szparagi asparagus
szpinak spinach
sztuka mięsa boiled beef
szynka ham
śledź herring
śliwki plums
śmietana sour cream
śmietanka cream
truskawki strawberries
tuńczyk tuna fish
twarożek soft white cream cheese
tymianek thyme
uszka ravioli filled with cabbage and
  mushrooms
wafle wafers
wątroba liver
wędzony smoked
węgorz eel
wieprzowina pork
winogrona grapes
wiśnie cherries
woda water
woda mineralna mineral water
wołowina beef
zając hare
zakąski snacks
zalewajka potato and rye soup
ziemniaki potatoes
zioła herbs
zrazy naturalne fillets of beef
zsiadłe mleko sour milk
zupa soup
z rusztu broiled
z wody poached
żeberka spareribs
żurawina cranberries
żurek sour rye-flour soup

# PORTUGUESE

## CONTENTS

INTRODUCTION                   314
USEFUL PHRASES                 316
DAYS, MONTHS, SEASONS          321
NUMBERS                        322
TIME                           323
COMMUNICATIONS                 325
HOTELS                         328
SHOPPING                       332
EATING OUT                     333
MENU GUIDE                     337

# PRONUNCIATION

When reading the imitated pronunciation, stress the part that is underlined. Pronounce each syllable as if it formed part of an English word, and you will be understood sufficiently well. Avoid pauses between the syllables. The Portuguese tend to link the sound of a terminal vowel with the beginning of the next word. They have a "soft" pronunciation and will often swallow word endings. Given this complex sound structure, it is not always easy to transcribe Portuguese in terms of English spelling. Remember the points below, and your pronunciation will be even closer to the correct Portuguese.

*j*    As in *ajood̲a̲hr* (for **ajudar**): this should be sounded as you would the s in "pleasure", soft not hard.

*ng*    As in *nowng* (for **não**): it represents the nasal sound made when the vowels a, e, i, o, or u precede m or n, and the nasal diphthongs ão, ãe, ãi, and õe. If you are familiar with the French pronunciation of words like "monter" and "environ", then the Portuguese nasal sound should be no problem for you. Don't give the *g* of *ng* its full (hard) value as in "sing" – treat the letter combination as a symbol of the nasal sound.

*r*    As in *rake̲ttuh* (for **raqueta**): the initial r of a word should be rolled and aspirated, to create a "hrr" sound from the back of the throat.

*u*    As in *ka̲h-zuh duh ba̲hn-yoo* (for **casa de banho**): this is a dull u sound, as in the o in "mother"

## BRAZILIAN PORTUGUESE

For Brazilian Portuguese, word endings are not swallowed as
in Portuguese, and vowel sounds are clearly pronounced. The
ão sound is heavily nasalized as in Portugal. The letter r at the
beginning of a word is pronounced as an h, so Rio (as in Rio de
Janeiro) actually sounds like hee-oo. A double r, in the middle
of a word, also sounds like the English h. The s as in **cortes** is
more like a z, whereas in Portuguese it is like the English sh.

Where the Portuguese word differs from the Brazilian, the
Brazilian equivalent has been given next to it, as in the
following example (**levantar** is the Portuguese and **tirar** the
Brazilian equivalent;)

**Posso levantar/tirar** (*Braz*) **dinheiro com este cartão de crédito?**

Where the whole sentence (or most of the sentence) is different,
the Brazilian equivalent will be repeated on a separate line and
have (*Braz*) preceding it:

**Desculpe, enganei-me no número**
*dushkoolp, enganay-muh noo noomeroo*

(*Braz*) **Desculpe, foi engano**
*dushkoolp, foy en-gah-noh*

In Things You'll See or Hear, the whole Brazilian phrase has
been given afterward:

| | |
|---|---|
| **casa de banho/banheiro** (*Braz*) | bathroom |
| **não fumadores/não fumantes** (*Braz*) | nonsmokers |

# USEFUL PHRASES  .

**Yes/No**
Sim/Não
*seeng/nowng*

**Thank you**
Obrigado *(said by a man)*
*obreegah-doo*

Obrigada *(said by a woman)*
*obreegah-duh*

**No, thank you**
Não obrigado *(said by a man)*
*nowng obreegah-doo*

Não obrigada *(said by a woman)*
*nowng obreegah-duh*

**Please**
Por favor
*poor fuh-vor*

**I don't understand**
Não compreendo/entendo *(Braz)*
*nowng kompree-endoo/ain-taing-doh*

**Do you speak English/French/Spanish?**
Fala inglês/francês/espanhol?
*fah-luh eenglesh/fransesh/shpan-yoll*

**I can't speak Portuguese**
Eu não falo português
*eh-oo nowng fah-loo poortoo-gesh*

**Please speak more slowly**
Por favor, fale mais devagar
*poor fuh-vor, fahl mysh duvagahr*

**Please write it down for me**
Não se importa de me escrever isso?
*nowng see eemportuh duh mushkrevair eessoo*

**Good morning**
Bom dia
*bong dee-uh*

**Good afternoon**
Boa tarde
*boh-uh tard*

**Good night**
Boa noite
*boh-uh noyt*

**Goodbye**
Adeus/Até logo (Braz)
*adeh-oosh/ahteh loh-guh*

**How are you?**
Como está?/Como vai? (Braz)
*koh-moo shta/koh-moo vaee*

**Excuse me, please**
Se faz favor/Com licença (Braz)
*suh fash fuh-vor/kong lee-saing-sah*

**Sorry!**
Desculpe!
*Dushkoolp*

**I'm really sorry**
Tenho muita pena/Sinto muito (Braz)
te̠nyo mwe̠entuh pe̠h-nuh/se̠ento mwe̠entoo

**Can you help me?**
Pode-me ajudar?
po̠d-muh ajooda̠r

**Can you tell me …?**
Pode-me dizer …?
po̠d-muh deeza̠ir

**May I have …?**
Dá-me …?/Me dá …? (Braz)
da̠-muh/meh dah

**I would like …**
Queria …/Gostaria … (Braz)
kre̠e-uh/gos-tah-re̠e-uh

**Is there … here?**
Há … aqui?
ah … ake̠e

**Where is the restroom?**
Onde é a casa de banho?
o̠ndeh uh ka̠h-zuh duh ba̠hn-yoo

(Braz) Onde é o banheiro
o̠ng-deh er oh bang-e̠h-roh

**Is there a highchair/crib/baby changing room?**
Há uma cadeira alta/um berço/um vestiário para bébés?
ah oomah kah-day-ruh al-tuh/oom behr-su/oom vesh-tee-aree-oo
   pahr-uh beh-besh

**Where can I get …?**
Onde posso arranjar …?
*onduh possoo arranjahr*

**How much is it?**
Quanto custa?
*kwantoo kooshtuh*

**Do you take credit cards?**
Aceitam cartões de crédito?
*assay-towng kartoyngsh duh kredditoo*

**May I pay by check?**
Posso pagar com cheque?
*possoo pagahr kong shek*

**What time is it?**
Que horas são?
*kee orush sowng*

**I must go now**
Tenho que me ir embora
*tenyo kuh muh eer emboruh*

*(Braz)* Tenho que ir embora
*teng-ho keh eer eng-boh-rah*

**Cheers!** *(toast)*
Saúde!
*sa-ood*

**Go away!**
Vá-se/Vai *(Braz)* embora!
*vassuh/vaee emboruh*

**Is there wheelchair access?**
Têm acesso para cadeiras de rodas?
*tay-ayng asseh-soo pahr-uh kah-day-rash deh ro-dash*

**Are guide dogs allowed?**
Permitem cães de guia?
*per-mee-tang kaingsh deh guahr-duh*

---

### THINGS YOU'LL SEE OR HEAR

| | |
|---|---|
| aberto | open |
| casa de banho/ banheiros (*Braz*) | restroom |
| com licença | excuse me |
| de nada | don't mention it |
| empurre | push |
| encerrado | closed |
| entrada | entrance |
| fechado | closed |
| homens | men |
| horário de abertura | opening times |
| lavabos | restrooms |
| muito prazer! | pleased to meet you! |
| não falo inglês | I don't speak English |
| não faz mal | never mind |
| não fumar | no smoking |
| obrigado | thank you |
| perdão | sorry |
| perigo de morte | danger |
| proibida a entrada | no admittance |
| puxe | pull |
| saída | exit |
| sanitários/WC | restrooms |
| senhoras | women |
| um momento, por favor | one moment, please |

# DAYS, MONTHS, SEASONS

| | | |
|---|---|---|
| **Sunday** | Domingo | *doomeengo* |
| **Monday** | Segunda-feira | *segoonduh fay-ruh* |
| **Tuesday** | Terça-feira | *tairsuh fay-ruh* |
| **Wednesday** | Quarta-feira | *kwartuh fay-ruh* |
| **Thursday** | Quinta-feira | *keentuh fay-ruh* |
| **Friday** | Sexta-feira | *sayshtuh fay-ruh* |
| **Saturday** | Sábado | *sabadoo* |
| | | |
| **January** | Janeiro | *janay-roo* |
| **February** | Fevereiro | *fuvray-roo* |
| **March** | Março | *marsoo* |
| **April** | Abril | *abreel* |
| **May** | Maio | *my-oo* |
| **June** | Junho | *joon-yoo* |
| **July** | Julho | *jool-yoo* |
| **August** | Agosto | *agoshtoo* |
| **September** | Setembro | *setembroo* |
| **October** | Outubro | *oh-toobroo* |
| **November** | Novembro | *noovembroo* |
| **December** | Dezembro | *dezembroo* |
| | | |
| **Spring** | Primavera | *preema-vairuh* |
| **Summer** | Verão | *verowng* |
| **Fall** | Outono | *otoh-noo* |
| **Winter** | Inverno | *eemvairnoo* |
| | | |
| **Christmas** | Natal | *natahl* |
| **Christmas Eve** | Véspera de Natal | *veshpurruh duh natahl* |
| **Good Friday** | Sexta-feira Santa | *seshtuh fay-ruh santuh* |
| **Easter** | Páscoa, | *pahsh-kwuh-wuh,* |
| | Semana Santa | *seman-uh santuh* |
| **New Year** | Ano Novo | *ah-noo noh-voo* |
| **New Year's Eve** | Véspera de Ano | *veshpuh-ruh dah-noo* |
| | Novo | *noh-voo* |

# NUMBERS

| | | | |
|---|---|---|---|
| 0 | zero *zairoo* | 5 | cinco *seeng-koo* |
| 1 | um *oom* | 6 | seis *saysh* |
| 2 | dois *doysh* | 7 | sete *set* |
| 3 | três *tresh* | 8 | oito *oytoo* |
| 4 | quatro *kwatroo* | 9 | nove *nov* |

10  dez *desh*
11  onze *onz*
12  doze *doze*
13  treze *trez*
14  catorze/quatorze (Braz) *katorz/katorzeh*
15  quinze *keenz*
16  dezasseis/dezesseis (Braz) *dezassaysh/dez-eh-seh-is*
17  dezassete/dezessete (Braz) *dezaset/dez-eh-setee*
18  dezoito *dezoytoo*
19  dezanove/dezenove (Braz) *dezanov/dez-eh-noh-vee*
20  vinte *veent*
21  vinte e um *veent ee oom*
22  vinte e dois *veent ee doysh*
30  trinta *treentuh*
31  trinta e um *treentuh ee oom*
32  trinta e dois *treentuh ee doysh*
40  quarenta *kwarentuh*
50  cinquenta *seeng-kwentuh*
60  sessenta *sessentuh*
70  setenta *setentuh*
80  oitenta *oytentuh*
90  noventa *nooventuh*
100  cem *sayng*
110  cento e dez *sentoo ee desh*
200  duzentos *doozentoosh*
1,000  mil *meel*
1,000,000  um milhão *oom meel-yowng*

# TIME

| today | hoje | _o_je |
| --- | --- | --- |
| yesterday | ontem | _o_ntayng |
| tomorrow | amanhã | amany_a_ng |
| this week | esta semana | _e_shtuh sem_a_h-nuh |
| last week | a semana passada | uh sem_a_h-nuh<br>   pass_a_h-duh |
| next week | a semana que vem | uh sem_a_h-nuh kuh<br>   vayng |
| this morning | esta manhã/<br>hoje de manhã (Braz) | _e_shtuh many_a_ng/<br>hoe-gee deh many_a_ng |
| this afternoon | esta tarde/<br>hoje à tarde (Braz) | _e_shtuh tard<br>hoe-gee ah tard |
| this evening | esta noite/<br>hoje de noite (Braz) | _e_shtuh noyt<br>hoe-gee deh noyt |
| tonight | esta noite | _e_shtuh noyt |
| in three days | dentro de três dias/ | d_e_ntroo duh tresh<br>   d_ee_-ush |
| | em três dias (Braz) | ehm tresh d_ee_-ush |
| three days ago | há três dias | ah tresh d_ee_-ush |
| late | tarde | tard |
| early | cedo | s_e_h-doo |
| soon | em breve | ayng brev |
| second | segundo | seg_oo_ndoo |
| minute | minuto | meen_oo_too |
| ten minutes | dez minutos | desh meen_oo_toosh |
| quarter of<br>  an hour | um quarto de hora/<br>quinze minutos (Braz) | oom kw_a_rtoo d_o_ruh/<br>king-zeh mee-_noo_-toes |
| half an hour | meia hora | may-yuh _o_ruh |
| hour | a hora | _o_ruh |
| day | o dia | d_ee_-uh |
| week | a semana | sem_a_h-nuh |
| two weeks | a quinzena | keenz_a_ynuh |
| month | o mês | mesh |
| year | o ano | _a_h-noo |

## TELLING TIME

In Portuguese you always put the hour first when talking about minutes past the hour. Use the word **e** for "past" (eg 3:20 = **três e vinte** or "three and twenty"). For minutes to the hour the minutes come first. Use the word **para** for "to" (eg 6:40 = **vinte para as sete** or "twenty to seven"). The 24-hour clock is used officially in timetables and inquiry offices.

In Brazilian Portuguese you never use the word "quarter" when telling the time, instead you say fifteen to the hour or fifteen past the hour (eg 2:15 = **duas e quinze** and 2:45 = **quinze para as três**).

| | | |
|---|---|---|
| **one o'clock** | uma hora | <u>oo</u>muh <u>o</u>ruh |
| **ten past one** | uma e dez | <u>oo</u>muh ee desh |
| **quarter past one** | uma e um quarto/ uma e quinze (Braz) | <u>oo</u>muh ee oom kw<u>a</u>rtoo/oomah eh <u>king</u>-zeh |
| **twenty past one** | uma e vinte | <u>oo</u>muh ee veent |
| **half past one** | uma e meia | <u>oo</u>muh ee m<u>a</u>y-yuh |
| **twenty to two** | vinte para as duas | veent prash d<u>oo</u>-ush |
| **quarter to two** | um quarto para as duas/quinze para as duas (Braz) | oom kw<u>a</u>rtoo prash d<u>oo</u>-ush/<u>king</u>-seh pah-rah as d<u>oo</u>-as |
| **ten to two** | dez para as duas | desh prash d<u>oo</u>-ush |
| **two o'clock** | duas horas | d<u>oo</u>-uz <u>o</u>rush |
| **13:00 (1 pm)** | treze horas | tr<u>e</u>zee <u>o</u>rush |
| **16:30/4:30 pm** | dezasseis e trinta/ dezesseis e trinta (Braz) | dezass<u>a</u>yz ee tr<u>e</u>entuh dez-eh-<u>seh</u>-is ee tr<u>e</u>entuh |
| **20:10/8:10 pm** | vinte e dez | veent ee desh |
| **at half past five** | às cinco e meia | ash s<u>ee</u>ng-koo ee m<u>a</u>y-yuh |
| **at seven o'clock** | às sete horas | ash set <u>o</u>rush |
| **noon** | meio-dia | m<u>a</u>y-yoo-d<u>ee</u>-uh |
| **midnight** | meia-noite | m<u>a</u>y-yuh-n<u>o</u>yt |

324

# COMMUNICATIONS

## Useful Words and Phrases

| | | |
|---|---|---|
| **code** | o indicativo/ | eendeekuh-_teevoo_/ |
| | o código (Braz) | _coh_-de-go |
| **collect call** | a chamada paga | shamah-duh _pah_-guh |
| | no destinatário/ | noo dushteenatar-yoo/ |
| | a chamada a cobrar (Braz) | sha-_mah_-da ah _ko_-bra- |
| **dial tone** | o sinal de chamada | seenal deh shumah-duh |
| **email address** | o endereço de email | endeh-re-soo deh ee-mayl |
| **emergency** | a emergência | eemer-_jenss_-yuh |
| **extension** | a extensão | eeshtensowng |
| **number** | o número | noomeroo |
| **operator** | a telefonista | tulluh-fooneeshtuh |
| **payphone** | o telefone público/ | tulluh-fonn _pooblikoo_/ |
| | o orelhão (Braz) | oh-reh-lee-aw |
| **telephone** | o telefone | tulluh-_fonn_ |
| **phone booth** | a cabina telefónica/ | kabeenuh tulluh- |
| | | fonnikuh/ |
| | o orelhão (Braz) | oh-reh-lee-aw |
| **phone book** | a lista telefónica/ | leeshtuh tulluh- |
| | a lista telefônica (Braz) | fonnikuh/lees-tah |
| | | teh-leh-_foh_-nee-ka |

## Where is the nearest phone booth?
Onde fica a cabina telefónica/o orelhão(Braz) mais próxima?
_onduh feekuh uh kabeenuh tulluh-fonnikuh/oo oh-reh-lee-aw mysh
prossimuh_

## I would like a number in …
Queria um número em …
_kree-uh oom noomeroo ayng_

## I would like to speak to …
Queria falar com …
_kree-uh falahr kong_

**My number is …**
O meu número de telefone é o …
*oo meh-oo noomeroo duh tulluh-fonn eh oo*

**Hello, this is … speaking**
Está, é o/a …
*shtah, eh oo/uh*

*(Braz)* Alô, aqui é o/a …
*ah-low, a-key eh oh/ah*

**Is that …?**
É o/a …?
*eh oo/uh*

**Could you leave him a message?**
Pode-lhe deixar um recado?
*podl-yuh dayshahr oom rekah-doo*

**Sorry, I've got the wrong number**
Desculpe, enganei-me no número
*dushkoolp, enganay-muh noo noomeroo*

*(Braz)* Desculpe, foi engano
*dushkoolp, foy en-gah-noh*

**I'll call back later**
Volto a telefonar mais tarde
*voltoo uh tulluh-foonar mysh tard*

**What's your fax number/email address?**
Qual é o seu número de fax/endereço de email?
*kwal eh oo she-oo noo-meyro deh fax/endeh-re-soo deh ee-mayl*

**Can I send an email/fax from here?**
Posso enviar um email/um fax daqui?
*possoo envee-ahr oom ee-mayl/man-dahr oom fax duh-kee*

## THINGS YOU'LL HEAR

**Com quem quer falar?**
Whom would you like to speak to?

**Quem fala?**
Who's speaking?

**De que número fala?**
What is your number?

**Desculpe, mas ele não está**
*(Braz)* **Sinto muito, mas ele não está**
Sorry, he's not in

**Volte a telefonar amanhã, por favor**
Please call again tomorrow

**Eu digo-lhe que telefonou**
I'll tell him you called

## THINGS YOU'LL SEE

| | |
|---|---|
| **avariado/não funciona** *(Braz)* | out of order |
| **cabina telefónica** | phone booth |
| **cartão telefónico** | phonecard |
| **chamada internacional** | international call |
| **chamada local** | local call |
| **correio electrónico** | email |
| **endereço de email** | email address |
| **fax** | fax machine |
| **informações** | inquiries |
| **página na internet/web site** *(Braz)* | website |
| **serviço internacional** | international calls |
| **tarifas** | charges |
| **telefone** | telephone |
| **telemóvel/cellular** *(Braz)* | mobile phone |

## HOTELS

| | | |
|---|---|---|
| balcony | a varanda | *varanduh* |
| bathroom | a casa de banho/ | *kah-zuh duh bahn-yoo/* |
| | o banheiro (Braz) | *bang-eh-roh* |
| bed | a cama | *kah-muh* |
| bedroom | o quarto | *kwartoo* |
| bill | a conta | *kontuh* |
| breakfast | o pequeno almoço/ | *pekeh-noo almoh-soo/* |
| | o café da manhã (Braz) | *café dah mang-nya* |
| dining room | a sala de jantar | *sah-lah duh jantahr* |
| dinner | o jantar | *jantahr* |
| double room | o quarto de casal | *kwartoo duh kazal* |
| elevator | o ascensor/ | *ash-sayng-sor/* |
| | o elevador (Braz) | *eh-lev-ah-door* |
| full board | pensão completa | *payng-sowng komplettuh* |
| half board | meia-pensão | *may-yuh payng-sowng* |
| hotel | o hotel | *oh-tell* |
| key | a chave | *shahv* |
| lobby | o foyer/o salaõ (Braz) | *fwy-ay/sahlang* |
| lounge | a sala | *sah-luh* |
| lunch | o almoço | *almoh-soo* |
| manager | o gerente | *jerrent* |
| reception | a recepção | *russepsowng* |
| receptionist | o recepcionista | *russepss-yooneeshtuh* |
| restaurant | o restaurante | *rushtoh-rant* |
| restroom | a casa de banho/ | *kah-zuh duh bahn-yoo/* |
| | banheiro (Braz) | *bah-nhei-roh* |
| room | o quarto | *kwartoo* |
| room service | o serviço de quartos | *sur-veeso duh kwartoosh* |
| shower | o duche/o chuveiro (Braz) | *doo-sh sho-veh-roh* |
| single room | o quarto individual/ | *kwartoo eendeeveedwal/* |
| | de solteiro (Braz) | *duh sol-teh-roh* |
| twin room | o quarto com duas | *kwartoo kong doo-ush* |
| | camas | *kah-mush* |

**Do you have any vacancies?**
Têm vagas?
*tay-ayng vah-gush*

**I have a reservation**
Eu fiz uma reserva
*eh-oo feez ooma rezairvuh*

**I'd like a single/double room**
Queria um quarto individual/de casal
*kree-uh oom kwartoo eendeeveedwal/duh kazal*

(*Braz*) Queria um quarto de solteiro/de casal
*kree-uh oom kwartoo dee sol-teh-roh/duh kazal*

**I'd like a twin room**
Queria um quarto com duas camas
*kree-uh oom kwartoo kong doo-ush kah-mush*

**I'd like a room with a bathroom/balcony**
Queria um quarto com casa de banho/com varanda
*kree-uh oom kwartoo kong kah-zuh duh banhyoo/kong varanduh*

(*Braz*) Queria um quarto com o banheiro/com varanda
*kree-uh oom kwartoo kong oh bang-eh-roh/kong varanduh*

**I'd like a room for one night/three nights**
Queria um quarto só por uma noite/três noites
*kree-uh oom kwartoo soh poor oomuh noyt/poor tresh noytsh*

**Is there satellite/cable TV in the rooms?**
Os quartos têm tv via satélite/tv por cabo?
*osh kwartoosh tay-ayng teh-vea vee-uh sateh-lee-tuh/teh-vee poor ka-bu*

**What is the charge per night?**
Qual é o preço por noite?
*kwal eh oo preh-soo poor noyt*

**When is breakfast/dinner?**
A que horas é o pequeno almoço/o jantar?
*uh kee oruz eh oo pekeh-noo almoh-soo/oo jantahr*

*(Braz)* A que horas é o café da manhã/o jantar?
*uh kee oruz eh oo café deh mang-nya/oo jantahr*

**Would you have my luggage brought up, please?**
Pode-me/Poderia *(Braz)* levar a bagagem, por favor?
*pod-muh/poh-deh-ree-ah luhvahr uh bagah-jayng, poor fuh-vor*

**Please call me at … o'clock**
Chame-me às … horas, por favor
*shamu-muh ash … orush, poor fuh-vor*

**May I have breakfast in my room?**
Posso tomar o pequeno almoço no quarto?
*possoo toomahr oo pekeh-noo almoh-soo/noo kwartoo*

*(Braz)* Posso tomar o café da manhã no quarto?
*possoo toomahr oo café deh mang-nya noo kwartoo*

**My room number is …**
O número do meu quarto é o …
*oo noomeh-roo doo meh-oo kwartoo eh oo*

**I'm leaving tomorrow**
Vou-me embora amanhã
*voh-muh emboruh amanyang*

**May I have the bill, please?**
A conta, por favor
*uh kontuh, poor fuh-vor*

**Can you get me a taxi?**
Pode-me chamar um taxi?
*pod-muh shamahr oom taksee*

## Things You'll See

| | |
|---|---|
| água fria | cold water |
| água quente | hot water |
| almoço | lunch |
| banheira | bathtub |
| casa de banho/ | bathroom, toilet |
| banheiro (*Braz*) | |
| chuveiro | shower |
| conta | check |
| elevador | elevator |
| jantar | dinner |
| pequeno almoço/ | breakfast |
| café da manhã (*Braz*) | |
| recepção | reception |
| reserva | reservation |
| restaurante | restaurant |
| saída de emergência | emergency exit |
| telefonista | switchboard operator |

## Things You'll Hear

**Tenho muita pena, mas estamos cheios**
**(*Braz*) Sinto muito, mas estamos cheios**
I'm very sorry, but we're full

**Não temos quartos individuais**
**(*Braz*) Não temos quarto de solteiros**
There are no single rooms left

**Não há vagas**
No vacancies

**É/Por (*Braz*) favor pagar adiantado**
Please pay in advance

# SHOPPING

**Where is the ... department?**
Onde é a secção de ...?
*ondeh uh seksowng duh*

**Do you have ...?**
Tem ...?
*tayng*

**How much is this?**
Quanto é que isto custa?
*kwantoo eh kee eeshtoo kooshtuh*

**Where do I pay?**
Onde é que se paga?
*ondeh kuh suh pah-guh*

**Do you take credit cards?**
Aceita cartões de crédito?
*asay-tuh car-tow-eensh de credee-too*

**May I have a receipt?**
Pode-me/Poderia (Braz) dar uma factura/um recibo (Braz),
  por favor?
*pod-muh/poh-deh-ree-ah dar oomuh faktooruh/oom heh-see-bow,
  poor fuh-vor*

**May I have a refund?**
Pode-me/Pode (Braz) devolver o dinheiro?
*pod-muh/poh-deh duvvolvair oo deen-yay-roo*

**That's fine**
Está bem
*shtah bayng*

# EATING OUT

Portugal and Brazil offer a variety of places to eat:

Café:                    A general café that sells all kinds of food and drinks and is well worth trying for a quick snack. Full meals are also often available.

Churrascaria:            A restaurant specializing in barbecued dishes.

Confeitaria (*Braz*):    A bakery/café that sells bread and cakes, and also serves snacks, juices, milkshakes, and coffee.

Esplanada:               Pavement café

Lanchonete (*Braz*):     A café-bar selling sandwiches and light meals as well as cakes, candy, and drinks.

Pastelaria:              A bakery that also serves tea, coffee, beer, sandwiches and light snacks. In Brazil, this is a place specializing in **pasteis** (savory pastries with fillings), and other snacks, but not cakes or sweet pastries.

Restaurante:             Restaurant.

Snack-bar:               A combined café, bar, and restaurant, not to be confused with the American idea of a snack bar. Service is provided at the counter or, for a little extra, at a table. There is usually a good variety of fixed-price menus at reasonable prices (look for **pratos combinados** or, in Brazil, **pratos do dia** – dish of the day.)

## Useful Words and Phrases

| | | |
|---|---|---|
| beer | a cerveja | serv_ay_-juh |
| bottle | a garrafa | garr_ah_-fuh |
| bowl | a tigela | teej_e_lluh |
| cake | o bolo | b_oh_-loo |
| check | a conta | k_o_ntuh |
| chef | o cozinheiro | koozeen-y_ay_-roo |
| coffee | o café | kuff_eh_ |
| cup | a chávena/a xícara (Braz) | sh_a_venuh/she-_ka-rah_ |
| fork | o garfo | g_a_rfoo |
| glass | o copo | k_o_poo |
| knife | a faca | f_ah_-kuh |
| menu | a ementa/o cardápio (Braz) | eem_e_ntuh/car-_dap_-eo |
| milk | o leite | layt |
| napkin | o guardanapo | gwarduh-n_a_poo |
| plate | o prato | pr_ah_-too |
| receipt | o recibo | russ_ee_boo |
| restaurant | o restaurante | rushtoh-r_a_nt |
| sandwich | a sandes/ | s_a_ndj/ |
| | o sanduíche (Braz) | sand-_weech_-eh |
| snack | a refeição ligeira/ | refay-s_ow_ng leej_a_yruh/ |
| | o lanche (Braz) | lang-sheh |
| soup | a sopa | s_o_hppuh |
| spoon | a colher | kool-y_ai_r |
| sugar | o açúcar | ass_oo_kar |
| table | a mesa | m_e_zuh |
| tea | o chá | sha |
| teaspoon | a colher de chá | kool-y_ai_r duh sha |
| tip | a gorjeta | goorj_e_tuh |
| waiter | o empregado de mesa/ | empreg_a_h-doo duh m_e_zuh |
| | a garçom (Braz) | gah-_song_ |
| waitress | a empregada de mesa/ | empreg_a_h-duh duh m_e_zuh |
| | a garçonete (Braz) | gah-song-_etche_ |
| water | a água | _a_hg-wuh |
| wine | o vinho | v_ee_nyoo |
| wine list | a lista dos vinhos | l_ee_shtuh doosh v_ee_nyoosh |

**A table for one, please**
Uma mesa para uma pessoa, por favor
*oomuh mezuh par-uh oomuh pessoh-uh, poor fuh-vor*

**A table for two/three, please**
Uma mesa para duas/três pessoas, por favor
*oomuh mezuh par-uh doo-ush/tresh pessoh-ush, poor fuh-vor*

**May we see the menu, please?**
Pode trazer a ementa/o cardápio (Braz), por favor?
*pod trazair uh eementuh/oh car-dap-eo, poor fuh-vor*

**May we see the wine list, please?**
Pode trazer a lista dos vinhos, por favor?
*pod trazair uh leeshtuh doosh veenyoosh, poor fuh-vor*

**Do you have children's portions?**
Servem porções para crianças?
*servaing poo-soyngsh pahr-uh kree-ang-sash*

**What would you recommend?**
O que é que nos aconselha?
*oo kee eh kuh nooz akonsell-yuh*

(Braz) O que pode sugerir?
*oo kee pohdeh soojeh-reer*

**Is this suitable for vegetarians?**
Isto é apropriado para vegetarianos?
*eeshtoo eh aproo-pree-ahdoo pahr-uh veh-jeh-tah-ree-ahnoos*

**I'd like …**
Queria …
*kree-uh*

**Just a cup of coffee, please**
Só um café, por favor
*soh oom kuffeh, poor fuh-vor*

**Waiter!/Waitress!**
Se faz favor!
*suh fash fuh-vor*

(*Braz*) Garçom! Garçonete!
*gah-song gah-song-etche*

**May we have the check, please?**
Pode trazer a conta, por favor?
*pod trazair uh kontuh, poor fuh-vor*

**I only want a snack**
Só quero uma refeição ligeira
*soh kairoo oomuh ruffay-sowng leejay-ruh*

(*Braz*) Só quero lanchar
*soh kairoo lang-shah*

**Is there a fixed-price menu?**
Qual é o prato do dia?
*kwal eh prato doh dea*

**I didn't order this**
Eu não pedi isto
*eh-oo nowng pedee eeshtoo*

**May we have some more …?**
Pode trazer mais …?
*pod trazair mysh*

**The meal was very good, thank you**
A comida estava óptima/ótima, obrigado
*uh koomeeduh shtah-vuh ottimmuh/oh-ti-moh, obrigah-doo*

# MENU GUIDE

**açorda** thick bread soup
**açúcar** sugar
**aipo** celery
**alcachofras** artichokes
**alface** lettuce
**alho** garlic
**alho francês** leek
**almôndegas** meatballs
**alperces** apricots
**amêijoas** clams
**ameixas** plums
**amêndoas** almonds
**ao natural** plain
**arroz** rice
**arroz doce** sweet rice dessert
**atum** tuna
**avelãs** hazelnuts
**azeitonas** olives
**bacalhau** cod
**bacalhau à Zé do Pipo** cod in egg sauce
**batata assada** baked potato
**batata palha** thinly cut french fries
**batatas** potatoes
**batatas cozidas** boiled potatoes
**batatas fritas** french fries
**batidos/batida** (*Braz*) milk shakes
**bem passado** well done
**berbigão** clamlike shellfish
**beringelas** eggplant
**besugos** sea bream (fish)
**beterraba** beets
**bica** small black coffee
**bifanas** pork slice in a roll
**bife** steak
**bife à cortador** thick, tender steak
**bife de alcatra** rump steak
**bife de atum** tuna steak
**bife grelhado** broiled steak

**bifes de peru** turkey steaks
**bifinhos de porco** small slices of pork
**bola de carne** meatball cooked in dough
**bolo** cake
**borrego à moda do Minho** marinated lamb in the Minho style
**branco** white
**cachorros/cachorro quente** (*Braz*) hot dogs
**café** coffee
**café pingado** espresso coffee with a touch of milk
**caldeirada** fish stew
**caldo** soup
**camarões** shrimp
**canela** cinnamon
**canja de galinha** chicken soup
**caracóis** snails
**caranguejos** crab
**carapaus** mackerel
**caril** curry
**carioca** small weak black coffee
**carne à jardineira** meat and vegetable stew
**carne de vaca assada** roasted beef
**carne de vaca guisada** stewed beef
**carne estufada** stewed meat
**carneiro** mutton
**carnes** meats
**carnes frias** selection of cold meats
**castanhas** chestnuts
**cerejas** cherries
**cerveja** beer
**chá de limão** lemon tea
**chá de mentol** mint tea
**chanfana de porco** pork casserole
**chocolate quente** hot chocolate
**chocos** cuttlefish

**chouriço** spiced sausage
**churros** long, tube-shaped fritters
**cimbalino** espresso coffee
**codorniz** quail
**coelho** rabbit
**cogumelos** mushrooms
**compota** stewed fruit
**conquilhas** baby clams
**coração** heart
**corvina** large sea fish
**costeletas** chops
**couve branca** white cabbage
**couve-flor** cauliflower
**couve roxa** red cabbage
**couves de bruxelas** Brussels sprouts
**couves guisadas com salsichas** stewed cabbage and sausage
**cozido à portuguesa** Portuguese stew (with chicken, sausage etc)
**creme de marisco** cream of shellfish soup
**doce** dessert; jam; dessert made from eggs and sugar
**doce de ovos** custardlike dessert made from eggs and sugar
**dourada** dory (sea fish)
**ementa** menu
**empadão de carne** large meat pie
**empadão de peixe** large fish pie
**encharcada** dessert made of almonds and eggs
**enguias** eels
**ensopado de borrego** lamb stew
**ensopado de enguias** eel stew
**entrecosto** entrecôte
**ervilhas** peas
**escalope panado** breaded escalope
**espargos** asparagus
**esparguete à bolonhesa** spaghetti bolognese
**esparregado** puréed spinach

**espetada** kabob
**faisão** pheasant
**farófias** whipped egg white with cinnamon
**farturas** long, tube-shaped fritters
**fatias recheadas** slices of bread with fried ground meat
**febras de porco** thin pork slices
**feijão verde** French beans
**feijoada** bean stew
**figos** figs
**filete** fillet
**filhozes** sugared buns
**folhado de carne** meat roll with puff pastry
**folhado de salsicha** sausage roll
**frango** chicken
**frango assado** roasted chicken
**frango na púcara** chicken casserole with port and almonds
**fruta** fruit
**funcho** fennel
**galão** large milky coffee
**galinha de África** guinea fowl
**galinha de fricassé** chicken fricassee
**gambas** shrimp
**garoto** small milky coffee
**gelado** ice cream
**gelado de baunilha** vanilla ice cream
**geleia** preserves
**groselha** currant similar to blackcurrant
**iogurte** yogurt
**iscas à portuguesa** fried liver and boiled potatoes
**lagosta** lobster
**lagostins** crayfish
**lampreia à moda do Minho** marinated lamprey served in the Minho style
**lampreia de ovos** egg dessert shaped as a lamprey
**laranjas** oranges

lasanha lasagne

leitão à Bairrada suckling pig from Bairrada

leite milk

leite creme light custard with cinnamon

língua tongue

linguado à meunière sole meunière

linguado grelhado/frito/no forno broiled/fried/baked sole

lista menu

lombo de porco loin of pork

lombo de vaca sirloin

lulas squid

maçã assada baked apple

maçãs apples

macedónia de frutas fruit cocktail

mal passado rare

manteiga butter

marinada marinade

marisco shellfish

marmelos quince

mazagrin iced coffee with lemon

meia de leite large white coffee

meia desfeita cod and chickpeas with olive oil and vinegar

melancia watermelon

melão melon

mexilhões mussels

migas à alentejana thick bread soup

mil folhas sweet, flaky pastry

molho sauce

molho branco white sauce

molho holandês hollandaise sauce

molho inglês brown sauce

molho veloutée white sauce made from egg yolks and cream

morangos strawberries

morena beer

mousse de fiambre ham mousse

napolitanas long, flat cookies

nêsperas loquats (fruit)

nozes walnuts

omolete/omelete (Braz) omelette

ovo estrelado fried egg

ovo quente soft-boiled egg

ovos escalfados poached eggs

ovos mexidos scrambled eggs

ovos verdes stuffed eggs

pão de centeio rye bread

pão de milho corn bread

pão integral whole wheat bread

pão torrado toasted bread

pargo sea bream

parrilhada fish grill

pastéis de nata puff pastry with egg custard filling

pastéis de Tentugal custard pie with almonds and nuts

pastelinhos de bacalhau cod fishcakes

pataniscas salted cod fritter

pato assado roasted duck

pato com laranja duck à l'orange

peixe fish

peixe espada swordfish

pequeno almoço continental breakfast

pêras pears

perdizes na púcara partridge casserole

perna de carneiro leg of lamb

peru turkey

pescada cozida boiled hake

pêssego careca nectarine

pêssegos peaches

pimenta pepper

pimentos peppers (red or green)

piperate pepper stew

pratos combinados mixed dishes

pregos thin slice of steak in a roll

pudim de laranja orange flan

pudim de ovos egg pudding

pudim flan type of crème caramel

puré de batata mashed potatoes

puré de castanhas chestnut purée

queijo cheese
rabanadas French toast
raia skate
remoulade dressing with mustard and herbs
requeijão curd cheese
rillete potted pork and goose meat
rins kidneys
rissol rissole
robalo rock bass
rolo de carne meatloaf
sabayon dessert with egg yolks and white wine
sal salt
salada salad
salada mista mixed salad
salmão salmon
salmão fumado smoked salmon
salmonetes grelhados broiled mullet
salsicha sausage
sandes sandwich
santola spider crab
santola gratinada spider crab au gratin
sapateira spider crab
sardinhas assadas broiled sardines
sobremesas desserts
solha flounder
sonhos dried dough with cinnamon
sopa soup
sumo juice
toranja grapefruit
torresmos small rashers of bacon
tortilha Spanish omelette (with potato)
tosta toasted sandwich
toucinho do céu egg dessert
truta trout
uvas brancas/pretas white/black grapes
veado assado roast venison
vieiras recheadas stuffed scallops
vinagre de estragão tarragon vinegar
xarope syrup

## BRAZILIAN MENU GUIDE

abacaxi pineapple
acarajé fried bean dumpling
angu polenta
bacalhoada baked salt cod with potato
bife steak
bobó de camarão cassava and shrimp
caldo de cana sugarcane juice
carne de boi/vaca beef
carne de sol dried salt beef
churrasco barbecued meat
cocada dessert made of coconut
couve a mineira chopped spring greens
coxinha de galinha chicken dumplings
damasco apricot
dendê palm oil
empadinha pie
farofa side dish of cassava flour and eggs
feijão preto black beans
feijoada black bean and meat stew
galinha/frango chicken
goiaba guava
linguiça sausage
mamão papaya
mandioca/aipim cassava
maracujá passion fruit
moqueca fish or shrimp stew
palmito palm heart
pão de queijo cheese bread
pastel thin fried pasty
pirão savory cream
porco pork
pudim creme caramel
quibe deep fried ground meat
quindim coconut dessert
salgadinho savory filled pastries
siri crab
tutu mashed beans with eggs and bacon
vatapá spicy thick cream
xinxim de galinha chicken with shrimp

# SPANISH

## CONTENTS

| | |
|---|---|
| INTRODUCTION | 342 |
| USEFUL PHRASES | 343 |
| DAYS, MONTHS, SEASONS | 349 |
| NUMBERS | 350 |
| TIME | 351 |
| COMMUNICATIONS | 353 |
| EMERGENCIES | 355 |
| HOTELS | 356 |
| SHOPPING | 360 |
| EATING OUT | 361 |
| MENU GUIDE | 365 |

# INTRODUCTION

## PRONUNCIATION

When reading the imitated pronunciation, stress the part that is underlined. Pronounce each syllable as if it formed part of an English word and you will be understood sufficiently well. Remember the points below, and your pronunciation will be even closer to the correct Spanish.

| | |
|---|---|
| g | always hard as in "get" |
| H | represents the guttural sound of "ch" |
| I | pronounced as "eye" |
| ow | as in "cow" |
| s | always sound the Spanish "s" as a double "ss" as in "missing," *never* like the "s" in "easy" |
| th | as in "thin," *not* as in "they" |
| y | always as in "yet," *not* as in "eye" (eg **bien** *byen*, **siento** *syentoh*) |

Don't be worried by the varying pronunciations you are certain to hear in some parts of Spain. An example is the sounding of "z" (and of "c" before e or i) like an English "s" – in this instance we recommend that you don't copy it, but lisp the sound as we have imitated it. Similarly, in certain circumstances, the Spanish "v" can be pronounced as either a "v" or a "b," so that **vaca** sounds like "baca."

## GENDERS AND ARTICLES

Spanish has two genders for nouns – masculine and feminine. We generally give the definite article ("the") – **el** for masculine nouns, **la** for feminine nouns, **los** for masculine plural nouns, and **las** for feminine plural nouns. Where the indefinite article ("a, an") is more appropriate, we have given **un** for masculine nouns and **una** for feminine nouns, or the words for "some" – **unos** (masculine) and **unas** (feminine.)

# USEFUL PHRASES

### Yes, No, OK etc

**Yes/No**
Sí/No
*see/noh*

**OK**
Vale
*baleh*

**That's fine**
Está bien
*esta byen*

**That's right**
Eso es
*essoh ess*

### Greetings, Introductions

**How do you do? Pleased to meet you**
¿Qué tal?, mucho gusto
*keh tal, mootchoh goostoh*

**Good morning/good evening/good night**
Buenos días/buenas tardes/buenas noches
*bweh-noss dee-ass/bweh-nass tardess/bweh-nass notchess*

**Goodbye/Bye**
Adiós
*ad-yoss*

**How are you?**
¿Cómo está usted?
*koh-moh esta oosteh*

*(familiar)*
¿Cómo estás?
*koh-moh estass*

**My name is …**
Me llamo …
*meh yah-moh*

**What's your name?** *(familiar)*
¿Cómo se llama usted?   ¿Cómo te llamas?
*koh-moh seh yah-ma oosteh*   *koh-moh teh yah-mass*

**This is …** *(introducing a man/woman)*
Éste/ésta es …
*esteh/esta ess*

**Hello/Hi!**
¡Hola!
*oh-la*

PLEASE, THANK YOU, APOLOGIES

**Thank you/No, thank you**
Gracias/No, gracias
*grath-yass/noh grath-yass*

**Please**
Por favor
*por fa-vor*

**Excuse me!** *(when sneezing, etc.)*
¡Perdón!
*pair-don*

**Sorry!**
¡Perdón!/Lo siento
*pair-don/loh syentoh*

WHERE, HOW, ASKING

**Excuse me, please** *(to get past)*
¿Me hace el favor?
*meh ah-theh el fa-vor*

**Can you tell me …?**
¿Puede decirme …?
*pweh-deh detheer-meh*

**Would you like a …?** (familiar)
¿Quiere un/una …? ¿Quieres un/una …?
*kyeh-reh oon/oona* *kyeh-rehs oon/oona*

**Would you like to …?** (familiar)
¿Le gustaría …? ¿Te gustaría …?
*leh goostaree-a* *teh goostaree-a*

**Is there … here?**
¿Hay … aquí?
*I … akee*

**What's that?**
¿Qué es eso?
*keh ess esso*

**How much is it?**
¿Cuánto es?
*kwantoh ess*

**Where is the …?**
¿Dónde está el/la …?
*dondeh esta el/la*

**Is there wheelchair access?**
¿Hay acceso para sillas de ruedas?
*I akthesoh a parra seeyahs de rooedas*

**Are there facilities for the disabled?**
¿Hay acceso a minusválidos?
*I akthesoh a meenoosvaleedos*

**ABOUT ONESELF**

**I'm from …**
Soy de …
*soy deh*

**I'm … years old**
Tengo … años
*teng-goh … ahn-yoss*

**I'm a …**
Soy …
*soy*

**I'm married/divorced**
Estoy casado/divorciado
*estoy kas<u>a</u>doh/deevorss-y<u>a</u>h-doh*

**I'm single**
Soy soltero
*soy solt<u>ai</u>roh*

**I have … sisters/brothers/children**
Tengo … hermanas/hermanos/hijos
*t<u>e</u>ng-goh … airm<u>a</u>h-nass/airm<u>a</u>h-noss/<u>ee</u>-Hoss*

HELP, PROBLEMS

**Can you help me?**
¿Puede ayudarme?
*pw<u>e</u>h-deh ayood<u>a</u>rmeh*

**I don't understand**
No comprendo
*noh kompr<u>e</u>ndoh*

**Does anyone here speak English?**
¿Hay alguien aquí que hable inglés?
*i <u>a</u>lgyen ak<u>ee</u> keh <u>a</u>hbleh eengl<u>e</u>ss*

**I can't speak Spanish**
No hablo español
*noh <u>a</u>h-bloh esspan-y<u>o</u>ll*

**I don't know**
No sé
*noh seh*

**Please speak more slowly**
Por favor, hable más despacio
*por fa-v<u>o</u>r <u>a</u>h-bleh mass dessp<u>a</u>th-yoh*

**Please write it down for me**
Por favor, escríbamelo
*por fa-vor eskreeba-meh-loh*

**I've lost my way**
Me he perdido
*meh eh pairdeedoh*

**Go away!**
¡Váyase!
*vah-ya-seh*

## LIKES, DISLIKES, SOCIALIZING

**I like/love …**
Me gusta/encanta el/la …
*meh goosta/enkanta el/la*

**I don't like …**
No me gusta el/la …
*noh meh goosta el/la*

**I hate …**
Detesto …
*detestoh*

**Do you like …?**
¿Le gusta …?
*leh goosta*

**It's delicious/awful!**
¡Es delicioso/horrible!
*ess deleeth-yohsoh/orreebleh*

**I don't drink/smoke**
No bebo/fumo
*noh beboh/foomoh*

**Do you mind if I smoke?**
¿Le importa que fume?
*leh eemporta keh foomeh*

**What would you like (to drink)?**
¿Qué quiere (beber/tomar)?
*keh kyeh-reh bebair/tomar*

**I would like a ...**
Quería ...
*keh-ree-a*

**Nothing for me, thanks**
No quiero nada, gracias
*noh kyeh-roh nada grath-yass*

**Cheers!** *(toast)*
¡Salud!
*saloo*

---

### THINGS YOU'LL HEAR

| | |
|---|---|
| ¡adelante! | come in! |
| aquí tiene | here you are |
| ¡bien! | good! |
| ¡buen viaje! | have a good trip! |
| ¿cómo? | excuse me? |
| ¡cuánto lo siento! | I'm so sorry! |
| ¡cuidado! | look out! |
| de acuerdo | OK |
| de nada | you're welcome, don't mention it |
| eso es | that's right |
| ¡hasta luego! | goodbye! see you later! |
| ¡hola! | hello! hi! |
| muchas gracias | thank you very much |
| por favor | please |
| ¿qué ha dicho? | what did you say? |
| sírvase usted mismo | help yourself |

# DAYS, MONTHS, SEASONS

| | | |
|---|---|---|
| Sunday | domingo | *dom<u>ee</u>ngoh* |
| Monday | lunes | *l<u>oo</u>ness* |
| Tuesday | martes | *m<u>a</u>rtess* |
| Wednesday | miércoles | *my<u>ai</u>rkoh-less* |
| Thursday | jueves | *H<u>weh</u>-vess* |
| Friday | viernes | *vy<u>ai</u>rness* |
| Saturday | sábado | *s<u>a</u>bbadoh* |
| | | |
| January | enero | *enn<u>eh</u>-roh* |
| February | febrero | *febr<u>eh</u>-roh* |
| March | marzo | *m<u>a</u>rthoh* |
| April | abril | *abr<u>ee</u>l* |
| May | mayo | *m<u>a</u>yyoh* |
| June | junio | *H<u>oo</u>n-yoh* |
| July | julio | *H<u>oo</u>l-yoh* |
| August | agosto | *ag<u>o</u>stoh* |
| September | septiembre | *set-y<u>e</u>mbreh* |
| October | octubre | *okt<u>oo</u>breh* |
| November | noviembre | *nov-y<u>e</u>mbreh* |
| December | diciembre | *deeth-y<u>e</u>mbreh* |
| | | |
| Spring | primavera | *preema-v<u>eh</u>-ra* |
| Summer | verano | *ver<u>a</u>h-noh* |
| Fall | otoño | *ot<u>o</u>n-yoh* |
| Winter | invierno | *eemb-y<u>ai</u>rnoh* |
| | | |
| Christmas | Navidad | *navee-d<u>a</u>* |
| Christmas Eve | Nochebuena | *notcheh-bw<u>eh</u>-na* |
| Easter | Pascua, | *p<u>a</u>skwa,* |
| | Semana Santa | *sem<u>a</u>h-na s<u>a</u>nta* |
| Good Friday | Viernes Santo | *vy<u>ai</u>rness s<u>a</u>ntoh* |
| New Year | Año Nuevo | *<u>a</u>hn-yoh nw<u>eh</u>-voh* |
| New Year's Eve | Nochevieja | *notcheh-vy<u>eh</u>-Ha* |

349

# NUMBERS

| | | | | |
|---|---|---|---|---|
| 0 | cero *theh-roh* | 10 | diez *dyeth* |
| 1 | uno, una* *oonoh, oona* | 11 | once *ontheh* |
| 2 | dos *doss* | 12 | doce *doh-theh* |
| 3 | tres *tress* | 13 | trece *treh-theh* |
| 4 | cuatro *kwatroh* | 14 | catorce *katortheh* |
| 5 | cinco *theenkoh* | 15 | quince *keentheh* |
| 6 | seis *sayss* | 16 | dieciséis *dyeth-ee-sayss* |
| 7 | siete *see-eh-teh* | 17 | diecisiete *dyeth-ee-see-eh-teh* |
| 8 | ocho *otchoh* | 18 | dieciocho *dyeth-ee-otchoh* |
| 9 | nueve *nweh-veh* | 19 | diecinueve *dyeth-ee-nweh-veh* |

20 veinte *vaynteh*
21 veintiuno *vayntee-oonoh*
22 veintidós *vayntee-doss*
30 treinta *traynta*
31 treinta y uno *trayntı oonoh*
32 treinta y dos *trayntı doss*
40 cuarenta *kwarenta*
50 cincuenta *theen-kwenta*
60 sesenta *sessenta*
70 setenta *setenta*
80 ochenta *otchenta*
90 noventa *noh-venta*
100 cien *thyen*
110 ciento diez *thyentoh dyeth*
200 doscientos, doscientas *doss-thyentoss, doss-thyentass*
500 quinientos, quinientas *keen-yentoss, keen-yentass*
1,000 mil *meel*
1,000,000 un millón *mee-yon*

\* When **uno** precedes a masculine noun, it loses the final o, e.g. "1 point" is **un punto**. Feminine nouns take **una**, e.g. "1 bag," **una bolsa**. Numbers in the hundreds, 200, 300, etc., use the form ending in **-as** with feminine nouns, e.g. "300 notes," **trescientos billetes**; " 300 weeks," **trescientas semanas**.

# TIME

| | | |
|---|---|---|
| today | hoy | *oy* |
| yesterday | ayer | *ayyair* |
| tomorrow | mañana | *man-yah-na* |
| this week | esta semana | *esta semah-na* |
| next week | la semana que viene | *la semah-na keh vyeh-neh* |
| this morning | esta mañana | *esta man-yah-na* |
| this afternoon | esta tarde | *esta tardeh* |
| this evening | esta tarde/noche | *esta tardeh/notcheh* |
| tonight | esta noche | *esta notcheh* |
| last night | anoche | *annotcheh* |
| tomorrow morning | mañana por la mañana | *man-yah-na por la man-yah-na* |
| in three days | dentro de tres días | *dentroh deh tress dee-ass* |
| three days ago | hace tres días | *ah-theh tress dee-ass* |
| late | tarde | *tardeh* |
| early | temprano | *temprah-noh* |
| soon | pronto | *prontoh* |
| later on | más tarde | *mass tardeh* |
| at the moment | en este momento | *en esteh momentoh* |
| second | un segundo | *segoondoh* |
| minute | un minuto | *meenootoh* |
| quarter of an hour | un cuarto de hora | *kwartoh deh ora* |
| half an hour | media hora | *meh-dya ora* |
| three quarters of an hour | tres cuartos de hora | *tress kwartoss deh ora* |
| hour | la hora | *ora* |
| day | el día | *dee-a* |
| every day | todos los días | *todoss loss dee-ass* |
| the next day | al día siguiente | *al dee-a seegyenteh* |
| week | la semana | *semah-na* |
| month | el mes | *mess* |
| year | el año | *ahn-yoh* |

351

## TELLING TIME

"O'clock" is not normally translated in Spanish unless it is for emphasis, when **en punto** would be used. For example: (**es**) **la una** (**en punto**) is "(it's) one o'clock." The plural form of the verb is used for all other hours, eg (**son**) **las cinco** (**en punto**) is "(it's) five o'clock."

The word "past" is translated as **y** (= "and"). In order to express minutes after the hour, state the hour followed by **y** plus the number of minutes: so **las seis y diez** is "ten past six." The word "to" is translated as **menos** (= "less"). So, for example, **las diez menos veinte** is "twenty to ten." The word for "quarter" is **cuarto**; **las siete menos cuarto** is "quarter to seven" and **las cinco y cuarto** is "quarter past five." The half hour is expressed using **y media**, so **las seis y media** is "6:30."

The word "at" is translated as **a** followed by **las**. For example, **a las tres y cuarto** is "at quarter past three." Remember to change **las** to **la** when using "one," thus "at 1:30" becomes **a la una y media**.

| what time is it? | ¿qué hora es? | keh ora ess |
|---|---|---|
| am | de la mañana | deh la man-yah-na |
| pm (*up to 8 pm*) | de la tarde | deh la tardeh |
| (*from 8 pm*) | de la noche | deh la notcheh |
| one o'clock | la una | la oona |
| ten past one | la una y diez | la oona ee dyeth |
| quarter past one | la una y cuarto | la oona ee kwartoh |
| 1:30 | la una y media | la oona ee meh-dya |
| twenty to two | las dos menos veinte | lass doss meh-noss vaynteh |
| quarter to two | las dos menos cuarto | lass doss meh-noss kwartoh |
| two o'clock | las dos (en punto) | lass doss (en poontoh) |
| at seven o'clock | a las siete | a lass see-eh-teh |
| noon | mediodía | meh-dyoh dee-a |
| midnight | medianoche | meh-dya notcheh |

# COMMUNICATIONS

**Useful Words and Phrases**

| code | el prefijo | *preh-fee-Hoh* |
|---|---|---|
| collect call | una llamada a cobro revertido | *yamah-da a kobroh reh-vair-teedoh* |
| dial tone | la señal para marcar | *sen-yal parra markar* |
| email address | la dirección de email | *deerektheeon deh eemail* |
| emergency | una emergencia | *emmair-Henth-ya* |
| extension | extensión | *ekstenth-yon* |
| fax machine | el fax | *fax* |
| internet | el internet | *internet* |
| mobile phone | el teléfono móvil | *teh-leffonoh mohbeel* |
| number | el número | *noomeh-roh* |
| operator | la operadora | *opeh-radora* |
| phonecard | una tarjeta de teléfono | *tar-Heh-ta deh teh-leffonoh* |
| telephone | un teléfono | *teh-leffonoh* |
| website | la web site | *'web site'* |
| wrong number | el número equivocado | *noomeh-roh eh-keevoh-kah-doh* |

**Where is the nearest phone booth?**
¿Dónde está la cabina telefónica más cercana?
*dondeh esta la kabeena tehleh-fonnika mass thair-kah-na*

**I would like a number in …**
Quiero un número de …
*kyeh-roh oon noomeh-roh deh*

**I would like to speak to …**
Quería hablar con …
*keh-ree-a ablar kon*

**Hello, this is … speaking**
Hola, soy …
*oh-la soy*

**Could you leave him/her a message?**
¿Podría dejarle un recado?
*podree-a deh-Harleh oon reh-kah-doh*

**I'll call back later**
Volveré a llamar luego
*volveh-reh a yamar lweh-goh*

**What's your fax number/email address?**
¿Cual es su número de fax/dirección de email?
*kwal ess soo noomeh-roh deh fax/deerektheeon de eemail*

**May I use the photocopier/fax machine?**
¿Puedo usar la fotocopiadora/el fax
*pweh-doh oosar la fotokopeeadora/el fax*

---

### THINGS YOU'LL HEAR

**¿Con quién quiere que le ponga?**
Whom would you like to speak to?

**Se ha equivocado de número**
You've got the wrong number

**¿Quién es?**
Who's speaking?

**Al aparato/Al habla/Soy yo**
Speaking

**¿Cuál es su teléfono?**
What is your number?

**Lo siento, no está**
Sorry, he/she's not in

**Vuelva a llamar mañana, por favor**
Please call again tomorrow

**Le diré que le/la ha llamado usted**
I'll tell him/her you called

---

# EMERGENCIES

### Useful Words and Phrases

| | | |
|---|---|---|
| accident | un accidente | *akthee-denteh* |
| ambulance | una ambulancia | *amboolanth-ya* |
| breakdown | una avería | *aveh-ree-a* |
| burglary | un robo | *roh-boh* |
| crash | un accidente | *akthee-denteh* |
| emergency | una emergencia | *emair-Henth-ya* |
| fire | un fuego | *fwehgoh* |
| (*large*) | un incendio | *eenthend-yoh* |
| fire department | los bomberos | *bombeh-ross* |
| police | la policía | *poleethee-a* |
| police station | la comisaria | *kommeessaree-a* |

**Help!**
¡Socorro!
*sokorroh*

**Stop!**
¡Pare!
*pareh*

**Get an ambulance!**
¡Llame a una ambulancia!
*yah-meh a oona amboolanth-ya*

**Hurry up!**
¡Dése prisa!
*deh-seh preessa*

**My address is …**
Mi dirección es …
*mee deerekth-yon ess*

**My passport/car has been stolen**
Me han robado el pasaporte/el coche
*meh an robah-doh el passaporteh/el kotcheh*

# HOTELS

## Useful Words and Phrases

| | | |
|---|---|---|
| balcony | el balcón | bal-kon |
| bathroom | el cuarto de baño | kwartoh deh bahn-yoh |
| bed | la cama | kah-ma |
| bed and breakfast | alojamiento y desayuno | aloh-Hamyentoh ee dessa-yoonoh |
| bedroom | la habitación | abbee-tath-yon |
| breakfast | el desayuno | dessa-yoonoh |
| car park | el aparcamiento | aparkamyentoh |
| check | la cuenta | kwenta |
| dining room | el comedor | kommeh-dor |
| dinner | la cena | theh-na |
| double bed | la cama doble | kah-ma doh-bleh |
| double room | una habitación doble | abbee-tath-yon doh-bleh |
| elevator | el ascensor | ass-then-sor |
| full board | pensión completa | penss-yon kompleh-ta |
| guesthouse | la pensión | penss-yon |
| half board | media pensión | meh-dya penss-yon |
| hotel | el hotel | oh-tell |
| key | la llave | yah-veh |
| lunch | la comida | komee-da |
| maid | la camarera | kamareh-ra |
| manager | el director | deerek-tor |
| reception | la recepción | reh-thepth-yon |
| restroom | los servicios | vattair, retreh-teh |
| room | la habitación | abbee-tath-yon |
| room service | el servicio de habitaciones | sairveeth-yoh deh abbeetath-yoh-ness |
| shower | la ducha | dootcha |
| single bed | la cama individual | kah-ma eendeeveed-wal |
| single room | una habitación individual | abbee-tath-yon eendeeveed-wal |
| twin room | una habitación con dos camas | abbee-tath-yon kon doss kah-mass |

**Do you have any vacancies?**
¿Tienen alguna habitación libre?
*tyeh-nen algoona abbee-tath-yon leebreh*

**I have a reservation**
He hecho una reserva
*eh etchoh oona reh-sairva*

**I'd like a single room**
Quería una habitación individual
*keh-ree-a oona abbee-tath-yon eendeeveed-wal*

**I'd like a room with a balcony/bathroom**
Quería una habitación con balcón/cuarto de baño
*keh-ree-a oona abbee-tath-yon kon bal-kon/kwartoh deh bahn-yoh*

**Is there satellite/cable TV in the rooms?**
¿Hay televisión por satélite/por cable en las habitaciones?
*i televeeseeon por sateleete/por kable en las abblee-tath-yoh-ness*

**I'd like a room for one night/three nights**
Quería una habitación para una noche/para tres noches
*keh-ree-a oona abbee-tath-yon parra oona notcheh/parra tress notchess*

**What is the charge per night?**
¿Cuál es la tarifa por noche?
*kwal ess la tarreefa por notcheh*

**When is breakfast/dinner?**
¿A qué hora es el desayuno/la cena?
*a keh ora ess el dessa-yoonoh/la theh-na*

**Please wake me at … o'clock**
Haga el favor de llamarme a las …
*ah-ga el fa-vor deh yamar-meh a lass*

**May I have breakfast in my room?**
¿Pueden servirme el desayuno en mi habitación?
*pweh-den sair-veermeh el dessa-yoonoh en mee abbee-tath-yon*

**My room number is …**
El número de mi habitación es …
*el noomeh-roh deh mee abbee-tath-yon ess*

**There is no toilet paper in the bathroom**
No hay papel higiénico en el cuarto de baño
*noh I papel ee-Hyeneekoh en el kwartoh deh bahn-yoh*

**The window won't open**
No se puede abrir la ventana
*noh seh pweh-deh abreer la ventah-na*

**There isn't any hot water**
No hay agua caliente
*noh I ahg-wa kalyenteh*

**I'm leaving tomorrow**
Me marcho mañana
*meh martchoh man-yah-na*

**When do I have to vacate the room?**
¿A qué hora tengo que desocupar la habitación?
*a keh ora teng-goh keh dessokoopar la abbee-tath-yon*

**May I have the check, please?**
¿Me da la cuenta, por favor?
*meh da la kwenta por fa-vor*

**I'll pay by credit card**
Pagaré con tarjeta (de crédito)
*pagareh kon tar-Heh-ta deh kredeetoh*

**I'll pay cash**
Pagaré al contado
*pagareh al kontahdoh*

**Can you get me a taxi?**
¿Puede llamar a un taxi?
*pweh-deh yamar a oon taksee*

## THINGS YOU'LL SEE

| | |
|---|---|
| almuerzo | lunch |
| ascensor | elevator |
| completo | no vacancies |
| cuarto de baño | bathroom |
| cuenta | check |
| desayuno | breakfast |
| empujar | push |
| entrada | entrance |
| prohibida la entrada | no admission |
| prohibido el paso | staff only |
| salida de emergencia | emergency exit |
| servicio | restroom |
| tirar | pull |

## THINGS YOU'LL HEAR

**Lo siento, está lleno**
I'm sorry, we're full

**No nos quedan habitaciones individuales/dobles**
There are no single/double rooms left

**¿Para cuántas noches?**
For how many nights?

**¿Va a pagar al contado, o con tarjeta?**
Will you be paying by cash or credit card?

**Haga el favor de pagar por adelantado**
Please pay in advance

**Tiene que desocupar la habitación antes de las doce**
You must vacate the room by noon

# SHOPPING

**Excuse me, where is/are …?** *(in a supermarket)*
Por favor, ¿dónde está/están …?
*por fa-vor dondeh esta/estan*

**Do you have …?**
¿Tienen …?
*tyeh-nen*

**How much is this?**
¿Cuánto es esto?
*kwantoh ess estoh*

**Where do I pay?**
¿Dónde se paga?
*dondeh seh pah-ga*

**Do you take credit cards?**
¿Puedo pagar con tarjeta de crédito?
*pweh-doh pagar kon tar-Heh-ta deh kredeetoh*

**May I have a receipt?**
¿Me da un recibo?
*meh da oon retheeboh*

**Do you have anything less expensive?**
¿Tiene usted algo más barato?
*tyeh-neh oosteh algoh mass barah-toh*

**May I have a refund?**
¿Pueden devolverme el dinero?
*pweh-den deh-volvair-meh el deeneh-roh*

**That's fine. I'll take it**
Está bien. Me lo llevo
*esta byen. meh loh yeh-voh*

**It isn't what I wanted**
No es lo que yo quería
*noh ess loh keh yoh keh-ree-a*

# EATING OUT

You can eat in a variety of places:

| | |
|---|---|
| **Restaurante:** | These have an official rating (1–5 forks), but this depends more on the variety of dishes served than on the quality. |
| **Cafetería:** | Not to be confused with the American term. It is a combined bar, café, and restaurant. Service is provided at the counter or, for a little extra, at a table. There is usually a good variety of set menus at reasonable prices (look for **platos combinados**). |
| **Fonda:** | Offers inexpensive, good food that is representative of regional dishes. |
| **Hostería** or **Hostal:** | A restaurant that usually specializes in regional dishes. |
| **Parador:** | Belonging to the previously state-run hotels, they offer a first-rate service in select surroundings. |
| **Café** or **Bar:** | Both are general cafés selling all kinds of food and drink (again, they are not to be confused with American establishments of the same name). Well worth trying if you just want a quick snack. In some places, they serve free **tapas** (appetizers) with alcoholic drinks. Full meals are often available. |
| **Merendero:** | Outdoor **café** on the coast or in the country. Usually inexpensive and a good buy. |

Generally, breakfast in Spain is at 8 am, lunch is at 2 pm, and dinner (the main evening meal) is at 10 pm.

## USEFUL WORDS AND PHRASES

| beer | una cerveza | *thairveh-tha* |
|---|---|---|
| **bottle** | la botella | *boh-tay-ya* |
| **bread** | el pan | *pan* |
| **butter** | la mantequilla | *manteh-kee-ya* |

| | | |
|---|---|---|
| cake | un pastel | *pastell* |
| carafe | una jarra | *Harra* |
| check | la cuenta | *kwenta* |
| chef | el cocinero | *kothee-neh-roh* |
| children's portion | una ración especial para niños | *rath-yon espethyal parra neen-yoss* |
| coffee | el café | *kaffeh* |
| cup | la taza | *tah-tha* |
| dessert | el postre | *postreh* |
| fork | el tenedor | *teneh-dor* |
| glass | el vaso | *vah-soh* |
| half liter | medio litro | *meh-dyoh leetroh* |
| knife | el cuchillo | *kootchee-yoh* |
| main course | el segundo plato | *segoondoh plah-toh* |
| menu | la carta | *karta* |
| milk | la leche | *letcheh* |
| napkin | la servilleta | *sairvee-yeh-ta* |
| pepper | la pimienta | *peemyenta* |
| plate | el plato | *plah-toh* |
| receipt | un recibo | *retheeboh* |
| salt | la sal | *sal* |
| sandwich (Spanish) | un sandwich | *sand-weetch* |
| | un bocadillo | *boh-kadee-yoh* |
| soup | la sopa | *soh-pa* |
| spoon | la cuchara | *kootchah-ra* |
| starter | el primer plato | *primair plah-toh* |
| sugar | el azúcar | *athookar* |
| table | una mesa | *meh-sa* |
| tea | el té | *teh* |
| teaspoon | la cucharilla | *kootcha-ree-ya* |
| tip | una propina | *propeena* |
| waiter | el camarero | *kamma-reh-roh* |
| waitress | la camarera | *kamma-reh-ra* |
| water | el agua | *ahg-wa* |
| wine | el vino | *veenoh* |
| wine list | la carta de vinos | *karta deh veenoss* |

**A table for one, please**
Una mesa para una persona, por favor
_oona meh-sa parra oona pairsoh-na por fa-vor_

**A table for two/three, please**
Una mesa para dos/tres personas, por favor
_oona meh-sa parra doss/tress pairsoh-nass por fa-vor_

**Is there a highchair?**
¿Hay sillita de niño?
_see-yeeta deh neen-yo_

**May we see the menu/wine list?**
¿Nos trae la carta/la carta de vinos?
_noss trah-eh la karta/la karta deh veenoss_

**What would you recommend?**
¿Qué recomendaría usted?
_keh rekomenda-ree-a oosteh_

**I'd like …**
Quería …
_keh-ree-a_

**Just a cup of coffee, please**
Un café nada más, por favor
_oon kaffeh nah-da mass por fa-vor_

**I only want a snack**
Sólo quiero una comida ligera
_soh-loh kee-eh-roh oona kommeeda lee-Heh-ra_

**Is there a fixed-price menu?**
¿Hay menú del día?
_i meh-noo dell dee-a_

**A liter carafe of house red, please**
Una jarra de litro de tinto de la casa, por favor
_oona Harra deh leetroh deh teentoh deh la kah-sa por fa-vor_

**Do you have any vegetarian dishes?**
¿Tiene algún plato vegetariano?
*tyeh-neh algoon plah-toh veh-Hetaryah-noh*

**May we have some water?**
¿Nos trae agua, por favor?
*noss trah-eh ahg-wa por fa-vor*

**Can you warm this bottle/baby food for me?**
¿Podría calentar este biberón/comida para niño?
*po-dreea kalentar este beeberon/komeeda parra neen-yoh*

**Waiter/waitress!**
¡Oiga, por favor!
*oy-gah por fa-vor*

**I didn't order this**
No he pedido esto
*noh eh pedeedoh estoh*

**May we have some more …?**
¿Nos trae más …?
*noss trah-eh mass*

**May I have another knife/fork?**
¿Me trae otro cuchillo/tenedor?
*meh trah-eh otroh kootchee-yoh/teneh-dor*

**May we have the check, please?**
¿Nos trae la cuenta, por favor?
*noss trah-eh la kwenta por fa-vor*

**May I have a receipt, please?**
¿Me puede dar un recibo, por favor?
*meh pweh-deh dar oon retheeboh por fa-vor*

**The meal was very good, thank you**
La comida ha sido muy buena, gracias
*la kommeeda a seedoh mwee bweh-na grath-yass*

# MENU GUIDE

aceitunas olives
aguacate avocado
ahumados smoked fish
ajo garlic
albaricoques apricots
albóndigas meatballs
alcachofas artichokes
alcaparras capers
almejas clams
almendras almonds
alubias con … beans with …
anchoas anchovies
anguila eel
arenque herring
arroz rice
arroz con leche rice pudding
asados roasted meat
atún tuna
avellanas hazelnuts
azúcar sugar
bacalao cod
batido milk shake
bebidas drinks
berenjenas eggplant
besugo al horno baked sea bream
bistec de ternera veal steak
bizcochos sponge fingers
bonito al horno baked tuna
bonito con tomate tuna with tomato
boquerones fritos fried anchovies
brazo gitano swiss roll
brevas figs
buñuelos light fried pastries
cachelada pork stew
calabacines zucchini
calabaza pumpkin
calamares squid
caldeirada fish soup

caldereta gallega vegetable stew
caldo de … … soup
camarones baby shrimp
canelones cannelloni
cangrejos de río river crabs
caracoles snails
caramelos candies
carnes meats
carro de queso cheese board
castañas chestnuts
cebolla onion
cebolletas spring onions
centollo spider crab
cerezas cherries
cerveza beer
cesta de frutas a selection of fresh fruits
champiñón mushrooms
chanquetes fish (similar to whitebait)
chipirones baby squid
chirimoyas custard apples
chocos squid
chuleta chop
chuletón large chop
churros deep-fried pastry strips
cigalas crayfish
ciruelas plums, greengages
ciruelas pasas prunes
cochinillo asado roasted suckling pig
cocido stew made with meat, chickpeas,
    and vegetables
cocktail de bogavante lobster cocktail
cocochas (de merluza) hake stew
codornices quail
col cabbage
coles de Bruselas Brussels sprouts
coliflor cauliflower
conejo asado roast rabbit
congrio conger eel

**contra de ternera con guisantes** veal stew with peas
**contrafilete de ternera** veal fillet
**copa ... ...** cup, glass of wine
**cordero asado** roasted lamb
**cordero chilindrón** lamb stew with onion, tomato, peppers, and eggs
**costillas de cerdo** pork ribs
**crema catalana** crème brûlée
**crema de cangrejos** cream of crab soup
**crema de espárragos** cream of asparagus soup
**crema de legumbres** cream of vegetable soup
**crocante** ice cream with chopped nuts
**croquetas** croquettes
**cuajada** curds
**dátiles** dates
**embutidos** sausages
**empanada gallega** fish pie
**empanada santiaguesa** fish pie
**empanadillas de bonito** small tuna pies
**empanadillas de carne** small meat pies
**ensalada** salad
**entrecot a la parrilla** broiled entrecôte
**entrecot de ternera** veal entrecôte
**escalope a la milanesa** breaded veal with cheese
**escalope a la plancha** broiled veal
**escalope de lomo de cerdo** escalope of pork fillet
**escalope de ternera** veal scallop
**escalope empanado** breaded scallops
**espadín a la toledana** kabob
**espaguetis italiana** spaghetti
**espárragos** asparagus
**espinacas** spinach
**estofado de ... ...** stew
**fabada (asturiana)** bean stew with sausage
**faisán** pheasant

**fiambres** cold meats
**fideos** thin pasta, noodles
**flan** crème caramel
**fresas con nata** strawberries and cream
**fruta** fruit
**gallina en pepitoria** chicken stewed with peppers
**gambas** shrimp
**garbanzos** chickpeas
**gazpacho andaluz** cold tomato soup from Andalusia
**gelatina de ... ...** gelatin
**gratén de ... ...** au gratin (baked in a cream and cheese sauce)
**grelo** turnip
**guisantes con jamón** peas with ham
**guisantes salteados** sautéed peas
**habas** broad beans
**habichuelas** beans
**helado** ice cream
**hígado** liver
**higos con miel y nueces** figs with honey and nuts
**higos secos** dried figs
**horchata (de chufas)** cold almond-flavored milk drink
**huevos** eggs
**huevos escalfados** poached eggs
**huevos fritos** fried eggs
**huevos rellenos** stuffed eggs
**huevos revueltos** scrambled eggs
**jamón** ham
**jerez** sherry
**judías verdes** green beans
**jugo** juice
**langosta** lobster
**langostinos** jumbo shrimp
**laurel** bay leaves
**leche frita** egg and milk pudding
**leche merengada** cold milk with meringues

lechuga lettuce
lengua tongue
lenguado sole
lentejas lentils
liebre estofada stewed hare
lombarda rellena stuffed red cabbage
lombarda salteada sautéed red cabbage
lomo curado pork loin sausage
lonchas de jamón sliced, cured ham
longaniza cooked Spanish sausage
lubina sea bass
macarrones macaroni
macedonia de fruta fruit salad
manises peanuts
manitas de cordero lamb shank
manos de cerdo pigs' feet
mantecadas small sponge cakes
mantequilla butter
manzanas apples
mariscada cold mixed shellfish
mariscos del día fresh shellfish
mariscos del tiempo seasonal shellfish
medallones de anguila eel steaks
medallones de merluza hake steaks
mejillones mussels
melocotón peach
melón melon
membrillo quince jelly
menestra de legumbres vegetable stew
menú de la casa set menu
menú del día menu of the day
merluza hake
mermelada jam
mero grouper (type of fish)
morcilla blood sausage
morros de cerdo pigs' cheeks
morros de vaca cows' cheeks
mortadela salami-type sausage
morteruelo kind of pâté
nabo turnip
naranjas oranges

natillas cold custard
níscalos wild mushrooms
nísperos medlars (similar to crab apple)
nueces walnuts
paella fried rice with various seafood
and chicken
paella castellana meat paella
paella de marisco shellfish paella
paella de pollo chicken paella
paella valenciana shellfish, rabbit, and
chicken paella
paleta de cordero lechal shoulder of
lamb
pan bread
pan de higos dried fig cake with
cinnamon
panache de verduras vegetable stew
panceta bacon
parrillada de caza mixed broiled game
parrillada de mariscos mixed broiled
shellfish
pasas raisins
pastel de ... ... cake
pastel de ternera veal pie
pasteles cakes
patatas potatoes
patatas fritas french fries
patitos rellenos stuffed duckling
pato duck
pavo turkey
pecho de ternera breast of veal
pechuga de pollo breast of chicken
pepinillos pickles
pepino cucumber
peras pears
perdices partridges
perejil parsley
pescaditos fritos fried fish
pestiños sugared pastries flavored
with aniseed
pez espada ahumado smoked swordfish

picadillo de ternera ground veal
pimienta black pepper
pimientos peppers
pimientos morrones bell peppers
pimientos rellenos stuffed peppers
pimientos verdes green peppers
piña pineapple
pinchos morunos kabobs
piñones pine nuts
pisto fried mixed vegetables
pisto manchego vegetable marrow with
  onion and tomato
plátanos bananas
pollo chicken
pomelo grapefruit
potaje castellano thick broth
potaje de garbanzos chickpea stew
potaje de habichuelas white bean stew
potaje de lentejas lentil stew
puchero canario casserole of meat,
  chickpeas, and corn
pulpitos con cebolla baby octopus with
  onions
pulpo octopus
puré de patatas mashed potatoes
purrusalda cod with leeks and potatoes
queso cheese
quisquillas shrimp
rábanos radish
rape monkfish
raya skate
remolacha beets
repollo cabbage
requesón cream cheese, cottage cheese
revuelto scrambled eggs
riñones kidneys
rodaballo turbot (fish)
romero rosemary
roscas sweet pastries
sal salt
salchichas sausages

salchichas de Frankfurt hot dogs
salchichón white sausage with pepper
salmón salmon
salmonetes red mullet
salsa sauce
salsa allioli/ali oli mayonnaise with
  garlic
sandía watermelon
sardinas sardines
setas a la plancha broiled mushrooms
setas rellenas stuffed mushrooms
sobreasada soft red sausage with
  cayenne pepper
solomillo fillet steak
solomillo frío cold roasted beef
sopa soup
sopa castellana vegetable soup
sopa de gallina chicken soup
sopa mallorquina soup with tomato,
  meat, and eggs
sopa sevillana fish soup
sorbete sorbet
tallarines noodles
tarta cake
tencas tench
ternera asada roasted veal
tocinillos del cielo crème caramel
tomates rellenos stuffed tomatoes
tomillo thyme
tordo thrush
torrijas sweet pastries
tortilla Alaska baked Alaska
tortilla Spanish omelette
tournedó tournedos (fillet steak)
trucha trout
turrón nougat
uvas grapes
vieiras scallops
zanahorias carrots
zarzuela de mariscos seafood stew
zumo de ... ... juice

# SWEDISH

## CONTENTS

INTRODUCTION 370

USEFUL PHRASES 371

DAYS, MONTHS, SEASONS 377

NUMBERS 378

TIME 379

COMMUNICATIONS 381

HOTELS 384

SHOPPING 388

EATING OUT 389

MENU GUIDE 393

# INTRODUCTION

## Pronunciation

When reading the imitated pronunciation, stress the part that is underlined. Pronounce each syllable as if it formed part of an English word, and you will be understood sufficiently well. Remember the points below, and your pronunciation will be even closer to the correct Swedish.

| | |
|---|---|
| *ai* | as in "fair" or "stair" |
| *ew* | like the sound in "dew" |
| *EW* | try to say "ee" with your lips rounded |
| *oo* | as in "book" or "soot" |
| *OO* | as in "spoon" or "groom" |
| *r* | should be strongly pronounced |

## Swedish Alphabetical Order

In the lists of *Things You'll See* and in the Menu Guide, we have followed Swedish alphabetical order. The following letters are listed after z: å, ä, ö.

## "You"

There are two words for **you**: **du** and **ni**. Ni is the polite form; **du** is the familiar form. But unlike in some other European countries, it is not necessarily impolite to address a complete stranger with the familiar form. In fact many Swedes consider the polite form to be old-fashioned. In many cases in this book, we have given you a choice.

## The Definite/Indefinite Articles

The most common form of the definite article ("the") in Swedish is as a suffix (eg **en**, **et**) added to the end of a word. When you see translations given in the form **hus**(et) or **bil**(en), the form **huset** will mean "the house" and **bilen** "the car." "A house" is **ett hus** and "a car" is **en bil**.

## USEFUL PHRASES

**Yes/no**
Ja/nej
*yah/nay*

**Thank you**
Tack
*tack*

**No, thank you**
Nej tack
*nay tack*

**Please** *(offering)*          *(asking for something, accepting something)*
Varsågod                 Tack
*vahrshawgood*            *tack*

**I don't understand**
Jag förstår inte
*yah furshtawr inteh*

**Do you speak English/French/German?**
Talar du engelska/franska/tyska?
*tahlar dEW engelska/franska/tEWska*

**I can't speak Swedish**
Jag talar inte svenska
*yah tahlar inteh svenska*

**I don't know**
Jag vet inte

*yah veat inteh*

**Please speak more slowly**
Kan du/ni tala långsammare, tack
*kan dew/nee tahla lawngssamareh tack*

**Please write it down for me**
Var snäll och skriv upp det för mig
*vahr snell ock skreev ewp deat fur may*

**My name is …**
Jag heter …
*yah heater*

**How do you do, pleased to meet you**
Hej, trevligt att träffas
*hay, treavligt att treffas*

**Good morning/good afternoon/good evening**
God morgon/goddag/god afton
*goo morron/goodahg/goo afton*

**Good night** *(when going to bed)*
Godnatt
*goonatt*

**Goodbye**
Adjö; *(informal word)* hejdå
*ahyur; haydaw*

**How are you?**
Hur mår du?
*hewr mawr dew*

**Excuse me, please**
Ursäkta
*ewrshekta*

**Sorry!**
Förlåt!
*furrlawt*

**I'm really sorry**
Jag är mycket ledsen
*yah air mEwkeh layssen*

**Can you help me?**
Kan du hjälpa mig?
*kan dEW yelpa may*

**Can you tell me …?**
Kan du säga mig …?
*kan dEW saya may*

**May I have …?**
Kan jag få …?
*kan yah faw*

**I would like a …**
Jag skulle vilja ha en/ett …
*yah skewleh vilya hah ehn/ett*

**Would you like a …?**
Vill du/ni ha en/ett …?
*vill dEW/nee hah ehn/ett*

**Is there … here?**
Finns det en/ett … här?
*finnss day ehn/ett … hair*

**Where can I get …?**
Var kan jag få …?
*vahr kan yah faw*

**How much is it?**
Hur mycket kostar det?
*hEwr mEwkeh kostar deat*

**What time is it?**
Hur mycket är klockan?
*hEwr mEwkeh air klockan*

**I must go now**
Jag måste gå nu
*yah mawsteh gaw nEW*

**I've lost my way**
Jag har tappat bort mig
*yah har tappat bort may*

**I've lost my passport/room key/traveler's checks**
Jag har förlorat mit pass/min rumsnyckel/mina resecheckar
*yah har furlorat mitt pass/min rewmssnEWckel/mina reasecheckar*

**Cheers!** *(toast)*
Skål!
*skawl*

**Do you take credit cards?**
Tar ni kreditkort?
*tahr ni kredeetkoort*

**Where is the restroom?**
Var är toaletten?
*vahr air too-aletten*

**Excellent!**
Utmärkt!
*EWtmerkt*

## THINGS YOU'LL HEAR

| | |
|---|---|
| adjö | goodbye |
| akta dig! | look out! |
| bra | good |
| förlåt | sorry |
| hej | hi; hello |
| hej, trevligt att träffas | how do you do, nice to meet you |
| hur står det till? | how are you? |
| hursa? | excuse me? |
| ja | yes |
| jag förstår inte | I don't understand |
| jag vet inte | I don't know |
| just det | that's right |
| lycklig resa | bon voyage |
| nej | no |
| stig in | get in |
| tack | thanks |
| tack, bra | very well, thank you |
| tack så mycket | thank you very much |
| ursäkta | excuse me |
| varsågod | please; you're welcome; here you are |
| vi ses senare | see you later |
| välkommen | welcome |

## THINGS YOU'LL SEE

| | |
|---|---|
| att hyra | to rent |
| damer | women |
| drag | pull |
| ej ... | no ..., do not ... |
| ej ingång/utgång | no entrance/exit |
| fritt inträde | admission free |
| fullsatt | no vacancies |

→

| | |
|---|---|
| förbjudet | forbidden |
| gata | street |
| herrar | men |
| hiss | elevator |
| ingång | entrance |
| inte | not |
| kassa | cash register, sales counter |
| korvkiosk | hot dog stand |
| ledigt | vacant/free |
| livsfara | danger |
| luciadagen | St Lucia's Day (13th December) |
| lägenhet att hyra | apartment for rent |
| nymålat | wet paint |
| nödutgång | emergency exit |
| polis | police |
| privat | private |
| rabatt | reduced prices |
| rea | sale |
| reserverad | reserved |
| semesterstängt | closed for holidays |
| skjut | push |
| stängt | closed |
| till salu | for sale |
| tillträde förbjudet | no admittance |
| toaletter | restrooms |
| tystnad | silence, quiet |
| upplysningar | information |
| upptaget | occupied |
| utförsäljning | sale |
| utgång | exit |
| utsålt | sold out |
| väg | road |
| öppet | open |

# DAYS, MONTHS, SEASONS

| Sunday | söndag | *s<u>u</u>rndahg* |
|---|---|---|
| Monday | måndag | *m<u>a</u>wndahg* |
| Tuesday | tisdag | *t<u>ee</u>ssdahg* |
| Wednesday | onsdag | *<u>oo</u>nssdahg* |
| Thursday | torsdag | *t<u>oo</u>rshdahg* |
| Friday | fredag | *fr<u>a</u>ydahg* |
| Saturday | lördag | *l<u>u</u>rrdahg* |

| January | januari | *y<u>a</u>newahree* |
|---|---|---|
| February | februari | *f<u>e</u>brewahree* |
| March | mars | *m<u>a</u>hrsh* |
| April | april | *ahpr<u>ee</u>l* |
| May | maj | *m<u>a</u>h-ee* |
| June | juni | *y<u>EW</u>nee* |
| July | juli | *y<u>EW</u>lee* |
| August | augusti | *ahg<u>ew</u>stee* |
| September | september | *sept<u>e</u>mberr* |
| October | oktober | *okt<u>oo</u>berr* |
| November | november | *noov<u>e</u>mberr* |
| December | december | *dess<u>e</u>mberr* |

| Spring | vår | *vawr* |
|---|---|---|
| Summer | sommar | *s<u>o</u>mmahr* |
| Fall | höst | *hurst* |
| Winter | vinter | *v<u>i</u>nter* |

| Christmas | jul | *yEWl* |
|---|---|---|
| Christmas Eve | julafton | *y<u>EW</u>lafton* |
| Good Friday | långfredag | *l<u>a</u>wngfraydahg* |
| Easter | påsk | *pawsk* |
| Pentecost | pingst | *pingst* |
| New Year | nyår | *n<u>EW</u>-awr* |
| New Year's Eve | nyårsafton | *n<u>EW</u>-awrsh-afton* |
| Midsummer | midsommarafton | *m<u>i</u>dsommahrafton* |

# NUMBERS

| | | | |
|---|---|---|---|
| 0 | noll *noll* | 5 | fem *fem* |
| 1 | ett *ett* | 6 | sex *sex* |
| 2 | två *tvaw* | 7 | sju *shEW* |
| 3 | tre *tray* | 8 | åtta *otta* |
| 4 | fyra *fEWra* | 9 | nio *nee-oo* |

10 tio *tee-oo*
11 elva *elva*
12 tolv *tolv*
13 tretton *tretton*
14 fjorton *f-yoorton*
15 femton *femton*
16 sexton *sexton*
17 sjutton *shewton*
18 arton *ahrton*
19 nitton *nitton*
20 tjugo *chEWgoo*
21 tjugoett *chEWgo-ett*
22 tjugotvå *chEWgo-tvaw*
30 trettio *tretti*
31 trettioett *tretti-ett*
32 trettiotvå *tretti-tvaw*
40 fyrtio *furrti*
50 femtio *femti*
60 sextio *sexti*
70 sjuttio *shewti*
80 åttio *otti*
90 nittio *nitti*
100 (ett) hundra *(ett) hewndra*
110 (ett) hundratio *(ett) hewndra-teeoo*
200 tvåhundra *tvawhewndra*
1,000 (ett) tusen *(ett) tEWssen*
100,000 (ett) hundra tusen *(ett) hewndra tEWssen*
1,000,000 en miljon *ayn milyoon*

# TIME

| today | i dag | *ee dahg* |
|---|---|---|
| yesterday | i går | *ee gawr* |
| tomorrow | i morgon | *ee morron* |
| the day before yesterday | i förrgår | *ee furrgawr* |
| the day after tomorrow | i övermorgon | *ee urvermorron* |
| this week | den här veckan | *dayn hair veckan* |
| last week | förra veckan | *furra veckan* |
| next week | nästa vecka | *nesta vecka* |
| this morning | i morse | *ee morsheh* |
| this afternoon | i eftermiddag | *ee eftermiddahg* |
| this evening | i kväll | *ee kvell* |
| tonight | i natt | *ee natt* |
| yesterday afternoon | i går eftermiddag | *ee gawr eftermiddahg* |
| last night | i går kväll | *ee gawr kvell* |
| tomorrow morning | i morgon bitti | *ee morron bittee* |
| tomorrow night | i morgon kväll | *ee morron kvell* |
| in three days | om tre dagar | *om trea dahgar* |
| three days ago | för tre dagar sedan | *furr trea dahgar seadan* |
| late | sen | *sean* |
| early | tidig | *teedig* |
| soon | snart | *snahrt* |
| later on | senare | *seanareh* |
| at the moment | just nu | *yewst NEW* |
| second | en sekund | *sekewnd* |
| minute | en minut | *meenEWt* |
| two minutes | två minuter | *tvaw meenEWter* |
| quarter of an hour | en kvart | *ehn kvahrt* |
| half an hour | en halvtimme | *ehn halvtimmeh* |
| three quarters of an hour | tre kvart | *trea kvahrt* |

| hour | en timme | *timmeh* |
|---|---|---|
| every day | varje dag | *vahryeh dahg* |
| all day | hela dagen | *heala dahgen* |
| the next day | nästa dag | *nesta dahg* |
| week | vecka | *vecka* |
| month | månad | *mawnad* |
| year | år | *awr* |

## TELLING TIME

Sweden conforms to Central European time, which is one hour ahead of GMT. The Swedes put their clocks forward by an hour from the end of March until the end of October.

In telling the time it is important to note that, instead of saying "half past" an hour, the Swedes refer to the next hour coming (for example, "half past one" is said in Swedish as "half two"). Also, the 24-hour clock is commonly used, both in the written form, as in timetables, and verbally, as when using an information desk or when making appointments.

| am | förmiddag(en) | *furmiddahg* |
|---|---|---|
| pm | eftermiddag(en) | *eftermiddahg* |
| one o'clock | klockan ett | *klockan ett* |
| ten past one | tio över ett | *teeoo urver ett* |
| quarter past one | kvart över ett | *kvahrt urver ett* |
| half past one | halv två | *halv tvaw* |
| twenty to two | tjugo i två | *chewgoo ee tvaw* |
| quarter to two | kvart i två | *kvahrt ee tvaw* |
| two o'clock | klockan två | *klockan tvaw* |
| 13:00 | klockan tretton | *klockan tretton* |
| 16:30 | sexton och trettio | *sexton ock tretti* |
| at half past five | halv sex | *halv sex* |
| at seven o'clock | klockan sju | *klockan shEW* |
| noon | klockan tolv | *klockan tolv* |
| midnight | midnatt | *meednatt* |

# COMMUNICATIONS

## Useful Words and Phrases

| | | |
|---|---|---|
| **code** | riktnummer | riktnewmer |
| **collect call** | b-a samtal (-numret) | bea-ah samtahl |
| **dial tone** | kopplingston | kopplingston |
| **email address** | email-adress | ee-mail adress |
| **emergency** | nödfall | nurdfall |
| **extension** | anknytning(en) | ank-nEWtning |
| **mobile phone** | mobiltelefon(en) | mobiltelefawn |
| **number** | nummer (numret) | newmer |
| **operator** | växel(n) | vexel |
| *(in hotel)* | telefonist(en) | telefawneest |
| **phonecard** | telefonkort(et) | telefawnkoort |
| **telephone** | en telefon | telefawn |
| **telephone booth** | en telefonkiosk | telefawn-cheeosk |
| **wrong number** | fel nummer | fayl newmer |

### Where is the nearest phone booth?
Var finns närmaste telefonkiosk?
*vahr finnss nairmasteh telefawn-cheeosk*

### I would like a number in …
Jag skulle vilja ha ett nummer i …
*yah skewleh vilya hah ett newmer ee*

### I would like to speak to …
Kan jag få tala med …?
*kan yah faw tahla med*

### My number is …
Mitt nummer är …
*mitt newmer air*

**Could you leave him a message?**
Får jag lämna ett meddelande?
*fawr yah lemna ett meadealandeh*

**I'll call back later**
Jag ringer senare
*yah ringer seanareh*

**What's your fax number/email address?**
Vad har du för faxnummer/email-adress?
*vahd hahr dew fur faxnewmmer/ee-mail adress*

**May I send an email/fax from here?**
Kan jag skicka et email/fax härifrån?
*kan yah skicka ett eemail/fax hair-eefrawn*

---

### THINGS YOU'LL SEE

| | |
|---|---|
| direktval | direct dialing |
| email | email |
| email addres | email address |
| faxmaskin | fax machine |
| information | inquiries |
| internationell | international |
| internationellt samtal | international call |
| i olag | out of order |
| lokalsamtal | local call |
| lyft luren | lift receiver |
| nödsamtal | emergency call |
| rikssamtal | long-distance call |
| riktnummer | code |
| Tele | public telephone office |
| telefonsvarare | answering machine |
| telefonkiosk | telephone booth |
| websida | website |

## THINGS YOU'LL HEAR

**Vem vill du tala med?**
Whom would you like to speak to?

**Du har fått fel nummer**
You've got the wrong number

**Vem är det som talar?**
Who's speaking?

**Jag kopplar vidare**
I'll put you through

**Vad har du for nummer?**
What is your number?

**Tyvärr, han är inte anträffbar**
Sorry, he's not in

**Han kommer tillbaka klockan …**
He'll be back at … o'clock

**Ring på nytt i morgon**
Please call again tomorrow

**Jag skall meddela honom att du har ringt**
I'll tell him you called

**Tyvärr är alla linjer upptagna**
Sorry, all lines are busy

**Försök på nytt senare**
Please try later

# HOTELS

## USEFUL WORDS AND PHRASES

| | | |
|---|---|---|
| balcony | en balkong | *balkong* |
| bathroom | ett badrum | *bahdrewm* |
| bed | en säng | *seng* |
| bedroom | ett sovrum | *sawvrewm* |
| breakfast | frukost(en) | *frewkost* |
| check | räkning(en) | *raikning* |
| dining room | matsal(en) | *mahtssahl* |
| dinner | middag | *middahg* |
| double room | ett dubbelrum | *doobelrewm* |
| elevator | en hiss | *hiss* |
| full board | helpension | *haylpangshoon* |
| half board | halvpension | *halvpangshoon* |
| hotel | ett hotell | *hootell* |
| key | nyckel(n) | *newckel* |
| lobby | lobby(n) | *lobbee* |
| lounge | sällskapsrum(met) | *sellskahps-rewm* |
| lunch | lunch(en) | *lewnch* |
| manager | direktör(en) | *direkturr* |
| reception | reception(en) | *resseptshoon* |
| receptionist | receptionist(en) | *ressept-shooneest* |
| restaurant | en restaurang | *restawrang* |
| restroom | en toalett | *too-alett* |
| room | ett rum | *rewm* |
| room service | rumsbetjäning(en) | *rewmss-bechaining* |
| shower | en dusch | *dewsh* |
| single room | ett enkelrum | *enkelrewm* |
| twin room | ett rum med två sängar | *rewm med tvaw sengar* |

**Do you have any vacancies?**
Har ni några lediga rum?
*hahr nee noorgra laydiga rewm*

**I have a reservation**
Jag har beställt rum
*yah hahr bestellt rewm*

**I'd like a single/double room**
Jag skulle vilja ha ett enkelrum/dubbelrum
*yah skewleh vilya hah ett enkelrewm/doobelrewm*

**I'd like a room with a bathroom/balcony**
Jag skulle vilja ha ett rum med bad/balkong
*yah skewleh vilya hah ett rewm med bahd/balkong*

**I'd like a room for one night/three nights**
Jag skulle vilja ha ett rum för en natt/tre nätter
*yah skewleh vilya hah ett rewm furr ehn natt/tray netter*

**Is there satellite/cable TV in the rooms?**
Finns det satellit/kabel TV på rummen?
*finns deat sateleet/kahbel teavea paw rewmmen*

**What is the charge per night?**
Vad kostar det per natt?
*vah kostar deat pair natt*

**Is there wheelchair access?**
Är det rullstolsvänligt?
*air deat rewllstoolsvainligt*

**Are there facilities for the disabled?**
Är det anpassat för rörelsehindrade?
*air deat anpassat fur rurelsehindrade*

**When is breakfast/dinner?**
När serveras frukosten/middagen?
*nair sairvearass frewkosten/middahgen*

**Please call me at … o'clock**
Kan ni/du väcka mig klockan … tack
*kan nee/dEW vaikka may klockan … tack*

**May I have breakfast in my room?**
Kan jag få frukost på rummet?
*kan yah faw frewkost paw rewmmet*

**My room number is …**
Mitt rumsnummer är …
*mitt rewmss-newmmer ay*

**I'm leaving tomorrow**
Jag reser i morgon
*yah raysser ee morron*

**May I have the check, please?**
Kan jag få räkningen?
*kan yah faw raikningen*

**I'll pay by credit card**
Jag betalar med kreditkort
*yah betahlar med kredeetkoort*

**I'll pay cash**
Jag betalar kontant
*yah betahlar kontant*

**Can you get me a taxi?**
Kan jag få en taxi?
*kan yah faw ehn taxee*

## THINGS YOU'LL SEE

| | |
|---|---|
| bottenvåning | ground floor |
| drag | pull |
| fullbelagt, fullbokat | no vacancies |
| nödutgång | emergency exit |
| rum med frukost | bed and breakfast |
| räkning | check |
| skjut, tryck | push |

## THINGS YOU'LL HEAR

**Tyvärr, vi är fullbokade**
I'm sorry, we're full

**Vi har inga lediga enkelrum/dubbelrum**
There are no single rooms/double rooms left

**För hur många nätter?**
For how many nights?

**För hur många personer?**
For how many people?

**Hur betalar ni?**
How will you be paying?

**Fyll i den här blanketten**
Please fill in this form

**Var snäll och skriv under här**
Please sign your name here

**Var vänlig och betala i förskott**
Please pay in advance

# SHOPPING

**Where is the … department?**
Var ligger … avdelningen?
*vahr ligger … ahvdealningen*

**Do you have …?**
Har du/ni …?
*hahr dEW/nee*

**How much is this?**
Hur mycket kostar den här?
*hEWr mEWkeh kostar dehn hair*

**Do you have any more of these?**
Har du/ni fler av den här sorten?
*hahr dEW/nee flear ahv dehn hair sorten*

**Where do I pay?**
Var kan jag betala?
*vahr kan yah betahla*

**Do you have anything less expensive?**
Finns det någonting billigare?
*finnss deat nawgonting billigareh*

**May I have a receipt?**
Kan jag få ett kvitto, tack?
*kan yah faw ett kvitto, tack*

**May I have a refund?**
Kan jag få pengarna tillbaka?
*kan yah faw pengarna tillbahka*

**I'm just looking**
Jag ser mig bara omkring
*yah sear may bahra omkring*

# EATING OUT

Swedish restaurants range from the expense-account variety to smallish cafeterias. Look for the **dagens rätt** (*dahgens rett*), the special dish of the day, which usually includes a main course, salad, soft drink, and coffee.

The gratuity is always included in the check, so any additional tipping is up to you.

You should try the traditional **smörgåsbord** (*smurrgawssboord*) but, to do it justice, choose a day when you have a hearty appetite. You start off with herring or some other salt fish, move on to cold meats and salads then to hot dishes. Athough there is no dessert as such, you can finish off with cheeses and fruit.

In most towns you'll find fast food outlets serving hamburgers and pizzas. A typical Swedish institution is the **korvkiosk**, a hot-dog stand, open very late, serving different varieties of hamburgers and hot dogs.

The Swedes eat early. Lunch starts around 11:30 and dinner from 5 pm (or 7–8 pm if you are eating out).

Beer is Sweden's favorite drink and it comes in three categories: **lättöl** (*letturl*) which is class I, the weakest; **mellanöl** (*mellanurl*) or **folköl** (*follkurl*), which is class II and the most popular; and **starköl**, which is class III and the strongest. **Snaps** is an aquavit flavored with various herbs and drunk ice-cold, and **punsch** is a sweet arrack liqueur served with coffee after dinner. If you are not in a restaurant, alcoholic beverages – apart from **lättöl**, which can be bought from grocery shops – are sold only by state-controlled shops called **Systembolaget** (*sewsteamboolahget*). You have to be at least 20 years old in order to be able to shop in these.

## USEFUL WORDS AND PHRASES

| | | |
|---|---|---|
| **beer** | en öl | *url* |
| **bottle** | en flaska | *flaska* |
| **cake** | tårta(n) | *tawrta* |
| **check** | nota(n) | *noota* |

| | | |
|---|---|---|
| coffee | kaffe(t) | *kaffeh* |
| cup | kopp(en) | *kopp* |
| dessert | efterätt | *efterett* |
| fork | gaffel(n) | *gaffel* |
| glass | ett glas | *glahss* |
| knife | kniv(en) | *k-neev* |
| main course | huvudrätt | *hEWvEWdrett* |
| menu | meny(n), | *menEW,* |
| | matsedel(n) | *mahtseadel* |
| milk | mjölk(en) | *m-yurlk* |
| napkin | en servett | *sairvett* |
| plate | tallrik(en) | *tallreek* |
| receipt | kvitto(t) | *kvitto* |
| sandwich | en smörgås | *smurrgawss* |
| snack | matbit(en) | *mahtbeet* |
| soup | soppa(n) | *soppa* |
| spoon | sked(en) | *shead* |
| starter | förätt | *furrett* |
| sugar | socker(et) | *socker* |
| table | ett bord | *boord* |
| tea | te(et) | *tea* |
| teaspoon | tesked(en) | *teashead* |
| tip | dricks(en) | *dricks* |
| waiter | hovmästare(en) | *hawvmestareh* |
| waitress | servitris | *sairvitreess* |
| water | vatten(et) | *vatten* |
| wine | vin(et) | *veen* |
| wine list | vinlista(n) | *veenlista* |

**A table for one, please**
Kan jag få ett bord för en person, tack?
*kan yah faw ett boord fur ehn pairshoon, tack*

**A table for two, please**
Kan jag få ett bord för två, tack?
*kan yah faw ett boord fur tvaw, tack*

**May I see the menu/wine list?**
Kan jag få se menyn/vinlistan, tack?
*kan yah faw sea men_EW_n/v_ee_nlistan, tack*

**What would you recommend?**
Vad rekommenderar ni/du?
*vah rekommend_ay_rar nee/d_EW_*

**Do you do children's portions?**
Går det att få barnportion?
*gawr deat att faw barnportsh_oo_n*

**Is this suitable for vegetarians?**
Är det här lämpligt för vegetarianer?
*air deat hair laimplit fur vehgetaree-_ah_ner*

**I'd like …**
Jag skulle vilja ha …
*yah sk_ew_leh v_i_lya hah*

**Just a cup of coffee, please**
Bara en kopp kaffe, tack
*b_ah_ra ehn kopp k_a_ffeh, tack*

**Waiter/waitress!** *(to get attention)*
Ursäkta!
*_EW_rshekta*

**I only want a snack**
Jag vill bara något litet att äta
*yah vill b_ah_ra nawgot leeteht att aita*

**Is there a fixed-price menu?**
Har ni en dagens rätt?
*hahr nee ehn d_ah_gens rett*

**I didn't order this**
Jag beställde inte det här
*yah bestelldeh inteh deat hair*

**May we have some more …?**
Kan vi få litet mer av …?
*kan vee faw leeteh mear ahv*

**May I have another knife, please?** *(a different one)*
Kan jag få en annan kniv, tack?
*kan jah faw ehn annan k-neev tack*

*(an extra one)*
Kan jag få en kniv till, tack?
*kan jah faw en k-neev till tack*

**May we have the check, please?**
Kan vi få notan?
*kan vee faw nootan*

**Can we pay together/separately?**
Kan vi betala tillsammans/var för sig?
*kan vee betahla tillsammans/vahr fur say*

**The meal was very good, thank you**
Det var mycket gott, tack
*deat vahr mewkeh gott, tack*

---

### THINGS YOU'LL HEAR

**Vad får det vara att dricka?**
What would you like to drink?

**Smaklig måltid**
Enjoy your meal

---

# MENU GUIDE

**abborre** perch
**anka** duck
**apelsin** orange
**bakelse** cake, pastry, tart
**biff** beef
**biffgryta** beef casserole
**biffpaj** beef pie
**bigarrå** white-heart cherries
**björnbär** blackberries, brambles
**blekselleri** celery
**blodpudding** black pudding
**blomkål** cauliflower
**blåbär** blueberries
**braxen** bream
**bruna bönor** brown beans
**brylépudding** caramel custard
**brynt vitkålsoppa** white cabbage soup
**brysselkål** Brussels sprouts
**bräckt** fried
**bröd** bread
**buljong** consommé
**bullar** sweet buns
**bär** berries
**böckling** smoked Baltic herring
**bönor** beans
**chips** potato chips
**dadlar** dates
**druvor** grapes
**duva** pigeon
**falukorv** fried pork sausage
**fasan** pheasant
**fisk** fish
**fiskbullar** fish balls
**fiskfärs** ground fish
**fiskgryta** fish casserole
**fiskpinnar** fishfingers
**flundra** flounder
**fläsk** pork

**fläskkorv** spicy boiled pork sausage
**forell** trout
**frukostflingor** cereal
**frukt** fruit
**fullkornsbröd** wholemeal bread
**fyllda stekta äpplen** stuffed roasted apples
**förlorat ägg** poached egg
**getost** goat's cheese
**glasmästarsill** salt herring marinated with horseradish and carrots
**glass** ice cream
**grahamsbröd** brown bread
**gravad lax/gravlax** raw spiced salmon
**griljerad skinka** glazed ham
**gräslök** chives
**gröna ärter** green peas
**grönkål** kale
**grönsaker** vegetables
**grönsallad** lettuce
**grön ärtpuré** green pea purée
**gul lök** yellow onion
**gurka** cucumber
**gås** goose
**gädda** pike
**gös** pike-perch
**hallon** raspberries
**hare** hare
**hasselnötter** hazelnuts
**helstekt** whole roast
**hjortron** cloudberries
**hummer** lobster
**hälleflundra** halibut
**höns** chicken
**inkokt** cold boiled
**inlagda rödbetor** pickled beets
**inlagd gurka** pickles
**inlagd sill** marinated salt herring

**isterband** lightly smoked sausage, made from barley, pork, and lard
**jordgubbar** strawberries
**jordärtskockspuré** artichoke purée
**jos/juice** juice
**järpe** hazel-grouse
**kaffe** coffee
**kalkon** turkey
**kallskuret** cold meats
**kalops** beef stew
**kalvbräss** calves' sweetbreads
**kalvfilé** fillet of veal
**kalvfricassé** veal fricassee
**kalvgryta** veal stew
**kalvlever** calf's liver
**kalvrulader** veal roulades
**kalvschnitzel** veal cutlet
**kalvstek** joint of veal
**kalvsylta** calves' head
**kanin** rabbit
**karp** carp
**kassler** smoked tenderloin of pork
**katrinplommon** prunes
**kavring** pumpernickel-type bread
**knäckebröd** crispbread
**kokosnöt** coconut
**kokt** boiled, poached
**kokta majskolvar** corn on the cob
**kolja** haddock
**korv** sausage
**korvgryta** sausage casserole
**korvkaka** oven-baked sausage and oatmeal dish
**korvlåda** sliced baked sausages
**kotlett** cutlet, chop
**krabba** crab
**kronärtskockor** artichokes
**kroppkakor** potato dumplings stuffed with chopped pork
**krusbär** gooseberries
**kryddost** cheese with caraway seeds

**kräftor** crayfish
**kummel** hake
**kyckling** chicken
**kycklinglever** chicken liver
**kål** cabbage
**kåldolmar** cabbage rolls stuffed with ground meat and rice
**kålpudding** cabbage and mince pudding
**kålrötter** rutabaga
**kålsoppa** cabbage soup
**körsbär** cherries
**köttbullar** meatballs
**köttfärs** ground beef
**köttfärslimpa** ground beef loaf
**köttfärsrulader** roulades of ground beef
**köttgryta** beef casserole
**köttsoppa** clear beef soup with meat and vegetables
**lake** burbot
**lammfricassé** lamb fricasse
**lammsadel** saddle of lamb
**lammstek** joint of lamb
**lapskojs** lobscouse, beef stew with mashed potatoes
**lax** salmon
**laxpudding** layers of salmon and potatoes baked in the oven
**laxöring** sea trout
**legymsallad** green vegetable salad
**lever** liver
**leverbiff** sliced fried liver
**levergryta** liver casserole
**leverpastej** liver paté
**lutfisk** dried fish, soaked in lye and cooked
**löjrom** roe from small whitefish
**lök** onion
**lövbiff** sliced beef fried with onions
**majs** maize, corn
**makaroner** macaroni
**makrill** mackerel

**mald leverbiff** hamburger made of ground liver
**margarin** margarine
**marängsviss (hovdessert)** meringue layered with whipped cream and melted plain chocolate
**matjessill** a type of salt herring
**mesost** sweet brown cheese
**mjukost** soft white cheese
**mjöl** flour
**mjölk** milk
**morkulla** woodcock
**morötter** carrots
**musslor** mussels
**nejonögon** lampreys
**njure** kidney
**njursauté** sautéed kidneys
**nyponsoppa** rose-hip soup
**nässelsoppa** nettle soup
**nötter** nuts
**olja** oil
**orre** blackcock
**ost** cheese
**ostron** oysters
**oststänger** cheese sticks
**oxfilé** fillet of beef
**oxjärpe** type of cylindrical meatball
**oxragu** beef ragout
**oxrulader** rolled beef with stuffing
**oxstek** joint of beef
**oxsvanssoppa** oxtail soup
**palsternacka** parsnip
**paltbröd** black pudding
**pannbiff** beefburger
**pannkakor** pancakes
**paprika** green or red pepper
**peppar** pepper
**pepparkakor** ginger cookies
**pepparrotskött** boiled beef with horseradish sauce
**persika** peach

**piggvar** freshwater cod
**plommon** plum
**pocherad forell** poached trout
**potatis** potatoes
**potatismos** mashed potatoes
**pressad potatis** puréed potatoes
**prinskorv** mini-sausages
**purjolök** leek
**pyttipanna** hash of meat, potato, and onion
**päron** pears
**pölsa** barley and meat hash
**rabarber** rhubarb
**raggmunkar** potato pancakes
**rapphöns** partridge
**renkött** reindeer
**renstek** joint of reindeer
**revbensspjäll** spareribs
**rimmad skinka** salted ham
**ripa** ptarmigan (grouse)
**ris** rice
**risgrynspudding** rice pudding
**rostat bröd** toast
**rotmos** mashed turnips
**russin** raisins
**råbiff** steak tartare
**rådjursstek** joint of roedeer
**rågbröd** rye bread
**rårivna morötter** grated carrots
**räkor** shrimp
**röda vinbär** redcurrants
**rödbetor** beet
**röding** char
**rödkål** red cabbage
**rödlök** red onion
**rödspätta** plaice
**rökt** smoked
**salt** salt
**saltgurka** salt pickle
**salt sill** salt herring
**sardiner** sardines

schalottenlök shallot
selleri celery
sellerikål celeriac
senap mustard
sik whitefish
sikrom whitefish roe
sill herring
sillbullar herring fish cakes
sillpudding herring soufflé
sjömansbiff beef, onions, and potatoes casseroled in beer
skorpor rusks
slåtvar brill
smultron wild strawberries
småbröd sweet cookies
smör butter
smörgås sandwich
smörgåsbord the famous Scandinavian buffet table
sniglar snails
socker sugar
soppa soup
sotare tench
sparris asparagus
spenat spinach
sprängd anka salted duck
sprängd gås salted goose
squash pumpkin
stekt fried, roasted
strömming Baltic herring
stuvad(e) in a white sauce
surkål sauerkraut
surstek marinated roasted beef
surströmming fermented Baltic herring
svampgratinerad oxfilé fillet of beef and mushrooms au gratin
svarta vinbär blackcurrants
svartsoppa black soup made of goose blood
syltomelett sweet omelette with jam
te tea

tjäder capercailzie (grouse)
tomat tomato
torsk cod
tranbär cranberries
tunga tongue
tårta gateau
ugnsbakad skinka oven-baked ham
ugnskokt fiskfilé oven-baked fillet of fish
ugnsstekt revbensspjäll roasted spare-ribs
valnöt walnuts
vingelé currant gelatine
vinkokt cooked in wine
vispgrädde whipped cream
vitkål white cabbage
vitling whiting
vitlök garlic
vitt formbröd white (British-style) bread
vitt matbröd white bread
våfflor waffles
wienerbröd Danish pastry
wienerkorv hot dog
ål eel
åkerbär arctic brambles
ångkokt salt sill steamed salt herring
ägg egg
äggröra scrambled eggs
älg elk
älgstek joint of elk
äppelkaka med vaniljsås apple crumble with vanilla sauce
äppelkräm apple compote
äppelmos apple purée
äpple apple
ärter peas
ärtsoppa (yellow) pea soup
ättika vinegar
ättikssill soused herring
ättiksströmming soused Baltic herring
öl beer

## TRAVEL GUIDES PHRASE BOOKS

ARABIC • CZECH • DUTCH • EUROPEAN • FRENCH
GERMAN • GREEK • HEBREW • INDONESIAN
ITALIAN • JAPANESE • LATIN AMERICAN SPANISH
POLISH • PORTUGUESE • ROMANIAN • RUSSIAN
SPANISH • THAI • TURKISH

## TRAVEL PACKS

DUTCH • FRENCH • GERMAN • GREEK • HEBREW
LATIN AMERICAN SPANISH • ITALIAN • PORTUGUESE
RUSSIAN • SPANISH

## DK/HUGO IN THREE MONTHS
## LANGUAGE COURSES

ARABIC • CHINESE • CZECH • DUTCH • FRENCH • GERMAN
GREEK • HEBREW • HINDI • ITALIAN • JAPANESE
LATIN AMERICAN SPANISH • NORWEGIAN • POLISH
PORTUGUESE • RUSSIAN • SCOTTISH GAELIC
SPANISH • SWEDISH • TURKISH • WELSH

## COUNTRY GUIDES

AUSTRALIA • CANADA • CROATIA • CUBA • EGYPT • FRANCE
GERMANY • GREAT BRITAIN • GREECE: ATHENS & THE MAINLAND
HOLLAND • INDIA • IRELAND • ITALY • JAPAN • MEXICO • MOROCCO
NEW ZEALAND • NORWAY • POLAND • PORTUGAL • SCOTLAND
SINGAPORE • SOUTH AFRICA • SPAIN • THAILAND • TURKEY

## REGIONAL GUIDES

BALI & LOMBOK • BARCELONA & CATALONIA • BRITTANY
CALIFORNIA • CANARY ISLANDS • CORSICA • CRUISE GUIDE TO
EUROPE & THE MEDITERRANEAN • EUROPE • FLORENCE AND TUSCANY
FLORIDA • HAWAII • JERUSALEM & THE HOLY LAND
GREAT PLACES TO STAY IN EUROPE • GREEK ISLANDS • LOIRE VALLEY
MILAN & THE LAKES • MUNICH & THE BAVARIAN ALPS
NAPLES WITH POMPEII & THE AMALFI COAST • NEW ENGLAND
PROVENCE & THE CÔTE D'AZUR • SARDINIA • SEVILLE & ANDALUCIA
SICILY • SOUTHWEST USA & LAS VEGAS • A TASTE OF TUSCANY
VENICE & THE VENETO

## CITY GUIDES

AMSTERDAM • BERLIN • BOSTON • BRUSSELS • BUDAPEST
CHICAGO • CRACOW • DELHI, AGRA & JAIPUR • DUBLIN
ISTANBUL • LISBON • LONDON • MADRID • MOSCOW
NAPLES • NEW ORLEANS • NEW YORK • PARIS • PRAGUE • ROME
SAN FRANCISCO • STOCKHOLM • ST PETERSBURG
SYDNEY • VIENNA • WARSAW • WASHINGTON, D.C.

Algarve • Amsterdam

Barcelona • Berlin • Boston

Cancun & the Yucatan • Crete

Dublin • Hong Kong • London

Madrid • Mallorca • Miami & the Keys

Milan & the Lakes • New York

Orlando • Paris • Prague

Provence & the Côte D'Azur

Rome • San Francisco • Scotland

Sicily • Tuscany • Venice

Vienna • Washington D.C.